INJUSTICE FOR ALL

AARON,

Thank you for your support!

Mary Lyn Derr

A SPECIAL REPORT FROM THE DESK OF
MARY LYN HAMMER

INJUSTICE FOR ALL
THE TRUTH ABOUT THE ANNIHILATION
OF AMERICAN EDUCATION IDEALS

CHAMPION EMPOWERMENT INSTITUTE, PHOENIX

INJUSTICE FOR ALL: The Truth about the Annihilation of American Education Ideals

Copyright © 2016 Mary Lyn Hammer.

Data, analysis, and source materials accuracy verification by "Independent Accountant Reports" conducted by Kaiser and Carolin, P.C. When the source material presented in this book is based upon open source information, those sources are referenced. All hyperlinks, unless notated, were valid at the time of publication, but we cannot ensure the hyperlinks remain valid post-publication.

Editors: Ja-lene Clark, C Diane Ealy, and Joanne Sprott

Index: Joanne Sprott

Project development, cover and interior design: Ja-lene Clark

Photography: Author photographs on back cover, pages 15, 188, and 293 by Sydney Peterson; pages 48, 76, 104, 142, 200, 226, and 252 from123RF.com; page 160 from Unsplash.com; page 282 from Wikimedia Commons.

Published by Champion Empowerment Institute

Box 97001
3920 E Thomas Rd
Phoenix, AZ 85018

ISBN: 978-0-9970978-0-1 (paperback)

ISBN: 978-0-9970978-1-8 (ebook)

PRINTED IN CANADA

10 9 8 7 6 5 4 3 2 1

1st Edition, January 2016

Dedication

Sometimes we must look beyond ourselves, beyond our fears, and beyond what is right in front of us to find out why we are here. My journey to write *Injustice for All* has been about overcoming my fears for the greater good, elevating what I have always known—that I am here to teach, mentor, and represent children and young adults especially those who are underprivileged—those who are at risk. I know the power of having someone say that they believe in you and having that make all the difference. I am an at-risk student and my education experience at Brooks College in Long Beach, California (a proprietary school) was the first time that people said to me, "We believe in you," and those simple words changed my destiny.

This book, my life, my mission are dedicated to encouraging the children of America into greatness and nurturing their gifts of ingenuity, insight, inspiration, enthusiasm, passion, and power to revitalize America. My quest is to empower children with appropriate and amazing opportunities, provoking meaningful actions to rise above adversities and become, once again, proud to be American. I believe in you.

This book is dedicated to an America that, with and through quality education, can become again one of the greatest countries on Earth. I believe in America.

INJUSTICE FOR ALL TABLE OF CONTENTS

INJUSTICE FOR ALL LIST OF TABLES

VI. SECTOR–LEVEL PERFORMANCE DATA

VII. 2015 ICDR SHOWS ONE POINT OF CONSISTENCY

VIII. THE IMPACT

IX. LEGISLATIVE SOLUTIONS THAT PROMOTE ACCOUNTABILITY

INJUSTICE FOR ALL

Gratitudes

To Ja-lene Clark, my editor, my mentor, and my friend—thank you for sharing your amazing gifts with me. Your insight, enthusiasm, support, criticism, and love have made *Injustice for All* a work that I am proud of. Thank you for being my confidante and friend. I love working with you and love being your friend. Thank you for embracing this opportunity for I know that your heart is in this just as deeply as is my own.

I'd like to thank the Obama Administration and the U.S. Department of Education for making the adjustments to the 2014 Official Institution Cohort Default Rates. This action drove my detailed examination of databases and reporting that led to the discovery of the DOE's data manipulation and erroneous reporting and was the catalyst which inspired me to write *Injustice for All*. You helped me find the truth.

A special thanks to Chairman John Kline (MN), Chairwoman Virginia Foxx (NC), Chairman Todd Rokita (IN) and the professional staff at the U.S. House of Representatives Committee on Education and the Workforce for taking time to examine and understand the evidence that is documented in *Injustice for All*. That was not an easy task. The questions that you have posed to the Department of Education are important not only for proprietary schools but to all students because they clear a path toward accountability and quality education opportunities for all students at all schools.

I would also like to thank many members of the U.S. House of Representatives and the Senate for working with me over the years to meld quality standards with opportunities for students, beginning with Chairman Pat Williams (D-MT) who ironically was in office when I began my journey in Washington, DC; Chairman Jim Jeffords (R-VT); Senator John McCain (R-AZ); Congressman John J. Rhodes III (R-AZ); Congressman Mo Udall (D-AZ); Senator Jon Kyl (R-AZ) for supporting my legislative efforts and hikes up Camelback; Senator Dennis DeConcini (D-AZ); Chairman Ted Kennedy (D-MA); Chairman Bill Ford (D-MI); Chairman Bill Goodling (R-PA); Congressman Dale Kildee (D-MI); Speaker John Boehner (R-OH) for your honesty, integrity, and mentorship from when you were Chairman of the House Education and the Workforce Committee through all these years—it has been an honor, pleasure, and a joy; Chairman Buck McKeon (R-CA); Senator Mike Enzi (R-WY); Chairman George Miller (D-CA); Chairman Tom Harkin (D-IA); Ranking Member Bobby Scott (D-VA); Chairman Lamar

Alexander (R-TN), and all of your respective professional staff. Please, forgive me if I have forgotten anyone, which I'm sure that I have, because there have been so many people in Washington who have been supportive. You have all shown me that an at-risk girl from Montana can make a difference in education. Thank you for the privilege and honor of working with you throughout the years.

Thank you, Chuck Collins (deceased), who was my boss when I was developing the original "Hands On" Default Management Program. When you told me that I would go on to do big things, I didn't understand your vision of me. I was young. When you first told me that I could copyright the program in my own name, I didn't realize what a blessing that was. You were my greatest supporter. Thank you for believing in me.

Very special thanks to Joan and Dick Smith. You believed in me, and I never would have gone down this path without your support and love. You changed my life and the lives of millions of students after me. I will forever be grateful.

Thank you to Debbie T, a former student whom I took to Washington, DC in 1988 to tell her story to Senators and Congressmen. That story of how you had given up your beautiful 2-year-old daughter for a year so you could complete your education and give her a better life gave me clarity on my life mission.

My gratitude is endless for my amazing staff, past and present, at Champion College Services. Thank you for emulating teamwork, honor, and integrity. You have been essential in changing the lives of millions of students. You are truly champions! I am honored to be your leader.

Special thanks to my friend and colleague, Tom Netting, who has been by my side in Washington since the 1992 reauthorization. It has been a wonderful journey making a difference for students and watching our girls grow up. Thank you for supporting me professionally and personally.

Special thanks to my family, friends, and colleagues who are too many to name and who have been my family, my friends, my comrades and who have stood by me through good times and bad. Your love and support have made all the difference in my life. Thank you so much!

And a very special thank you goes to the Salgado family, who has taken care of Elizabeth and me for many years. You are our family and our friends. You have showed me what family and love is. We will forever be grateful that we have you in our lives.

Thank you to C Diane Ealy and Joanne Sprott for your editorial support; to my former executive assistant and Karina Salgado for helping to collect and document evidence; to Kathe Carolin for completing the evidence and analysis audits; to my dear friends, Sydney Peterson for your amazing photography skills and Rachelle Peterson for getting Sydney from Alaska to Arizona to take the photos; to Larry Prather, Terry Zaleski and all the others who have encouraged me to share the truth. During times when I felt overwhelmed, your support sustained me.

I would also like to acknowledge my dear friend, Phil Rosen (deceased), who mentored me from the moment that I decided to go into business, even taught me how to set up my first booth. Phil took me on many adventures and supported me through every tragedy and accomplishment that I had professionally and personally until the day God's angels took him for his next adventure. I miss you every day.

Last but not least, a big thank you goes to the two great loves of my life. First, to my amazing child, Elizabeth, who inspires me every day. You are by far the greatest gift that has ever been given me and I thank God for you every day. Elizabeth—thank you for the honor of being your mom. I am so very proud of you. Second, to my love and best friend, Chuck Curry, who provides constant and undying support in everything that I do especially through listening, advising, and reading numerous versions of *Injustice for All* along the way. Thank you both for allowing me to work crazy hours to complete this work. You both have made me a better person and I am grateful beyond words. I believe in both of you. Thank you for believing in me.

I. MANIFESTO

Injustice for All
The Truth about the Annihilation of American
Education Ideals

PRAECIPIO PRUDENTIA

LIBERTAS

The data, analysis, and source materials used in *Injustice for All* have been verified for accuracy in "Independent Accountant Reports" conducted by Kaiser and Carolin, P.C.

America has become a nation where the majority of our citizens base their beliefs and opinions upon the spin from media coverage and news feeds that often regurgitate unverified facts; in particular regarding data. People usually gravitate toward or seek out media sources that support their most familiar opinions and views—which ultimately become a belief system.

After eliminating the private Federal Family Education Loan Program (FFELP) community in 2010, the U.S. Department of Education (DOE) now controls a growing majority of student loans. In 2014, the DOE decided to make unauthorized "adjustments" to a long-standing law for quality measures based on the student loan cohort default rates (CDRs). I KNEW something was terribly wrong. I examined various publicly-available data and reports to determine exactly what had been "adjusted" and found a plethora of manipulated data and inaccurate reporting for private (FFELP) and Federal Direct Student Loan Program (FDSLP) CDRs and for sector-level institution CDRs and gainful employment rates.

The greatest illusionists have used sleight-of-hand methods to distract people from seeing what they are actually doing. In many ways, constant media focus on extreme examples of certain publicly-traded proprietary institutions is a seductive distraction: the sleight-of-hand that keeps the U.S. Department of Education's epic failures out of the headlines.

Almost silently with a whisper...a horrible fate is occurring in the United States—the annihilation of our higher education system through manipulation of facts presented to the public that provide false impressions of outcomes and performance metrics for ALL institutions of higher education. This situation wields the power to quickly turn America from a country lauded for ingenuity and leadership into one of growing ignorance and lacking self-reliance.

Analysis Reveals the Manipulative Agendas

During my analysis (especially over the last year while examining numerous national databases, reports, and press releases), the patterns exposed what can clearly be seen as agendas that have little to do with actually educating Americans. Instead, these agendas have everything to do with carrying out a tragic injustice by reducing or eliminating free enterprise within higher education—something that will ultimately lead to the annihilation of American educational ideals *if we do not take actions now.*

AGENDA ITEM #1: First, came the elimination of the private sector of federal student loans—the FFELP or FFEL Program community; many of these lenders, secondary markets, guarantee agencies and servicers were for-profit companies. Within a month of being sworn into office after the 2008 presidential election, Barack Obama introduced his first budget proposal, which ultimately succeeded in the elimination of the FFEL Program and many companies in the FFELP community.

Ironically, the performance for loans under the DOE's direct management (direct loans, FDSL Program, or FDSLP) have either been misreported or underreported for EVERY 3-year cohort default rate since Obama has been in office. At the same time, the performance for the private sector FFEL Program has been misreported as performing worse than they have actually performed.

Table 1: DOE Loan Program Reporting vs Data Reality

Discrepancies in DOE Reporting for Loan Programs				
Loan Program	FFELP Reporting & Data		FDSLP Reporting & Data	
Information Source	DOE Briefing	DOE Data	DOE Briefing	DOE Data
FY 2009 3-year Default Rates by Loan Program	14.6%	**10.6%**	8.6%	**23.9%**
FY 2010 3-year Default Rates by Loan Program	not released	9.6%	12.8%	**16.5%**
Information Source	DOE Data for Loan Holders	Other Publicly Available Data	DOE Data for Loan Holders	Other Publicly Available Data
FY 2011 3-year Default Rates by Loan Program	9.1%	9.1%	10.7%	**15.0%**
FY 2012 3-year Default Rates by Loan Program	8.6%	8.6%	6.6%	**12.2%**

Publicly available data shows that the private sector still outperforms the direct loan program even with diminishing returns on the loan portfolios these companies still manage.

For example, in September 2012 the U.S. Department of Education (DOE) released "briefings" for the first FFELP and FDSLP 3-year cohort default rates. The FY 2009 FFELP briefing reported the FFELP default rate as 14.6% when the 2014 loan holder data shows it to actually be 10.6%. The FY 2009 FDSLP briefing touted an 8.6% default rate when the 2014 loan holder data shows that the FY 2009 FDSLP rate was actually 23.9%. In other words, the DOE misreported the FFELP 3-year CDR to be higher than it actually was and its own FDSLP CDR to be much lower than it actually was. This has become the norm for the DOE's self-reporting of its loan portfolios.

AGENDA ITEM #2: The second agenda item is well underway to eliminate for-profit (proprietary) education by covering up an underperforming nonprofit sector while grossly misreporting information about the for-profit, proprietary sector.

Comprehensive data available in the College Navigator[1] in 2014–2015 when this research and analysis was completed contains pertinent information about each sector that had to be manually collected, most likely so that people wouldn't easily see the truth.

Table 2: Cost of Student Loans by School Sector

College Navigator Information for FY 2010 (available on the College Navigator at the time of this analysis in 2014)			
Sector	Average Median Student Loan Debt	Average Graduation Rate %	Cost of Ave. Student Loan per Grad %
Public Community Colleges	$ 5,182	26.6%	$ 195
Public Traditional Colleges	$ 6,857	45.6%	$ 150
Private Nonprofit Colleges	$ 10,506	55.6%	$ 189
Proprietary Colleges	$ 7,088	60.4%	$ 117

The cost of the average student loan is calculated by dividing the Average Median Student Loan Debt by the Average Graduation Rate %. This gives an apples-to-apples comparison for all schools in relation to the cost for students.

1. https://nces.ed.gov/collegenavigator/

The College Navigator data shows that community colleges are the lowest performing group in terms of graduation rates (26.6%) and are the most costly for students per graduation percent ($195). It also shows that the proprietary colleges are the highest performing of all groups in terms of graduation rates (60.4%) and are the least costly for students per graduation percent ($117).

Traditionally, the loan balance has always been used to drive the opinion that community colleges are the least expensive of all schools, while the truth is that the loan balances are high when considering the extremely low graduation rates.

In contrast, the proprietary colleges have slightly higher loan balances ($7,088) than community colleges ($5,182), while the proprietary sector graduates more than twice the students (60.4%) than community colleges graduate (26.6%)—and these schools are both serving students with similar socioeconomic backgrounds.

The cost for borrowers is higher at community colleges ($195) while the costs are the lowest ($117) at proprietary colleges. When you consider that proprietary schools do not get all of the state and federal grants that public colleges get, the cost of education at proprietary colleges is lower for taxpayers as well.

When we add cohort default rate data (CDRs are defined later in this chapter) to the mix, the data proves that misinformation about sector default rates has also been pushed upon the public. The following CDR information by sector (Table 3) is based on the September 2015 Official FY 2012 Institution Cohort Default Rate (iCDR) data contained in the comprehensive PEPS300 data file provided on the DOE's website.

Table 3: Sector Cohort Default Rate (iCDR) Good and Bad Quality Indicators

SECTORS and TOTALS	Schools with N/A (No Loans)		30 or More Borrowers			Average of iCDRs for Schools with Borrowers
2015 Official FY 2012 iCDR Data			Good Quality		Bad Quality	
	# Schools with N/A (No Loans)	% of Total Schools with No Loans	# Schools Under 15%	% Schools Under 15%	% Schools with Loans Subject to Sanctions	
PUBLIC	301	16.1%	909	58.0%	<1%	13.9%
COMMUNITY COLLEGES	296	22.1%	425	40.8%	<1%	17.1%
PROPRIETARY	439	21.3%	930	57.3%	<1%	13.9%

Additionally, the iCDR data for high quality schools with default rates under 15% shows that there are 909 schools or 58.0% of all public colleges with default rates under 15%, and there are 930 schools or 57.3% of all proprietary colleges with default rates under 15%. The data show that less than 1% of all institutions in every sector are subject to loss of federal student loan and grant funding—including the proprietary sector.

CDRs have always been reported for national and sector rates by taking the total number of borrowers in default divided by the total number of borrowers who entered repayment. This method of calculation reflects borrower activity and gives those institutions with larger numbers of borrowers a greater influence upon the sector. With the increase of mergers even among community college groups, large corporations and publicly-traded institutions, small schools' reputations are unfairly being measured by numbers that have nothing to do with school performance.

Since the CDR rates are reported by sector and the rates are being used to form perceptions of schools within each sector, the sector CDR rates should be based on school performance and not borrower performance; therefore, the average of all institutional rates better reflects how a sector performs because it gives each school equal consideration.

> *The 2015 Official FY 2012 Cohort Default Rate data shows the public and proprietary sectors have EXACTLY the same average cohort default rate of 13.9%.*

As the reputations of proprietary institutions are ruined through false information and the media's thirst for sensationalized tragedies that are atypical, at for-profit institutions, at-risk students are migrating to public institutions, and they will inherit the default rate and other issues that for-profit institutions have been experiencing for years because...

> *The primary contributor to high default rates and satisfactory progress issues is the socioeconomic background of the students served. In other words, these issues are at-risk-student-centric, NOT school-centric.*

If you compare this audited and independently verified information to the U.S. Department of Education publicly released Briefings for the FY 2012 institution cohort default rates, the data will not match. The information in the DOE's briefings has been manipulated and misreported in favor of public and private nonprofit institutions and to the detriment of for-profit institutions. Both financial rewards and sanctions *should be* based upon each individual school's performance and not on sectors as a whole.

> *The institution cohort default rate data (iCDR or PEPS300 data) shows that the number of borrowers in default in the public sector has increased from 4,230 fewer defaults than the proprietary sector in the FY 2009 CDR to 91,563 more defaults than the proprietary sector.*

Table 4: YOY iCDR Manipulation of # Borrowers in Default

Year-over-year Comparison of iCDR Manipulation # Defaults from Official Briefings and Institution iCDR (PEPS300) Data				
	FY 2009 #DFLT 2012 Release	FY 2010 #DFLT 2013 Release	FY 2011 #DFLT 2014 Release	FY 2012 #DFLT 2015 Release
PUBLIC				
Briefing Borrowers in Default	-8,700	-9,031	-11,276	-4,990
Briefing Borrowers Entered Repayment	-65,164	-65,700	-87,473	-47,273
PRIVATE				
Briefing Borrowers in Default	318	563	609	-8,034
Briefing Borrowers Entered Repayment	-449	917	-3,396	-56,028
PROPRIETARY				
Briefing Borrowers in Default	20,353	21,277	12,332	20,504
Briefing Borrowers Entered Repayment	81,679	87,181	39,520	86,737
DIFFERENCE BETWEEN THE NUMBER OF BORROWERS IN DEFAULT FOR PUBLIC vs PROPRIETARY				
Total # Borrowers in Default in Reporting Manipulation Between Public & Proprietary	29,053	30,308	23,608	25,494
DOE Reported Difference in # Borrowers in Default (Public vs Proprietary iCDR)	(33,283)	(26,427)	3,886	66,069
Actual Difference Number Default (Public vs Proprietary iCDR)	**(4,230)**	**3,881**	**27,494**	**91,563**

If collecting student loan default dollars is what serves the federal fiscal interest, why is the focus ALL on proprietary schools when the public nonprofit sector represents the lion's share of student loan defaults?

Additionally, if the nonprofit institutions are performing so much better than the proprietary institutions, why would the DOE have the need to falsely report the sector CDRs?

Table 5: YOY iCDR % of Manipulation by Sector

Year-over-year Comparison of iCDR Manipulation % from Official Briefings compared to Institution iCDR (PEPS300) Data				
	FY 2009 iCDR% 2012 Release	FY 2010 iCDR% 2013 Release	FY 2011 iCDR% 2014 Release	FY 2012 iCDR% 2015 Release
PUBLIC				
Briefing Borrowers in Default	-4%	-3%	-4%	-2%
Briefing Borrowers Entered Repayment	-4%	-3%	-4%	-2%
PRIVATE				
Briefing Borrowers in Default	+1%	+1%	+1%	-10%
Briefing Borrowers Entered Repayment	<1%	<1%	<1%	-5%
PROPRIETARY				
Briefing Borrowers in Default	+10%	+8%	+4%	+10%
Briefing Borrowers Entered Repayment	+9%	+7%	+3%	+6%

For the proprietary sector, when the percent of increase in the number of borrowers in default is greater than the percent of increase in borrowers entered repayment, the default rate calculation is inflated.

For the private sector's FY 2012 reported iCDR, when the percent of decrease in the number of borrowers in default is greater than the percent of decrease in the number of borrowers entered repayment, the default rate calculation is deflated.

The total percent of data manipulation between the numbers for public sector and proprietary sector borrowers in default and borrowers entered repayment represents the following:

Table 6: YOY Total % of Difference in iCDR Manipulation

3-Year CDR	Total % of Difference in # of Borrowers in Default	Total % of Difference in # of Borrowers Entered Repayment
FY 2009	14%	13%
FY 2010	11%	10%
FY 2011	8%	7%
FY 2012	12%	8%

Table 7: YOY Comparison of DOE iCDR Briefings to iCDR PEPS300 Data

Year-over-year Comparison of iCDR % from Official Briefings and Institution iCDR (PEPS300) Data				
	FY 2009 iCDR% 2012 Release	FY 2010 iCDR% 2013 Release	FY 2011 iCDR% 2014 Release	FY 2012 iCDR% 2015 Release
PUBLIC				
Official DOE Briefing	11.0%	13.0%	12.9%	11.7%
iCDR (PEPS300) Data	**11.1%**	**13.1%**	**13.0%**	**11.7%**
PRIVATE				
Official DOE Briefing	7.5%	8.2%	7.2%	**6.8%**
iCDR (PEPS300) Data	7.5%	8.2%	7.2%	**7.2%**
PROPRIETARY				
Official DOE Briefing	22.7%	21.8%	19.1%	**15.8%**
iCDR (PEPS300) Data	**22.6%**	**21.6%**	**18.9%**	**15.4%**

Prior to 2015, the reporting manipulation was limited to the public and proprietary sectors. In 2015, the private sector data also showed gross misrepresentation.

When big decisions are made about sectors as a whole, we risk forcing students into underperforming community colleges because they are "free" while many students miss opportunities for high-quality training and employment opportunities that result from education experiences at for-profit institutions.

The Obama Administration has eliminated the FFEL Program and is well on its way to eliminating the proprietary sector as a whole. Public support for these two agendas has been driven by inaccurate reporting and does not support quality in higher education for American citizens.

The Motivation Behind These Agendas

In February 2009, I was a negotiator in the Negotiated Rulemaking for the Team II Loan Issues that was a part of the 2008 Reauthorization of the Higher Education Act of 1965. Our negotiating team was holding our first round of negotiations in the U.S. Department of Education office when the budget was released. The room started to buzz with vibrating cell phones as news of this reached the public. The noise rose to a level where I felt we were sitting inside of a beehive. Because of the intensity, we stopped to look at the news coming in. The DOE representatives were just as shocked as the non-federal negotiators and spectators. We ended the negotiations early.

In September 2009, the House passed the Student Aid and Fiscal Responsibility Act[2] (SAFRA) to eliminate the FFEL Program. Although President Obama claimed it would save $87 billion, the bill never passed the Senate.

The following year, provisions in SAFRA that eliminated new bank-run loans for the FFEL Program as of July 1, 2010[3], were passed under the Health Care and Education Reconciliation Act (HCERA) of 2010. Yes, that's right—the elimination of FFELP was included in the law that brought us Obamacare. At the time of the HCERA enactment, the Congressional Budget Office (CBO) estimated the 10-year savings for student loans at $61 billion.

From the beginning of President Obama's campaign to date, he has publicly claimed that eliminating the FFELP community would save taxpayers money and reduce costs for students. Yet in April 2014, the CBO projected federal profits over the next ten years to be in excess of *$127 billion*[4]. Actual profits reported have shown these numbers to be grossly underestimated.

Government profits for federal student loans for 2013 alone were $41.3 billion, and this profit goes into the federal General Fund, not back into education!

How could this happen? Obama used his executive authority to implement repayment programs (Pay-As-You-Earn or PAYE and REPAY) that drop payments so low that, in most cases, the interest accruing is greater than the minimum payments required.

And, how do lenders make money? Through interest payments.

---

2. https://www.govtrack.us/congress/bills/111/hr3221

3. http://www.gpo.gov/fdsys/pkg/PLAW-111publ152/pdf/PLAW-111publ152.pdf

4. http://www.cbo.gov/sites/default/files/cbofiles/attachments/44198-2014-04-StudentLoan.pdf

These repayment plans that appear to be helpful to students, drop payments to levels where little to no principal will ever be paid; where payment schedules are increased from ten years to twenty or twenty-five years; and where students will have to pay lump sum amounts in the form of taxes when the loan balance, often larger than the original loans, is "forgiven" and reported as income. *If these students haven't paid down their loans in 20–25 years, how will they ever be able to pay a lump-sum debt to the IRS?*

Could this famous epic, *The Wizard of Oz*, have some commonality to what's been going on with higher education? Think back to the story…

> **Dorothy:** *"If you were really great and powerful, you'd keep your promises." (Tin Man, Cowardly Lion, and Scarecrow shake in fear.)*
>
> **Wizard:** *"Do you presume to criticize the great Oz? You ungrateful creatures! Think yourselves lucky that I am giving audience tomorrow instead of 20 years from now. The great Oz has spoken!"*
>
> *(Toto, the dog, runs over and pulls the curtain away to expose an ordinary man.)*
>
> **Wizard:** *"Pay no attention to the man behind the curtain! The great Oz has spoken!"*

It's not coincidental that many of the posts for this scene refer to President Obama and the way that the U.S. government is being run.

This book is written to provide evidence of the facts that are backed up by publicly available data and reports to show that the current belief system on education is misguided. Data are being manipulated, then pushed onto the public to support this erroneous belief system. This annihilates our American education system by allowing substandard quality to exist at nonprofit institutions while implementing extreme standards that often force closure of for-profit institutions that provide education and training for at-risk students who the nonprofit traditional colleges do not want to educate. The probable unintended consequences of these practices are limiting options for training and education of low- to middle-income students and creating the need to expand and establish new entitlement programs that support an uneducated people.

Look at the facts—all of the facts—and decide for yourself!

Student Loan Default Rates Are Used as a Measure of Quality Education

Since 1990, the U.S. Department of Education has used cohort default rates as a measure of quality in higher education. The premise is that there is quality when the students pay their loans. The DOE's regulatory definitions are based on laws primarily found in the Higher Education Act and its amendments.

The U.S. Department of Education released the most recent cohort default rate (CDR) information and data on September 22, 2014 that included CDRs for FY 2009, FY 2010, and FY 2011.

September 22, 2014

(Loans) Subject: FY 2011 3-Year Official Cohort Default Rates Distributed September 22, 2014 http://ifap.ed.gov/eannouncements/092214FY20113-YearOfficialCohort-DefaultRatesDistributedSept222014.html

The 3-year cohort default rate definition is based on the federal fiscal year which begins on October 1st of each year and ends on September 30th of the following year. Two data points are used. The first defines the "cohort" of borrowers as the number of borrowers who enter repayment in a federal fiscal year (FFY1). The second data point defines the number of those borrowers in repayment in FFY1 who default before the end of the third federal fiscal year (FFY3). The cohort default rate is the percent of defaulters divided by the number of borrowers who entered repayment.

The 3-year cohort default rate equals:

NUMERATOR: # of borrowers who entered repayment in FFY1 and who defaulted before the end of FFY3

DIVIDED BY

DENOMINATOR: # of borrowers who entered repayment in FFY1

The CDR rates determine if a college can continue eligibility for Title IV federal funding, including Pell Grants and federal student loans (Stafford Loans).

Schools face loss of eligibility to participate in these programs when they have one CDR rate over 40% or three consecutive years over 30%. CDRs also determine if a college is eligible for certain disbursement benefits that improve cash flow when they have three consecutive rates under 15%.

The first time that a 3-year cohort default rate could be used to determine eligibility was in 2014.

In prior years, a 2-year CDR definition was used.

In 2014, numerous public institutions would have lost eligibility if the DOE had not granted exceptions.

EXCEPTION #1: September 23, 2014—Adjustment of Calculation of Official Three Year Cohort Default Rates for Institutions Subject to Potential Loss of Eligibility.[5] Colleges subject to loss of Title IV Eligibility (federal student loans and grants), receive adjustments to change defaulted borrowers to non-default status (in repayment) in the three most recent 3-year cohort default rates when the borrower had multiple loans where at least one loan was in default and at least one loan was in good standing for a minimum of 60 consecutive days.

These circumstances noted in the announcement as reasons for the CDR adjustments—multiple loan programs, loan transfers, multiple loan servicers—have existed since 2010 when SAFRA legislation, part of the Health Care and Education Reconciliation Act of 2010, was passed; when a mass exit of lenders led to large numbers of loan transfers; and when the DOE was allowed to purchase FFELP loans made on or after October 1, 2007 as a way of keeping some lenders in business (known as "conduit" or "PUT" loans).

By the way, the FY 2012 CDRs released on September 28, 2015, have also been adjusted for schools facing sanctions; however, this was only disclosed in individual letters to those schools affected and not in an official DOE electronic announcement.

Why did the DOE change the CDR calculation criteria without Congressional approval?

---

5. http://ifap.ed.gov/eannouncements/092314AdjustmentofCalculationofOfc3YrCDRfor-InstitutSubtoPotentialLossofElig.html

How does the DOE know that students without multiple loans weren't adversely affected by the obvious loan servicing issues?

If the DOE thought it important enough to make these adjustments for schools facing sanctions, why wasn't it important enough to adjust the CDRs for ALL schools?

Many schools lost disbursement benefits as a result of the improper servicing and no longer had three consecutive rates under 15%. Many schools in California no longer qualified for state funding based on having default rates under the state's CDR threshold currently set at a 15.5% threshold. Additionally, the reputations of institutions are largely based upon the cohort default rates that make it into the news each year and that are mandated to be disclosed. Wouldn't it be prudent to correct this situation for all schools?

What did the DOE do to prevent these defaults?

I traveled to Washington, DC when the first huge group of conduit loans were purchased and transferred to DOE servicers, and took almost 10 months to appear on the new servicing system. I met with David Bergeron, a top official for postsecondary education and the U.S. Department of Education, and explained to him that every deferment, forbearance and special payment arrangement was dropped during the transfer and the loans immediately went into default. I asked him to find a solution so that these kids didn't wrongly suffer the consequences of default when they had done everything right in getting deferments, forbearances and alternate payment arrangements when they could not make timely payments. **The U.S. Department of Education did nothing.**

The students affected by the poor servicing for conduit loans have suffered tremendous adverse consequences to their credit and financial stability. Please, explain what the DOE has done to provide relief to the students affected by this? Has the DOE set up programs for the students to get out of default?

Is the DOE pursuing all normal means for collecting the defaulted loans that it would had the student actually knowingly defaulted? For example, is the DOE imposing wage garnishment in addition to requiring[6] voluntary on-time payments in 10 months for these affected students to rehabilitate their loans?

Has the DOE ever requested Congressional support for helping the students

---

6. More details are provided in *Chapter IV. 2014 Cohort Default Rates.*

in these high-CDR portfolios up to and including full rehabilitation, waiver of all interest and fees, and corrections to the students' credit reports?

At this point, we will have to rely upon Congressional action to get these kids out of default, repair their credit, and correct the cohort default rates of those institutions the affected borrowers attended.

EXCEPTION #2: Erroneous Data Appeal—Incorrect Borrower Enrollment.[7] Advised all data managers that received an Erroneous Data Appeal based on incorrect enrollment information to accept the appeal, if otherwise correct, without regard to when the enrollment change occurred.

Timely enrollment reporting is clearly defined in regulations, and exceptions have NEVER been allowed during adjustments or appeals. Current enrollment reporting requires schools to update enrollment status at least every 30 days. A waiver to this will allow schools to change data that would otherwise not be acceptable for the purpose of cohort default rate adjustments and appeals or, for that matter, any other reasons. Timely enrollment guidelines exist to keep databases accurate and to ensure that many laws and regulations can be upheld, such as the 150% rule, interest subsidy payments, and satisfactory progress standards to name a few. In other words, lack of enforcement for timely reporting will lead to fraudulent reporting to avoid CDR sanctions.

Is it all of a sudden OK to break the rules?

Why is the DOE accepting enrollment data changes *during* the appeal process that were not timely reported when the requirements and methods of appropriate reporting have been so clearly defined?

Cohort default rates have been defined by Congress and used as a measure of institutional quality since 1993. The schools allowed to "adjust" their default rates through the Erroneous Data Appeal process already have a high default rate bringing into question their administrative capabilities.

Why would the DOE then allow these schools to have adjustments to their default rates based on one more indicator of poor administrative capabilities with untimely enrollment reporting?

---

7. http://ifap.ed.gov/eannouncements/092314ErronousDataAppealIncorrectBorro wer-Enroll.html

The grace period and repayment schedules for student loans are based on the last date of at least half-time enrollment status. If enrollment statuses are not properly reported by an institution, that directly affects the servicing of the students' loans. Do federal student loan servicers accept enrollment changes that would change a student's repayment schedule when the enrollment change is not timely reported? For example, if a loan enters repayment based upon the anticipated graduation data but the student actually dropped prior to that date—and the change in enrollment was not timely reported—does the federal servicer change the repayment schedule, reapply the payments based on the change after the fact, and put the student into delinquent status? Or do they bring the loan current through administrative forbearance? And do they charge the student interest for these adjusted and unpaid loan payments?

Correct reporting of enrollment status obviously affects many things. How does allowing schools that don't comply with timely enrollment reporting help the students who attend their schools?

Have changes in enrollment dates that weren't timely reported been accepted for Erroneous Data Adjustments and Erroneous Data Appeals prior to the September 23, 2014 Electronic Announcement that mandated data managers accept Erroneous Data Appeals even when the enrollment reporting wasn't timely?

When erroneous data are corrected during the draft cohort default rate processes, is it permanently changed in the National Student Loan Data System (NSLDS) that is the data depository for loan servicing and CDR reporting?

When erroneous data are corrected during the official CDR appeal processes, are they permanently changed in the NSLDS?

Understanding that many of these data corrections move borrowers from one cohort to another, are the corrected data permanently changed in a school's cohort default rate?

If the untimely reported changes in enrollment status are not permanently changed in the NSLDS, is there risk that a student will incorrectly be counted in more than one CDR?

Will these schools get a "pass" in their audits when they have findings for these same enrollment updates that have not been submitted in a timely manner?

There are many unanswered questions related to the U.S. Department of Education's actions. Congress and the DOE insist that these CDR rates are backed by law and existing regulations are a measurement of the quality of education.

> *Why have exceptions been made since the U.S. Department of Education began managing the majority of federal student loans?*

Ironically, representatives for community colleges and other minority-serving institutions—*the same people who brought forth and supported 3-year cohort default rates*—had statements ready touting the importance of these CDR adjustments and appeal exceptions and supporting the DOE's decision.

At the same time, the proprietary schools knew nothing about this and several were so far down the road of closing their schools that when they received written communication that they actually had rates under the threshold and weren't subject to loss of eligibility, it was too late to turn back—they did the right thing and had numerous conversations with the DOE and were never told about the adjustments that gave rates under the threshold.

One such proprietary school in Erie, Pennsylvania, that had been in business for 150 years learned on September 22, 2014, <u>that it actually had three (3) cohort default rates under the threshold and was therefore not subject to sanctions</u>. At that time, most students would finish their programs before the school closed or had transferred out to other institutions to complete their programs as part of teach-out agreements the school had arranged. Most of the students would be able to pursue their dreams—except the 54 nursing students who could not find another school to attend to finish their education—54 nursing students, some with years invested in pursuit of their passion to help others, on the street with broken hearts and crushed dreams.

This story impacted me deeply when I heard it on September 22nd—when I knew there was nothing that I could do to help them. This story enraged me, made me cry for days, and became my motivation for writing this book.

Was saving a few schools from loss of Title IV Eligibility the only reason that default rates were adjusted? I say, "Hail, Dorothy!" Expose the man behind the curtain!

Everyone Sings: We're off to see the wizard, the Wonderful Wizard of Oz, We hear he is a whiz of a wiz, if ever a wiz there was, If ever, oh a wiz there was, the Wizard of Oz is one because, Because, because, because, because, because, BECAUSE of the wonderful things he does...

Let's take a look at some of these wonderful things.

On September 24, 2014, the DOE released its "National Default Rate Briefing for FY 2011 3-year Rates" (DOE Briefing or Briefing). The school CDR data (PEPS300) for all of the three most recent 3-year rates including FY 2009, FY 2010, and FY 2011 that support the DOE Briefing are also posted on the DOE's IFAP website.

In September and October 2014, I pulled down all relevant CDR data files and the DOE Briefing and began to analyze the information.

AGENDA ITEM #1: How has the government handled the transition to 100% direct lending? The government has over-promised, under-delivered, and now they are lying about it.

The first loan program default rates under the new Obama regime were published in 2012, right before the presidential election where Obama was re-elected. At the time, a "briefing" was published for both the FFEL Program and the Federal Direct Student Loan Program (FDSLP or FDSL Program). The only other documentation to support the briefing data was a "Top 100 Loan Holders" PDF document so, at the time, the briefing information could not be audited.

In September 2014, the DOE posted the comprehensive data for the FY 2009 3-year Cohort Default Rates by loan program and I was able to audit the briefings. In addition to the Official Loan Program Briefings discrepancies, a disturbing trend in default rates for loans transferred to the U.S. Department of Education emerged.

These "conduit loans," otherwise known as "PUT Loans" were purchased by the DOE to slow down the mass exit of FFELP lenders when they were eliminated from making new loans. These conduit loans included any FFELP loan disbursed on or after October 1, 2007.

The first transfers did not go well, and many students have been suffering the consequences ever since because their loans should never have gone into default.

Even though I told DOE officials early in the process that these loans had defaulted in error, the DOE officials chose to do nothing to correct the problems for the students or for the schools they attended.[8]

Table 8: DOE-Controlled Loan Portfolio Performance

	USDOE-Held Conduit Loan Performance					
LID	LENDER NAME PROVIDED BY DOE	COHORT YEAR	CURR RATE	CURR DEF	CURR REP	DOLLARS IN REPAY
899577	U.S. DEPT OF ED/ 2008-2009 LPCP	FY 2009-3YR	21.2%	148,171	697,298	$ 3,232,796,415
898577	US DEPT OF ED/ 2007-2008 STPP	FY 2009-3YR	27.1%	19,598	72,201	$ 359,620,740
895577	US DEPT OF ED/ABCP CONDUIT 09-10	FY 2009-3YR	59.8%	26,774	44,769	$ 346,999,081
897577	U.S. DEPT OF EDUCATION/ 2009-2010 LPCP	FY 2009-3YR	54.3%	1,294	2,381	$ 7,257,268.00
899577	U.S. DEPT OF ED/2008-2009 LPCP	FY 2010-3YR	14.5%	226,621	1,558,484	$ 3,549,408,535
895577	US DEPT OF ED/ABCP CONDUIT 09-10	FY 2010-3YR	56.6%	25,433	44,872	$ 388,261,027
897577	U.S. DEPT OF EDUCATION/ 2009-2010 LPCP	FY 2010-3YR	18.2%	148,636	815,265	$ 3,961,533,085
895577	US DEPT OF ED/ABCP CONDUIT 09-10	FY 2011-3YR	58.6%	14,455	24,666	$ 248,497,076
895577	US DEPT OF ED/ABCP CONDUIT 09-10	FY 2012-3YR	56.0%	3,916	6,998	$ 68,645,140

The DOE stopped reporting CDRs by loan program after the FY 2010 3-year CDRs were released in September 2013. They have also neglected to include their own data in the files posted on their website for loan holder default rates.

When the loan holder data is compared to the institution data contained in the PEPS300 data files (iCDR), I have been able to estimate the DOE-controlled and direct loan default rate.

---

8. https://studentaid.ed.gov/sa/sites/default/files/fsawg/datacenter/library/July-2011ECASLAReport.pdf

Table 9: YOY Comparison of DOE Loan Portfolio Reporting vs Available Data

3-YR CDR	DOE National Official iCDR Briefing	iCDR Data PEPS300	REPORTED DOE Loan Program CDRs	ACTUAL DOE-held CDRs	Estimated DOE % of Total iCDR Volume
FY 2009	13.4%	13.2%	8.6% DOE Briefing	23.9% 2014 Loan Holder Data	22.7%
FY 2010	14.7%	14.5%	12.8% DOE Briefing	16.5% 2014 Loan Holder Data	57.5%
FY 2011	13.7%	13.6%	10.7% 2014 DOE Loan Holder Data	15.0% 2014 Loan Holder Data plus iCDR PEPS300	75.8%
FY 2012	11.8%	11.7%	6.6% 2015 DOE Loan Holder Data	12.2% 2015 Loan Holder Data plus iCDR PEPS300	86.4%

AGENDA ITEM #2: Could the assault on the proprietary sector be a diversion for the DOE's own poor performance for managing student loan defaults?

There is no doubt in my mind that these default rates are what led to the "adjustment" of the CDRs released in 2014 and to the "exception" for timely reporting in CDR appeals. If schools don't have to do appeals to remain in the Title IV loan and grant programs, they don't have to look at the data. This thought gave me insight to continue to examine the 2014 Official CDR data.

Cohort Default Rates: The CDR information reported by the U.S. Department of Education is a little off—is it that big of a deal?

DOE-released information is used by the public and students to decide which schools are of good quality and which are of bad quality. The manipulation in this reporting seems to support "the story" that the Obama Administration and certain lawmakers want the public to believe: That all proprietary schools are predatory and should be eliminated. The DOE's own databases show otherwise.

Since the CDRs influence the public opinion, reputation and value of schools in addition to determining federal funding eligibility, shouldn't the U.S. Department of Education publish accurate calculations for these rates?

These patterns net results that support an agenda that has nothing to do with quality education or serving the students' best interest—the DOE and certain critics of the proprietary sector want politicians and the public to buy into their plan so they can move forward with eliminating proprietary schools through legislation and regulations known as Gainful Employment—their agenda is not the truth.

The Gainful Employment Agenda

Quality measures and metrics are a good idea when these are reasonably administered, are based upon fair and realistic measurements, and are applied to all institutions. Every institution has challenging students and this is not determined by tax status—it is determined by the physical location of the school and the socioeconomic background of the students served.

If the laws and regulations can't be applied to all institutions, the standards are likely not fair and equitable.

Another controversial subject where public perception in the higher education arena has been swayed by inaccurate data reporting is known as "Gainful Employment" (GE). This law requires higher education training to prepare students for gainful employment. The current definition, however, does not include all institutions and is limited to the for-profit proprietary schools and certain programs at private and public schools. The majority of programs offered by private and public nonprofit institutions are not included in the current definition!

Since 2009, the U.S. Department of Education has pushed implementation of federal regulations that are not backed by law onto a limited number of colleges and programs. The DOE insists that the GE regulations are a measurement of the quality of education yet isn't applying these rules to all institutions. Why? Because there is an agenda that has nothing to do with validating the quality of education—it is validating a misguided belief system.

If the Gainful Employment measures were applied to all institutions and all pro-

grams, would there be any support for the GE regulations at all? Let's take a look at what has happened so far...

Gainful Employment *Original* Federal Regulations:

- GE metrics and measures are not defined by law.

- In December 2009, a negotiated rulemaking team was unable to reach consensus on the proposed federal regulations for GE.

- Over 90,000 comments were submitted during the Notice of Proposed Rulemaking (NPRM) process.

- Final regulations were published on October 29, 2010.

- Association of Private Sector Colleges and Universities (APSCU), an organization representing proprietary colleges, filed a lawsuit against the DOE.

- On June 30, 2012, the DOE received a U.S. District Court for the District of Columbia ruling to vacate the rules because they were found to be arbitrary and capricious; however, the DOE's authority to write the rules was upheld.

- The DOE filed a motion to reinstate the rules.

- On March 19, 2013, the federal court issued a decision that denied the DOE reinstatement request including reporting requirements although it did not affect the GE disclosure requirements.

Gainful Employment 2.0 *Subsequent* Federal Regulations:

- On April 16, 2013, the DOE published a notice of intent to establish a Negotiated Rulemaking Committee that included GE.

- Negotiations for GE 2.0 began on September 13, 2013 with even harsher measures than originally written that include a "zone" threshold where programs can lose eligibility *beyond* the minimum standards set forth in the original GE measures.

- Consensus was not reached.

- Again, thousands of comments were submitted during the NPRM process.

- Against strong recommendations and requests from U.S. Congressional members to hold back publication of GE 2.0 final regulations, the DOE published the final rules on October 31, 2014.

- Meetings with those affected by the regulations as required by law were still being held when the final regulations were published.

- The DOE admitted that some of the language was problematic, and it published the regulations with the intent of correcting the language before the implementation date of July 1, 2015.

- APSCU and Association of Proprietary Colleges (APC), both representing proprietary institutions, filed lawsuits against the DOE— two different judges upheld the GE regulations.

- APSCU has filed an appeal.

Table 10: Gainful Employment Debt-to-Earnings (D/E) Definitions for Original and GE 2.0 Regulations

Gainful Employment Rate Definitions		
	GE 1.0	**GE 2.0**
Repayment Rates		
Passing	Over 35%	No longer eligibility measure and included in disclosures
Failing	Under 35%	
Annual Debt-to-earnings Rates		
Passing	12% or Less	8% or Less
Zone	n/a	Over 8% and Under 12%
Failing	Over 12%	Over 12%
Discretionary Debt-to-earnings Rates		
Passing	30% or Less	20% or Less
Zone	n/a	Over 20% and Under 30%
Failing	Over 30%	Over 30%

Reviewing Table 10 I find it's hard to imagine that this is the "short version" of the story, but it is. More details about the deception and manipulation behind these regulations are provided in this book in Chapter V. Gainful Employment Manipulation. I wanted to provide this basic history of gainful employment to show the extent of the work put into the Administration's efforts to enforce these gainful employment regulations on a limited number of institutions and programs.

Now, you'll get a taste of the rest of the story...

FY 2011 GE Informational Rates Were Incomplete, Inaccurate, and Misled Public Opinion about Results

There were two sets of data for the FY 2011 GE Informational Rates:

1. The **"Streamlined"** data released to the general public included rates for 3,787 programs.

2. The more comprehensive **"Final"** data not released to the general public included 13,587 programs and the data details behind the GE rates.

A disproportionate number of schools from each sector were reported in the "FY 2011 Streamlined Informational Data" that was released to the public compared to the comprehensive "FY 2011 Final Informational Data."

Table 11: GE Programs Included in Final vs Streamlined Data by Sector

SECTOR	# Programs in Final Data	# Programs in Streamlined Data	% of Streamlined to Final # Programs
PUBLIC	5,301	268	5.1%
PRIVATE	616	111	18.0%
PROPRIETARY	7,847	3,408	43.4%

The payments in the comprehensive "Final" FY 2011 GE Informational Rate data weren't calculated properly using the defined standard repayment schedules.

1. The payment calculations for programs where all sectors are compared were the most accurately reported ratios:

   ○ The UNDERGRADUATE program payments were consistent

with the average debt amount and the defined length of repayment period.

○ The POST BACCALEAUREATE program payments were similar to the payments calculated for the average debt amount and defined length of repayment period. The payments for the proprietary programs had the biggest discrepancy.

2. The payment calculations for credential levels where the proprietary schools had the only programs reported (foreign programs excepted), were inaccurately calculated too high. The average payments for these programs showed:

Proprietary Associate's Degree:	85% too high
Proprietary Bachelor's Degree:	160% too high
Proprietary Master's Degree:	45% too high
Proprietary Doctorate Degree:	149% too high
Proprietary First Professional Degree:	77% too high

Debt-to-earnings (DTE) calculations take the annual total of debt payments using defined standard repayment calculations and divide that total by the annual earnings (D/E). But these grossly inflated payments had a negative impact of significantly and erroneously increasing the debt-to-earnings calculations which made the results look much worse than they actually were. **Grossly exaggerated debt-to-earnings ratios based on inflated inaccurate payments gave the <u>false impression</u> that proprietary school programs left their students with high debt that they could not afford to pay.**

In fact, the proprietary sector had the following averages[9] when correct payments were applied to the gainful employment metrics:

Proprietary Undergraduate Certificate:	Pass 2 of 3 metrics
Proprietary Associate's Degree:	Pass 3 of 3 metrics
Proprietary Bachelor's Degree:	Pass 3 of 3 metrics
Proprietary Post Baccalaureate Certificate:	Pass 3 of 3 metrics
Proprietary Master's Degree:	Pass 3 of 3 metrics
Proprietary Doctorate Degree:	Pass 3 of 3 metrics
First Professional Degree:	Pass 3 of 3 metrics

9. The rates were calculated and based on available data in the FY 2011 Final GE Data.

When correct payments were applied to FY 2011 failing programs, only 6 of 193 proprietary programs remained failing.

Where did the "zone" definition come from in GE 2.0?

Just my theory:

1. After hearing my testimony in May 2013, about the inaccuracy of the data used in the FY 2011 GE Informational Rates, the DOE went back and recalculated the payments.

2. The DOE's misguided beliefs were not supported by the data when the appropriate payments were applied and rates were recalculated.

3. Even though the DOE used several hundred pages of preamble language to support the thresholds that it used in the original GE regulations, it decided to come up with a measure that would recapture those schools that were lost when correct payment calculations were applied.

4. The DOE developed the "zone" as another arbitrary and capricious method solely targeted at eliminating certain programs and having nothing to do with actually measuring the quality of education.

5. To ensure that its FY 2012 GE Informational Data would not be audited (by me) like the GE 1.0 data was, the "median debt" data was left out of the data, making it impossible to verify the accuracy of the rates that were used for publishing GE 2.0 final regulations.

Does There Appear to Be Another Agenda with GE?

If the GE 2.0 (FY 2012) Informational Rates are accurately calculated, why is the DOE withholding pertinent data that is needed to verify the accuracy of the calculations?

Is it because the calculations aren't accurate—again?

Is it because full disclosure of the accurate data wouldn't support their misguided belief system and would derail a plan to eliminate proprietary schools even when the majority of these schools are performing well?

The U.S. Department of Education published final regulations on October 31, 2014, knowing there were issues with the language, and saying it would pull them back or adjust the regulations, if needed, so that it could force implementation on July 1, 2015.

Am I the only one thinking this sounds way too similar to the broken promises that we live with under the Affordable Care Act?

Equal Application of Quality Metrics

Having quality standards for every sector would be appropriate for the students, schools, taxpayers, and America in general. As currently written, the GE regulations do not require the same quality standards for certain public and private colleges that would ensure positive outcomes and performance for all students. **This habit of writing laws and regulations that only apply to certain sectors or programs leads to a decline in quality education for students.** Requirements for cohort default rates, cash flow requirements (called 90/10 in higher education), graduation rates, and the ability to find gainful employment after graduating are all designed to protect the students and create fiscal responsibility. How can the students and fiscal interest truly be protected if certain institutions aren't held to the same quality measures?

If the quality metrics are good measures, they should be applied to all institutions.

Is Tax-Filing Status Really an Indicator of Good or Bad Quality in Education?

As an example, the following is a comparison of two colleges in Tucson, Arizona that serve students of similar socioeconomic backgrounds: Pima Community College (PCC) and Pima Medical Institute (PMI).

Table 12: Comparison of Performance Metrics for Public (PCC) and Proprietary (PMI)[10]

INSTITUTION COMPARISON FY 2010 STATISTICS	Pima Community College (PCC) College Scorecard *	Pima Medical Institute (PMI) School Disclosure Info
Tax Filing Status	Nonprofit	For-profit
Graduation Rate*	10.2%	75.0%
FY 2010 Default Rate	23%	11.5%
Tuition	$2,968 *	$11,070
Average Debt	$5,867	$7,000
Average Cost (Ave Debt/ Grad%)	$575 per % of Graduation*	$93 per % of Graduation

The College Scorecard for Pima Community College shows an average student loan debt of $5,827—high considering almost 90% of their students aren't completing in a timely manner. The average loan debt divided by the graduation rate, yields the cost per graduation percentage point (completion) of $575. Somehow in the current belief system, the statistics for Pima Community College are acceptable because it is a public nonprofit school.

By comparison, Pima Medical Institute does not have a College Scorecard

---

10. Referring to information in Table 12:

The College Scorecard is posted on http://www.whitehouse.gov/issues/education/higher-education/college-score-card. FY 2010 data was available at the time of our research.

Graduation Rate is the acceptable time for being counted as a "graduate" and for receiving federal student aid funds and benefits is when a student completes a program or degree within 150% of the original expected course length. For example, bachelor's degrees have a 4-year expected completion time; students who complete within 6 years count as graduates; and qualified students receive Title IV funding and interest subsidies on in-school deferments for up to 6 years.

Non-profit Tuition does not include state and federal grant money that is not available to for-profit colleges. When this is added to the average cost, PCC costs students and taxpayers much more than PMI, a comparable college servicing the same location and student clientele.

Dollars per % of Graduation is calculated by dividing the average loan debt by the graduation percentage to get a cost per percent of graduation—giving an apples-to-apples comparison of cost to the student for what is received.

A comprehensive analysis of school data is provided in Chapter V. Gainful Employment Manipulation of this book.

and was happy to provide their amazing statistics as required in disclosures to students. The average student loan debt is $7,000—low considering that 75% of their students are graduating in a timely manner. When the average loan debt is divided by the graduation rate, the cost per graduation percentage point (completion) is $93. Somehow in the current belief system, Pima Medical Institute is considered unacceptable because it is a for-profit or proprietary school.

According to the Federal Student Aid website:[11]

"In February 2013, the Administration released the College Scorecard, a new planning tool to help students and their families make more educated decisions about college.

"Using the college scorecard, students and their families can look up the cost and assess the value of colleges. Each scorecard highlights five key pieces of data about a college: costs, graduation rate, loan default rate, average amount borrowed, and employment."

Only 308 or 14.4% of all proprietary colleges were included in the College Scorecard website.

> **Scarecrow:** *Come along, Dorothy. You don't want any of "those" apples.*

The students, parents, press, lawmakers and public rely on the College Scorecard for pertinent information about colleges so that informed decisions can be made. When I told the owner of Pima Medical Institute that his school was missing from the College Scorecard site, Richard (Dick) Luebke, Jr. wasn't surprised and replied, "It must be because of our good numbers."

How can good decisions be made when certain good schools are missing from DOE websites and limited data is provided?

Since I began speaking publicly on this subject in January 2015, the College Scorecard data has disappeared twice.

---

11. https://studentaid.ed.gov/about/announcements/college-scorecard

The first time that the College Scorecard information disappeared was sometime between February 13, 2015 and March 18, 2015.[12]

Table 13: March 18, 2015 College Scorecard Search Results:
THIS PAGE CAN'T BE DISPLAYED (whitehouse.gov screenshot)

We tried to identify when the database had been removed using several companies that periodically archive snapshots of websites. Two sites shut down when the College Scorecard URL was entered and wouldn't show us anything for the College Scorecard URL. These were:

- https://screenshotmachine.com/

- http://snapito.com/index.html

At this time, we can only verify that the College Scorecard data were available on February 13, 2015 and were no longer available on March 18, 2015. Over a dozen DOE employees were present during my last speech on February 23, 2015.

Has the data been eliminated to cover this up?

The second time the College Scorecard information disappeared was on September 17, 2015, less than two weeks after its release on September 5, 2015.

---

12. The Wayback Machine website last archived the College Scorecard site on February 13th. The information is available at the following link: https://web.archive.org/web/20150213214414/http://www.whitehouse.gov/issues/education/higher-education/college-score-card

Luckily, I was able to capture some screenshots prior to the data being removed. The information was available in a downloadable zip file until September 17th. After I began downloading the file, the site went down. When it came back up, I tried looking at groups of schools and received an error message stating: "Error Forbidden." No matter what I put into the system for searches from individual schools to groups of schools, the same message occurs.

Widespread criticism of the new College Scorecard came from many different sources this fall when the public and interested parties found out that those schools reported did not include all schools, and when definitions of data provided were blatantly excluding certain students and statistics. I was no longer the only person questioning the Administration's and the DOE's intent.

Is it a coincidence that the "New" College Scorecard search began returning an "Error Forbidden" message for every search on September 17, 2015, after I began downloading the zip file with the College Scorecard data?

Table 14: September 17, 2015 College Scorecard Search Results:
ERROR FORBIDDEN (DOE screenshot)

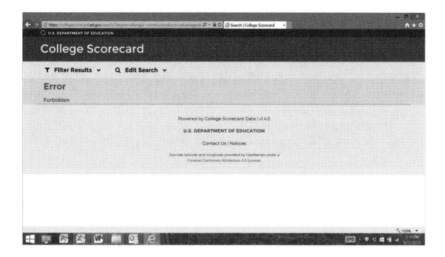

Freedom of Education Is Important

There are many reasons students choose to attend proprietary institutions and not public or private schools. I know, because I was an at-risk student who graduated from a proprietary institution when I was 19 years old. I grew up in a small town in Montana; one that was smaller in population than the public institutions that offered me scholarships to attend. I chose to forfeit the scholarships to attend a small proprietary school that I could quickly graduate from, one that had a limited population that I could emotionally handle at the time, and where I could study what drove my passion for a career. The education and support that I received from my proprietary school helped me break away from the abusive home where I grew up and shaped my future to help other at-risk students have access to higher education.

Proprietary institutions serve a very special niche, and the majority of institutions follow the laws and regulations that are mandated. There is no doubt that quality measures are needed to ensure good outcomes for students. But focusing on and manipulating facts and applying extreme examples to all will result in the loss of colleges that do a great job of educating the proprietary sector. Creating educational opportunities for all people requires that we develop a means to apply consistent quality standards to everyone and hold them accountable when they fail.

Manipulated facts undermine the value and importance of for-profit proprietary institutions that primarily serve at-risk students. These are the students for whom the Higher Education Act was written in the first place.

Without quality education, we have a people who do not have the education, training, or discernment to make good decisions that ensure America will be a safe, productive, financially stable, and healthy, happy nation in the future. Without it, dependency upon the government to tell us what to do, when to do it, and how to live will increase. Increased government control equates to fewer and diminished freedoms.

Education Is One of Many Freedoms Being Compromised

The most disturbing fact is that education is only one area where this is happening. When we consider the application of smoke and mirrors that cover up actual facts for education, healthcare, national security, missing money from government accounting, social security funds, welfare and entitlement programs, taxation, and all other areas of government control, the level of manipulation has the potential to end America as we know it. These injustices have already begun.

The DOE wants all citizens to believe that proprietary schools are greedy and have bad results while all the public schools do a better job.

It wants people to believe that community colleges can better educate at-risk students than proprietary institutions. This is spin, not fact.

I urge you to ask yourself, "What are you, as an American, going to do to protect your freedom while ensuring you know the factual truth so you can make sound, informed decisions about your life and the lives of your children?

How Many of Us Are Already Living the Life of a Zombie?

Kids talk about it on a regular basis, fearing the "zombie apocalypse." Look at the facts. Many are already there…

Until Americans take the time to research facts behind decisions that are being made on our behalf, we will continue to be led down the wrong path. Now is the time to question everything and assume nothing.

zombie [zom-bee]
Informal. A person whose behavior or responses are wooden, listless, or rote: automaton.

wooden [woo d-n]
Adjective. Expressionless, vacant, lifeless, impassive.

listless [list-lis]
Adjective. Having or showing little or no interest in anything; languid; spiritless; indifferent.

rote [roht]
Adjective. Proceeding mechanically and repetitiously; being mechanical and repetitious in nature; routine; habitual.

automaton [aw-tom-uh-ton]
Noun. A person or animal that acts in a monotonous, routine manner, without active intelligence.

Reference: dictionary.com

Did you know that PROFITS from federal student loans land in the U.S. Government's General Fund?

2013 profits were $41.3 BILLION!

II. HISTORY

Cohort Default Rates,
Gainful Employment
and Other Related Issues

*Sheer dollar volume in student loans can lead to fraud and cor-
ruption if the federal agencies and private companies involved
in the profit are not closely monitored. The lack of transparency
and oversight of federal agencies and private companies has led
students down a path that has nothing to do with education.*

How Did Defaulted Student Loan Dollars Land in the Government's General Fund?

It started with the noble intention of making higher education available to all U.S. citizens. The 1960s ushered in many movements to end discrimination in the United States. On the heels of enactment of the Civil Rights Act of 1964, intended to end discrimination based on race, color, religion, and national origin, came the Higher Education Act of 1965, also known as HEA. The HEA focused on providing equal opportunity for obtaining an education beyond high school, known as "higher education."

Title IV of the HEA directed assistance to students even though institutional aid still held the spotlight. Title IV formed the basis for the Guaranteed Student Loan Program, now known as the Stafford Loan. With the reauthorization of HEA in 1972, the foundation of today's student loan program was set. Federal student loans were backed by the federal government if students defaulted on the loans, including those students who didn't pay on their student loans for at least one year, those who died, who were determined to have total permanent disability, or who had loans forgiven through the bankruptcy courts. Little if anything was done to hold students accountable for the loans or collect on defaulted student loans. In fact, many students used the money to buy cars and other personal items, didn't pay for their education, and then defaulted on the loans. Most of these students experienced no consequences for their behavior.

Part of the reason for not enforcing penalties prior to 1986 was that the Internal Revenue Service was only able to seize federal tax refund money from students who filed taxes in the same region where they originated and defaulted on their student loans. There were nine regions in the United States. In 1986, the federal government had the ability to seize tax refunds from all regions regardless of where the student loan was originated. In 1986, the government had a national computer system that included all nine regions, and the U.S. Treasury collected $131 MILLION in tax refund offsets in addition to $37 MILLION in voluntary payments for education loans.[13]

At a time when the national budget was a focus of President Reagan and Congress as seen in the Balanced Budget and Emergency Deficit Control Act of 1985 and 1987 (better known as the "Gramm-Rudman-Hollings Act" or "Gramm-Rudman"), the collection of money to feed into the nation's *general fund* was very appealing. To reiterate, when the government started collecting on defaulted student loans, *the money recovered did NOT get reinvested in higher education*, it went into the general fund, and $131 million was significant to a country in financial crisis.

In 1987, the first requirements for default prevention required institutions to conduct exit interviews for student loans that reiterated the responsibilities and consequences of default to federal student loan borrowers.

Default rates at this time were based on dollars in default and were very controversial because the guarantee agencies who held the data admitted the data wasn't accurate but the data was used anyway because it was the only information available.

* * * * * * * *

---

13. http://www.gao.gov/assets/160/150497.pdf

History 1987–2009: Mary Lyn Hammer Is the First Known Default Manager. She Uncovers Program Abuse and Drafts Loan Management Regulatory Language

Mary Lyn Hammer was hired by the Al Collins Graphic Design School in Tempe, Arizona, in December 1987 to conduct exit interviews and manage the default rates. To the best of our knowledge, she was the first full-time default manager in the history of the country.

While developing her default prevention program, Ms. Hammer uncovered significant and devastating program abuse by lenders and servicers. She turned over evidence to and testified numerous times before the U.S. Congress and the U.S. Department of Education in 1988 and 1989. She played a significant part in bringing down fraudulent and criminal activities in the student loan industry. Details of the scam can be found in "Borrowed Trouble: Ineptitude Causes Biggest Mess Ever in Student Loan Program" by James Bates, published on April 2, 1989 in the *Los Angeles Times*.

> *United Education's servicing problems went far beyond Pierz's account and faulty computer programs. Last summer, a review of its operation by the U.S. Department of Education and other agencies uncovered the biggest mess ever in the nation's student-loan program, one that a federal report said "caused immeasurable hardship to hundreds of thousands of borrowers" such as Pierz. The fiasco may cost as much as $650 million to straighten out, according to one estimate...*[14]

The design school's default rate when Ms. Hammer was hired was 35%. After two years under her management, the rate had been reduced to less than 10%. In addition to providing effective borrower education to the student loan borrowers, significant reductions in rates were a result of correcting the fraud and abuse with the lenders and applying appropriate payment amounts and servicing for the loans. Ms. Hammer's innovative "Hands On" Default Management program was recognized in 1989 by the U.S. Department of Education for its results.

Ms. Hammer worked diligently with the Department of Educa-

---

14. http://articles.latimes.com/1989-04-02/business/fi-1560_1_student-loan-program

tion and Dewey Newman, Deputy Assistant Secretary for Student Financial Assistance at the time, to draft comprehensive default reduction regulations that were issued on June 5, 1989 as part of a major effort to reduce the default rate of Federal Stafford Loan (formerly GSL) and Federal Supplemental Loans for Students (SLS) borrowers. The regulations were originally found in the General Provisions regulations (Part 668) and in the Federal Family Education Loan Program (FFEL) Program regulations (Part 682). Schools with high FFEL Program cohort default rates were a major focus of the default reduction regulations and of subsequent legislation focusing on the problem of defaulted loans. These actions by law and regulation required schools to provide students with additional loan counseling and to take specific steps to reduce loan defaults.[15] A significant portion of the loan management regulatory language of "Appendix D" was based on Ms. Hammer's default reduction program. These regulations were mandatory from 1989 to 1996 and amended language exists today in Subpart M and Subpart N. Ms. Hammer participated in the 2009 negotiated rulemaking process for the rewrite of Appendix D into these subpart sections.

* * * * * * * *

Defining Cohort Default Rates and Early Amendments to Refine These Laws

The Omnibus Budget Act of 1990 (H.R. 5835) (Public Law No: 101-508) defined "cohort default rate" (CDR) as a measurement for federal student loan eligibility. The CDR definition is based on the federal fiscal year, which begins on October 1st of each year and ends on September 30th of the following year. Two data points are used. The first defines the "cohort" of borrowers as the number of borrowers who enter repayment in a federal fiscal year (FFY1). The second data point defines the number of those borrowers in repayment in FFY1 who default before the end of the second federal fiscal year (FFY2). The cohort default rate is the percent of defaulters divided by the number of borrowers who entered repayment.

---

15. https://ifap.ed.gov/fsahandbook/doc0374_bodyoftext.htm

> The cohort default rate percent equals:
>
> **The number of borrowers who entered repayment in FFY1 and who defaulted before the end of FFY2**
>
> **DIVIDED BY**
>
> **The number of borrowers who entered repayment in FFY1**

The threshold for federal government student loan (GSL) eligibility measures the three most recent federal fiscal years for which data are available as follows:

1. FY 1991 and 1992: 35%

2. 30% for any succeeding fiscal year

Historically Black Colleges and Universities (HBCU) and Tribally Controlled Community Colleges (TCU) were exempt from the default rate requirements until July 1, 1994. The Secretary of Education was also given authority to waive ineligibility and continue participation based on inaccurate data or mitigating circumstances.[16]

The Higher Education Amendments of 1992 (Public Law No: 102:325) (1992 HEA or 1992 Reauthorization), Part B, defined additional terms of eligibility and measurements for school cohort default rates. Beginning with fiscal year 1994, the threshold for cohort default rates was 25% for the three most recent years in which data were available or one year in excess of 40%.[17]

Provisions included a definition of low borrower schools with provisions for averaging those with fewer than 30 borrowers; a 30-day delayed certification for first-time borrowers; expanded and defined an institution's authority to limit or refuse certification of an individual students' loan amounts; defined eligibility and loan amounts for Supplemental Loans for Students (SLS); required students admitted on the basis of ability-to-benefit (ATB tests are given to potential students who did not graduate from high school or failed to obtain a GED) to pass an independently administered examination, approved by the Secretary, as a condition of their eligibility for any student aid under Title IV of

---

16. The CRS Bill Summary for the Omnibus Budget Reconciliation Act of 1990 can be found at http://thomas.loc.gov/cgi-bin/bdquery/z?d101:HR05835:@@@D& summ2=m&%7CTOM:/bss/d101query.html%7C.

17. http://www.gpo.gov/fdsys/pkg/STATUTE-106/pdf/STATUTE-106-Pg448.pdf

HEA; amended and expanded the federal bankruptcy code regarding eligibility; changed the criteria for paying guarantee agencies for pre-claims assistance; and extended the exemption for default rate loss of eligibility for historically black colleges and universities (HBCU), tribally controlled community colleges and Navajo community colleges to July 1, 1998.

In addition, the 1993 Technical Amendments to the HEA (Public Law No: 103-208) require the annual publication of a cohort default rate for lenders, guaranty agencies, and schools. Measures enacted to facilitate the exchange of information between lenders, guaranty agencies, and schools help in locating borrowers once borrowers leave school; keeping borrowers in touch with the lender is an effective means of avoiding delinquency and default.

The Omnibus Budget Reconciliation Act of 1993, often called the Student Loan Reform Act of 1993 (Public Law No: 103-66), significantly changed the FFEL Program and set requirements for the implementation of the Federal Direct Student Loan (FDSL) Program. The DOE issued several regulations so that this law could be implemented.[18]

Federal Regulations for Default Reduction Measures were written into 34 C.F.R. 668.17[19] and were published on December 1, 1994.

When the DOE was writing federal regulations for the 1992 HEA, the 1993 Technical Amendments and the Student Loan Reform Act of 1993, they developed the first extremely discriminatory language for the private, for-profit colleges. This language was not in any of the laws.

"For proprietary, non-degree-granting schools, a direct loan is also considered to be in default on the 271st day that a borrower's scheduled payments under the Income Contingent Repayment Plan (ICR) have been less than $15 per month and less than the monthly interest accruing on the loan."

* * * * * * * *

---

18. http://www.gpo.gov/fdsys/pkg/HJOURNAL-1993/html/HJOURNAL-1993-05-05-para50-19.htm

19. http://ifap.ed.gov/regcomps/doc1432_bodyoftext.htm

History 1992–1995: Mary Lyn Hammer's Work with DOE and U.S. Lawmakers

Mary Lyn Hammer actively worked with members of the U.S. House of Representatives, U.S. Senate, and officials at the U.S. Department of Education on the Higher Education Amendments of 1992, the 1993 Technical Amendments to the HEA of 1992, and the Omnibus Budget Reconciliation Act of 1993. Her efforts led to sharing of pertinent information among lenders, servicers, and schools; appeal rights for erroneous data, improper loan servicing and collection, exceptional mitigating circumstances, economically disadvantaged and completion rates, economically disadvantaged and placement criteria, and participation rate index; expansion of repayment schedule and deferment options; and continued participation for schools that successfully brought their default rates down by 5% each year. She worked with Department of Education officials to write the regulations in 34 C.F.R. 668.17 based on these laws and helped write the first *Official Cohort Default Rate Guide.* She also aided in the revisions for the *FY 1995 Official Cohort Default Rate Guide.* She fought against discriminatory CDR language that counted loans in current status that had payments approved by the Secretary for under $15/month or in negative amortization schedule for more than 270 days as defaulted loans—only for proprietary schools.

* * * * * * * *

INJUSTICE FOR ALL INSIGHT

Common Sense

Just as we, as a citizenship, wish to transcend discrimination in our society and provide excellent higher education opportunities to all Americans, we should also ensure that laws are written to protect private enterprise and educational venues from being punished or discriminated against for being profitable while providing a valuable service.

The 2000 Negotiated Rulemaking Committee

In 1996, the Default Reduction Measures contained in "Appendix D"(34 C.F.R. 668.17) were no longer mandatory for schools with CDRs in excess of 20% and were still in regulation as suggested language for default management plans.[20]

The Higher Education Amendments of 1998 (Public Law No: 105:244), Part B and Part D, established new limits for federal grants and student loans, new grant programs, a peer review process, new programs for disadvantaged students, new interest rates and loan terms, and additional disclosure and appeal criteria, among other subjects.[21] This law also defined eligibility loss to include both federal student loans and Pell Grants. Prior to this, schools only lost federal student loan eligibility and could continue Pell Grant participation. Schools were given a one-time option to opt-out of Title IV participation to retain Pell Grant participation.

New regulatory language in 34 C.F.R. 668.17 for Default Reduction and Prevention Measures was negotiated by the 1999 Negotiated Rulemaking Committee.[22] The 2000 Negotiated Rulemaking Committee produced the following final regulations:

> **November 1, 2000—Final Regulations Part VII:** Student Assistance General Provisions, Federal Family Education Loan Program, William D. Ford Federal Direct Loan Program, and Federal Pell Grant Program for Loan Default Reduction and Prevention[23]
>
> **November 1, 2000—Final Regulations Part X:** Federal Perkins Loan Program, Federal Family Education Loan Program, William D. Ford Federal Direct Loan Program to improve and strengthen the processes for granting loan discharges based on a borrower's death or total and permanent disability[24]

* * * * * * * *

---

20. http://ifap.ed.gov/regcomps/doc0160_bodyoftext.htm

21. http://www.gpo.gov/fdsys/pkg/PLAW-105publ244/pdf/PLAW-105publ244.pdf

22. http://ifap.ed.gov/regcomps/doc4075_bodyoftext.htm

23. http://ifap.ed.gov/drmaterials/attachments/03AppendixAfederalreg.pdf

24. http://ifap.ed.gov/fregisters/attachments/1101200010.pdf

HISTORY 1998–2000: Mary Lyn Hammer Champions the Removal of Discriminatory Language

Mary Lyn Hammer actively worked with members of the U.S. House of Representatives, U.S. Senate, and officials at the U.S. Department of Education on the Higher Education Amendments of 1998. She served as an alternate negotiator for the 1999 Negotiated Rulemaking Committee for Loan Issues and as a primary negotiator for the Career College Association for the 2000 Negotiated Rulemaking Committee. The latter included the rewrite of all default management language originally written by Ms. Hammer from Appendix D into Subpart M. There were 2 goals in these negotiations:

1. to define regulations based on the 1998 Higher Education Amendments

2. to rewrite the regulatory language into the new subsection, part of reorganizing the regulations for easier understanding by the public

During the 2000 Negotiated Rulemaking, Ms. Hammer fought to remove the discriminatory language for ICR loans in good standing with payments less than $15 or in negative amortization being counted as defaults for proprietary schools only. Again, this regulatory language was not backed by any law.

The federal negotiators told Ms. Hammer that, if she could get Congressional backing to remove the language, the negotiators would remove it.

She went up on the Hill and garnered Congressional support in both the House and Senate, from both Republicans and Demo-crats. Several lawmakers, including the chairman of the U.S. House Education and Workforce Committee, Buck McKeon, wrote letters and made calls telling the DOE to remove the language.

The negotiators returned for the next round of negotiations and then were told that the DOE was keeping the language. This did not go over well with Congressional members or with Ms. Hammer. She withheld consensus at a point when all negotiators must agree on the entire regulatory package for passage until a carve-out was agreed upon recognizing that she was not in agreement with this discriminatory language.

A carve-out is rare—this was the first time it had ever happened in higher education. Under normal procedure when consensus is not reached, the entire package is not passed. The federal agency can then write regulations as it wishes, possibly taking into consideration (but this is not guaranteed) the negotiations for those sections where there was agreement.

Because Ms. Hammer continued to work with Congressional members to put heat on the DOE, the discriminatory language was removed shortly afterward.[25]

* * * * * * * *

INJUSTICE FOR ALL INSIGHT

Many Levels of Accountability

Federal laws, federal regulations and state laws have some accountability in place for institutions, teachers, and students; however, there are many areas needing improvement including insufficient accountability measures and oversight for the U.S. Department of Education at a level that adequately considers the extraordinarily complex education and funding programs. The public, schools and uninformed Congressional, Senate and government servants need to have input from expert advocates like Mary Lyn Hammer to realize the hidden implications of haphazard rulemaking and ensure the successful education of Americans.

The Grijalva-Bishop Amendment

In November 2007, the subcommittee in the U.S. House Education and Labor Committee passed an amendment to the house reauthorization bill that became known as the "Grijalva-Bishop Amendment." This combined two amendments because the rules committee had set a limit on the number of amendments that could be offered. Grijalva's original amendment required

---

25. http://www2.ed.gov/offices/OPE/rulemaking/index.html

enhanced borrower education. Bishop wanted to add an amendment, supported by the community college association president and other public institutions, that changed the cohort default rate *from a 2-year definition to an intended 3-year definition* with the same thresholds of 3 years over 25% or 1 year over 40% for loss of eligibility.

Because of the limit set on the number of allowable amendments, Grijalva allowed Bishop to add his amendment language to Grijalva's original amendment. Bishop knew that most voting members wouldn't know the implications of his amendment language, there was no public knowledge of this amendment prior to it being introduced on the floor, and that it would likely pass because everyone supported increased borrower education.

> The new CDR definition in effect beginning with the FY 2009 CDRs was as follows:
>
> **The number of borrowers who entered repayment in FFY1 and who defaulted before the end of FFY3**
>
> **<ins>DIVIDED BY</ins>**
>
> **The number of borrowers who entered repayment in FFY1**

With the new 3-year CDR definition, the thresholds were changed to three (3) years over 30% or one (1) year over 40%. There were also provisions for remaining eligible based on compliance with DOE approved default management plans with measurable objectives.

* * * * * * * *

HISTORY 2007–2008: Mary Lyn Hammer Works to Clarify Definition of CDR Rates

In November 2007, Mary Lyn Hammer was watching the votes when the amendment was introduced, and she immediately began efforts to get it taken out of the bill. She was very clear in stating that she did not agree that schools should be accountable for defaults that long after the student left school and publicly fought against it.

Then, she clarified the intent because the amendment was written as a 4-year definition when the authors were presenting what was written as a 3-year definition. Although feedback was that it had already gone in front of legal counsel, Ms. Hammer's reputation for detail allowed her to gain access to decision-makers to explain why it was a 4-year definition and get it amended to the intended 3-year definition.

In December 2007, a top official at the U.S. Department of Education called Ms. Hammer, explaining that the DOE had no way to determine the impact of the 3-year CDR on the colleges in the U.S. and asked her if she could conduct an analysis for the officials. Of course, she obliged and provided the information to both the DOE and members of Congress.

In January 2008, the Chairman's office for the House Education and Labor Committee asked Ms. Hammer and two other people to negotiate a higher threshold for eligibility and limited language for appeals. She was told that, if she brought into the negotiation any person other than the two chosen by the Chairman, the deal would be off. Over a very intense weekend of negotiating and attempts for a 35% threshold for 3 years over and 50% for 1 year over, the end result was a threshold of 3 years over 30% with no movement for 1 year over 40%. The team was also successful in getting appeal rights that recognized a school's efforts to reduce their CDR rates. These terms along with the corrected language for the 3-year CDR definition were passed through full committee and into law during the 2008 reauthorization of the Higher Education Act of 1965.

Aside from the absurd fact that a 3-year CDR definition actually holds schools accountable for student behavior for up to 4 ½ years including the grace period, the unintended consequence from this legislation is that it puts access to education funding at risk for those institutions that serve the at-risk students whom the Higher Education Act was written for in the first place.

* * * * * * * *

October 2009 Rulemaking Committees Results

The Higher Education Opportunity Act of 2008 (Public Law No: 110:315) (HEOA), Part B and Part D, established new limits and terms for federal grants and student loans, created new disclosure and reporting guidelines, changed the definition for cohort default rates from 2 to 3 years, and modified criteria for default rate appeals, among other subjects.[26]

---

26. http://www.gpo.gov/fdsys/pkg/PLAW-110publ315/pdf/PLAW-110publ315.pdf

The Ensuring Continued Access to Student Loans Act of 2008 (Public Law No: 110:227) (ECASLA) set increased aggregate student limits and an additional $2,000 per academic year for undergraduate students, defined a grace period for Parent Plus Loans and authorized a GAO report about the impact of the increased loan limits.[27]

The 2009 Negotiated Rulemaking Committees for Loan Issues, Teams I and II, produced the following final regulations based on these laws:

- **October 29, 2009**—Final Rule; Perkins, FFEL, and Direct Loan Programs in PDF Format, 36 pages

- **October 28, 2009**—Final Rule; Institutions and Lender Requirements Relating to the Title IV Student Loan Programs in PDF Format, 44 pages

HISTORY 2009: Mary Lyn Hammer Goes Head to Head with the DOE Negotiator and Legal Counsel

Mary Lyn Hammer actively worked with members of the U.S. House of Representatives, U.S. Senate, and officials at the U.S. Department of Education on the Higher Education Opportunity Act of 2008 and the Ensuring Continued Access to Student Loans Act of 2008. She served as a primary negotiator for the 2009 Negotiated Rulemaking Committee for Loan Issues–Team II and offered relevant information as a special witness to Loan Issues–Team I. There were two goals in these negotiations: to define regulations based on the HEOA and ECASLA bills and to rewrite the regulatory sections into a format that would be easier for the public to understand, part of the performance based objectives established by the Performance Based Office (PBO) within the U.S. Department of Education.

During the 2009 Negotiated Rulemaking, Ms. Hammer worked diligently to develop language that was fair and equitable to all schools and all students. She had provided suggestions and draft language to the DOE and fellow negotiators prior to Round 1 to help negotiations go smoothly and stay on schedule. The cohort default rate language was scheduled as Issue 8. Suddenly, the DOE announced that it was moving the CDR negotiations up to the third package because the DOE had a "special witness" who would not be available at the next round when those discussions were scheduled. Ms. Hammer believed this was a deliberate attempt to

27. http://www.gpo.gov/fdsys/pkg/PLAW-110publ227/html/PLAW-110publ227.htm

throw her off guard because she was usually the primary person negotiating this particular language. The committee was given a break before the negotiations began and she asked a top DOE official who the special witness was. His reply was "our legal counsel."

After the break, the negotiations became very confrontational. The special witness and federal negotiator tried presenting information to the non-federal negotiators that was not factual. The feds were not prepared for Ms. Hammer's intimate knowledge of the laws and regulations which she could state off the top of her head. She had already prepared for the negotiations. She went head to head with the DOE's negotiator and legal counsel. After many of Ms. Hammer's responses, the DOE took time away from the table to look at the laws and regulations. The most common response to Ms. Hammer's requests and input was, "The Department chooses not to comment at this time." This went on for three and a half hours.

Non-federal observers in the room were shocked at the events. A reporter from the *Career Education Review* was following Ms. Hammer that day, researching an article about "A Day in the Life of a Negotiator." He documented the entire event.

When negotiators returned to Washington for the next round of negotiations, regulatory language presented had every item that Ms. Hammer had fought for except for one piece that was not critical.

During the February 2009 negotiations, the President's Budget was released. The room sounded like a giant beehive with blackberries buzzing furiously. President Obama announced that he intended to end the FFELP program and to fund the Perkins Loan Program that was an agenda item based on the HEOA language to end the program. The DOE was as surprised as the non-federal community and negotiations ended a day and a half early. The Perkins issues were never negotiated.

The group reached consensus on the package.[28]

* * * * * * * *

---

28. http://www2.ed.gov/policy/highered/reg/hearulemaking/2009/loans-school-based.html

The History of Gainful Employment

(From here forward, I will document events out of order because of the complexity of the content. There were multiple complex events occurring at the same time.)

Where Did Gainful Employment Begin?

In November 2009, the DOE began Negotiated Rulemaking for what became known as "Gainful Employment." These were not regulations based on law—the regulations were pushed by the Obama Administration and targeted primarily toward proprietary schools using the definition for Gainful Employment (GE) to further define programs providing education that lead to gainful employment in a recognized occupation.

Education programs under 34 C.F.R. 668.8(c)(3) or (d) include:

- **All Proprietary Institution Programs** *except* those with a baccalaureate degree in liberal arts that have been regionally accredited since October 1, 2007; or preparatory courses of study that provide course work necessary for enrollment in an eligible program.

- **Nonprofit, Public, and Private Institution Programs** *except* programs that lead to a degree; programs that are at least 2 years in length and fully transferable to a bachelor's degree program; or preparatory courses of study that provide course work necessary for enrollment in an eligible program.

- **Teacher Certification Program Exclusion** applies *if* the program does *not* lead to a certificate awarded by the institution.

Here's a short summary of the events and the deception I witnessed surrounding the blatant manipulation of GE:

Gainful Employment 1.0

- **November 2009**—The GE Negotiate Rulemaking Committee did not reach consensus

- **July 26, 2010**—The DOE published the Notice of Proposed Rulemaking (NPRM) for Gainful Employment and received a record number of comments totaling over 33,000 during the comment period. The NPRM contained concepts and language that was never discussed with the Negotiated Rulemaking Committee as required.[29]

○ Final regulations were released in two groups:

1. **October 28, 2010**—Final Regulations for Program Integrity

2. **June 13, 2011**—Additional Regulations Related to Program Eligibility Metrics

○ **June 22, 2012 (Friday)**—Gainful Employment Informational Rates were released and schools had 4 days to examine the data before these rates were publicly released. The data had many difficulties including:

- Letters and data were not consistently released and came in pieces.

- Data format was difficult to convert.

- Schools didn't have time to examine data thoroughly prior to its release to the press (public).

- Delivery to the press and analysts was done in a way that placed the schools at a disadvantage.

- A "Streamlined" set of GE rates containing limited information was easily available.

- A "Final" set of GE data was more comprehensive and difficult to find—it is also the data set released to the press and analysts.

○ **June 25, 2012 (Monday)**—The DOE published an electronic announcement late in the day regarding a "Live Internet Webinar—Gainful Employment: Just Released Rates" that was occurring at 8 the next morning.[30] Select public institutions, reporters, and Wall Street people were specifically notified of the webinar. I knew about it because my company watches the announcements every day.

○ **June 26, 2012 (Tuesday)**—The DOE released the data to the public. Most received the streamlined data, and it was apparent that some on the call had a more comprehensive set of data. While

---

29. http://www2.ed.gov/legislation/FedRegister/proprule/2010-3/072610a.html

30. http://ifap.ed.gov/dpcletters/ANN1215.html

I was on the webinar and emailing contacts on Wall Street and in Washington, the following occurred:

- The DOE claimed technical difficulties with having the webinar screen available while certain participants asked questions about comprehensive data that not all of us had access to.

- My Wall Street contact began to see the screen at about 20 minutes into the webinar.

- My Washington contact who represents proprietary schools and I began to see the screen about 30 minutes into the webinar. We were viewing the host screen that showed the questions being asked and who was asking them. It was obvious that the host had no idea that we could see what he was doing.

- The host overlooked all questions from proprietary schools, my Washington contact and me, then said, "We have answered all of the questions, so we will end this early." They ended the webinar after 40 minutes.

- I began to look for and found the other set of data. My analysis of that is provided in this book *Injustice for All*.

○ DOE continued to host webinars about Gainful Employment.

○ **June 30, 2012**—The U.S. District Court of the District of Columbia vacated most of the GE regulations while upholding DOE's authority to write the regulations.

- Basis for 35% threshold for repayment rates was vacated as being arbitrary and capricious.

- Department of Education's authority was upheld.

- Debt-to-earnings ratios and reporting were upheld in spirit and only vacated because these were so "intertwined" with repayment rates that the data couldn't be "untangled."

○ DOE filed a motion asking the court to amend its decision to reinstate reporting requirements as the DOE felt effective disclosures could only be provided to students if first reported to DOE. Because DOE filed this motion to amend, THE U.S. DISTRICT COURT RULING IS NOT FINAL.

- **September 24, 2012**—The court granted an extension for the filing of related briefing to the first week of November.

- **March 19, 2013**—The court issued a decision that denied a request from the department to reinstate certain GE provisions, including the reporting requirements. The decision did not affect the GE disclosure requirements for schools.

- **June 12, 2013**—The DOE announced its intent to form a negotiated rulemaking committee for gainful employment.[31]

- **September 11, 2013**—The GE 2.0 Negotiated Rulemaking began. Even though the prior GE rules had been thrown out by the court, these rules were the basis for starting this round of negotiations. Consensus was not reached.[32]

- **March 25, 2014**—The DOE published the GE 2.0 Notice of Proposed Rulemaking (219 pages).[33] The informational data provided this time was also incomplete—for some schools, data were missing for 40% to 60% of their programs—and the DOE intended to move forward anyway.

- **November 1, 2014**—Final rules were published even though some of the rules had not been vetted out. The DOE's attitude was to publish updates if the language needed to be changed or if it couldn't implement certain rules.

- **November 2014–May 2015**—APSCU and APC filed lawsuits against the DOE. Neither lawsuit was upheld even though the suits were filed in separate courts. APSCU filed an appeal which is still pending.

---

31. http://www.gpo.gov/fdsys/pkg/FR-2013-06-12/pdf/2013-13975.pdf

32. https://www.insidehighered.com/news/2013/12/16/feds-move-next-step-gainful-employment-negotiations-end-stalemate

33. http://ifap.ed.gov/fregisters/attachments/FR032514GENPRM.pdf

⊙ **July 2015** —The GE 2.0 regulations went into effect.

From November 2009 to the date this book was completed (November 2015), the DOE has moved forward with questionable GE 2.0 language; has continued to publish questionable data with missing information so that it can't be audited; has avoided answering direct questions from Congress about many issues with the rules; and has ignored numerous requests from Congress to the DOE asking it to delay GE 2.0 implementation until Congress can reauthorize the Higher Education Act of 1965, scheduled for completion in 2016. The DOE, under the direction of the Obama Administration, has moved forward without regard to obvious issues with the rules.

Blatant Manipulation Threatens to Annihilate American Higher Education Opportunities

Gainful Employment Manipulation

On June 25, 2012, the U.S. Department of Education publicly released the FY 2011 Gainful Employment "Streamlined" Informational Rates to the press, public, and Wall Street. *The streamlined data did not contain* the detailed information that the Gainful Employment "final" data had so, for those who didn't look at the final data, assumptions were made that the streamlined data were accurate.

First, the data do not support the theory that proprietary colleges force high loan debt on their students. In fact, debt is reasonable for the education level. For post baccalaureate certificate programs, the proprietary debt is significantly lower than public and private colleges. Second, the information was incorrectly calculated and the "proprietary schools are bad" theme was based on grossly incorrect data measures. At the same time, the information was incorrectly calculated in favor of public and private institutions giving the impression that these institutions perform better than the results show—some of these data calculations were also grossly incorrect. Debt-to-earnings calculations were based upon these incorrect payment amounts and metrics calculations. Public opinion was also based on these misrepresented "failing" programs for proprietary colleges and misrepresented "passing" programs for public and private colleges.

To the best of my knowledge, the DOE never printed a rescission or publicly corrected the data upon which many conclusions and opinions were based including EDU stock values. Indictments related to GE and for leaking (incorrect) information to Wall Street short sellers and other unethical behavior has been buried more than once for Robert Shireman, former Deputy Under-secretary at the U.S. Department of Education, who was overseeing Gainful Employment 1.0. (see Chapter V. GE Manipulation for more details)

On March 25, 2014, the DOE published the GE NPRM with a link to the 2012 GE Informational Rates. The data does not contain debt information needed to verify the accuracy of GE rates provided. We question the motivation because the rates released to the public were so inaccurate for the 2011 GE Informational Rates.

HISTORY 2013: The Truth Behind the Motivations to Keep Mary Lyn Hammer from Participating as a 2013 Rulemaker

When the DOE published the intent to establish a Negotiated Rulemaking Committee for Gainful Employment, Mary Lyn Hammer called the DOE and asked if the 2013 Rulemaking was going to go into her area of expertise. She was specifically told no, so she did not throw her hat into the ring. After seeing that the negotiations definitely went into Ms. Hammer's area of expertise, in a private conversation, her Washington contact was told by a top official at the DOE that she wasn't chosen because she was the only person who could unravel its plans.

Ms. Hammer wrote an article for the *Career Education Review* about the inaccuracies in the data and reporting for the 2012 GE Informational Rates titled, "Is the Wicked Witch Really Dead: A GE Epic."

On May 30, 2013, she provided oral and written testimony regarding the data issues at a U.S. Department of Education field hearing in San Francisco, CA. Ms. Hammer was not chosen as a negotiator for the 2013 GE Negotiated Rulemaking Committee.

At the September 11, 2013 GE Negotiated Rulemaking session, Ms. Hammer spoke during the public comment period at the end of the day. In an attempt to bring reality to the negotiators in seeing that cohort default rates were manipulated by large federal student loan servicers more than small for-profit proprietary institutions, she brought forth information that led to numerous investigations about the quality of servicing that eventually led to a change in the servicing contracts and criteria for loan allocations.

On May 27, 2014, Ms. Hammer provided written comments to the DOE for the March 25, 2014 GE NPRM for Docket ID: ED-2014-OPE-0039.

* * * * * * * *

At the Same Time, the Crisis with Transition to 100% Direct Lending Began

The Health Care and Education Reconciliation Act of 2010 (Public Law No: 111-152) (HERA or HCERA) eliminated the FFELP loan program and defined the transition to 100% Direct Student Loan lending, established an opportunity for nonprofit FFELP servicers and guarantee agencies to become servicers for the direct loans. It also established an income-based repayment (IBR) schedule that cut the monthly loan payment from 15% to 10% of discretionary income and accelerated loan forgiveness from 25 years to 20 years, effective July 1, 2014.[34]

In 2012, President Obama used his regulator authority to implement the new IBR terms starting on December 21, 2012.

Congress and the DOE planned to manage a gradual transition from dual programs (FFELP and FDSLP) to 100% direct lending (FDSLP only). Many of the private lenders, secondary markets, and servicers, however, experienced only financial losses and rapidly started closing and/or exiting the student loan arena. The DOE was not prepared to take on the large volume of student loans that it suddenly had on its plate. And, tragically, students were forced to take out loans with whatever lender was left at the time, leaving the students with multiple lenders, multiple servicers, multiple payments and a loan management mess that was difficult even for those who were organized and knew something about financial literacy.

Under ECASLA, Congress authorized the DOE to purchase loans from the FFELP lenders that were disbursed on or after October 1, 2007. This action was supposed to free up cash for the FFELP lenders and keep students' loans with one holder and servicer, if possible. Congress and the DOE were hoping

---

34. http://www.gpo.gov/fdsys/pkg/PLAW-111publ152/pdf/PLAW-111publ152.pdf

this would slow down the rapid and mass exit of FFELP lenders.

The DOE had to step into high gear to purchase loans and juggle loans with servicers. It was a disaster for everyone involved, most importantly and especially the students. Loans were being transferred in large numbers and the servicing of the loans suffered. Many loans were transferred and the payments and paperwork for deferments, forbearances, disability, death claims, and various other important items were lost. Students were incorrectly labeled delinquent when they had made payments or correctly completed required documentation.

During the eight months it took for the first big loan transfer that began in January 2011 and was completed in September 2011, students' loans were in limbo. The statuses were updated in the "old" servicer's database but when the loans were loaded into the "new" servicer's database, the deferment and forbearance and many loan payments were lost. These loans showed delinquent and many were automatically put into default status. **The students had done nothing wrong yet they were in default.** This was one of many loan transfers worth millions of dollars.

Delinquent rates skyrocketed nationwide. Many students had one or more loans in good standing while at least one other was in default. It was a complete nightmare and tragedy for the students.

Several of the larger lenders and guarantee agencies went bankrupt. To keep some nonprofit FFELP players in business, Congress authorized the nonprofit guarantors under HERA to service up to 100,000 loans a year. These servicers were "trained" by a member of the DOE default management task force who had never serviced a loan. Then the servicers were phased into the federal servicing allocation for nonprofit guarantors. The measurement of "success" was different than it was for the four large federal servicers. Many of these nonprofit servicers failed to meet quality standards for servicing, another tragedy for the students.

History 2011–2013: Mary Lyn Hammer Attempts to Thwart the Impending Disaster

In October 2011, Mary Lyn Hammer traveled to Washington, DC to meet with DOE officials and members of Congress to discuss the disaster that was unfolding. Officials had no idea how bad things were and worked with her to change the process and minimize these tragedies as much as possible under the circumstances. Unfortunately, the situation dictated hundreds of thousands of tragic financial outcomes for the students.

Ms. Hammer's company represented thousands of students caught in the financial disaster that was unfolding. Her staff hand-held students through many frustrating and costly phone calls. In fact, the call length for these students increased from approximately 3 minutes to 45 minutes because the students with her company had to make 3-way calls to EVERY servicer involved to manage each loan separately.

The process of helping the students caught in the transition from FFELP to 100% direct lending coupled with the extreme numbers of loan transfers to and from federal loan servicers and when companies went out of business caused immense stress to student borrowers and increased defaults for those who didn't have anyone who cared to hold the students' hands through the process. Luckily, Ms. Hammer and her staff pride themselves in doing so.

On August 28, 2013, Ms. Hammer provided written comments to loan issues contained in a Notice of Proposed Rulemaking with reference: Docket ID ED-2013-OPE-0063.[35]

On September 10, 2013, Mary Lyn Hammer spoke in open forum at the Gainful Employment 2.0 Negotiated Rulemaking session in Washington, DC about these statistics knowing that the people in the room were the people who would take action with this alarming information. This was in addition to recorded calls with students and other documentation that she had been providing to members of Congress and the DOE.

Investigations into the quality of servicing by those under contract for servicing federal direct student loans (Title IV Additional Servicers or TIVAS) escalated.

Many unethical and some illegal practices were brought to light

---

35. http://ifap.ed.gov/fregisters/FR072913ProposeRulemaking.html

although little action was taken, certainly not sufficient to repair the damage to the students and schools who suffered long-term consequences from their abhorrent practices. All of the companies are still receiving large percentages of student loans every year.

On August 29, 2014, the U.S. Department of Education announced that it had renegotiated contracts with the federal student loan servicers to strengthen the quality of servicing.[36]

* * * * * * * *

Expansion of the "Pay-As-You-Earn" Repayment Plan

On September 3, 2014, the DOE announced their intent to form a Negotiated Rulemaking Committee to expand the President's "Pay-As-You-Earn" (PAYE) repayment plan to more borrowers.[37]

HISTORY 2014: Mary Lyn Hammer Attempts to Protect the Best Interests of Students, Schools and Taxpayers

Ms. Hammer testified[38] at the October 23, 2014 hearing in Washington, DC to avail participants of the costly and devastating choices that often come from the Pay-As-You-Earn, Income Contingent Repayment, and Income Based Repayment plans. Those options are not always in the best interest of the borrower and should not be used as a "one size fits all" plan because each borrower's circumstances should be considered. Ms. Hammer's company often and regularly has instances where federal loan servicers say that the "Pay-As-You-Earn" program is their top initiative and the servicers try to put the borrowers into the program **even when the borrower understands** that action is not his or her best option or if the borrower has said no. Ms. Hammer has provided evidence of this to the DOE and members of Congress in hopes that the students' best interest will be protected.

---

36. http://www.ed.gov/news/press-releases/us-department-education-strengthens-federal-student-loan-servicing

37. https://www.federalregister.gov/articles/2014/09/03/2014-20977/negotiated-rulemaking-committee-public-hearings, and http://www.gpo.gov/fdsys/pkg/FR-2014-09-03/html/2014-20977.htm

38. Details that were used in Ms. Hammer's testimony are included within the book *Injustice for All*.

When the Government Is Running a "Direct Loan Program," Who Has Accountability Oversight?

On September 22, 2014, the DOE released the 3-year cohort default rates for FY 2009, FY 2010 and FY 2011. This was the first year to use three 3-year CDRs to determine eligibility.[39]

On September 23, 2014, the DOE published a notice announcing the "Adjustment of Calculation of Official Three Year Cohort Default Rates for Institutions Subject to Potential Loss of Eligibility."[40]

As the reason for doing so, the DOE explains the following which has existed since 2010 but has not been addressed until 2014:

> *In recent years there have been significant changes in the administration of the Federal student loan programs. Under the Ensuring Continued Access to Student Loans Act (ECASLA) of 2008, the Department acquired, and became responsible for the servicing of, more than 25 million Federal Family Education Loan (FFEL) Program loans for almost 12 million borrowers with an aggregate outstanding balance of more than $110 billion. In 2010, in accordance with SAFRA legislation, part of the Health Care and Education Reconciliation Act of 2010, on or after July 1, 2010 all federal student loans were required to be made under the direct loan program, with no new loan originations under the FFEL Program. As a result of these events, the incidence of borrowers with loans held by multiple lenders and serviced by more than one servicer has increased. Many borrowers, for example, have one or more Title IV student loans serviced by a FFEL Program lender/servicer and, at the same time, one or more loans serviced by a Federal loan servicer (split-servicing). This is particularly the case for the cohorts of borrowers who are included in the three-year Cohort Default Rate calculations. This is because these cohorts include many borrowers who took out loans both before and after the Department's acquisition of FFEL Program loans under ECASLA and the transition to 100% direct lending.*

---

39. http://ifap.ed.gov/eannouncements/092214FY20113YearOfficialCohortDefaultR atesDistributedSept222014.html

40. http://ifap.ed.gov/eannouncements/092314AdjustmentofCalculationofOfc3YrC DRforInstitutSubtoPotentialLossofElig.html

On September 23, 2014, the DOE published a notice announcing "Erroneous Data Appeal—Incorrect Borrower Enrollment," which instructs the data manager to accept corrections for erroneous and incorrect borrower enrollment even when the enrollment correction was not timely submitted as required. [41]

On September 30, 2015, the DOE published the 2015 Official FY 2012 iCDR Briefing and posted the relevant 2012 iCDR PEPS300 Data which included data for FY 2010–2012. The information didn't match—again—and an even more drastic manipulation of reporting emerged that now included the private sector.

The DOE didn't publish an electronic announcement advising of adjusted rates; however, schools received individual letters stating there were adjustments.

Additionally, the DOE has not included its own direct loan data in the Loan Holder Data posted on its website for the last two years. These unreported data and rates show very high rates when compared to the remaining FFELP portfolios that are included in the national iCDR rates—so the direct loan iCDRs are driving the national rates and institution rates up and it will soon be evident that this is happening as fewer and fewer FFELP loans are included in the national rates.

Certain conduit and PUT Loan iCDRs over the last four years have been just under 60% iCDRs and represent hundreds of thousands of students who have suffered and are still suffering the consequences of defaulted loans when the onus is on the government's poor management of the transition to 100% direct lending—could this be the real reason the Obama Administration and the DOE are grossly misreporting CDR information for loan programs and institutions and trying so hard to blame everything on the proprietary sector? Please, examine all of the evidence in *Injustice for All* and decide for yourself.

---

41. http://ifap.ed.gov/eannouncements/092314ErronousDataAppealIncorrectBorrow erEnroll.html

The Bottom Line:
Quality Oversight for Everyone

Information provided in the Manifesto and throughout this book documents purposeful actions by the Obama Administration to use the U.S. Department of Education to eliminate the FFEL Program so that loans are now government run. This authority has also been used to tarnish the reputations of all proprietary schools through deceitful reporting to the public to gain support for extreme federal regulations that most nonprofit institutions would fail.

The DOE's misreporting for loan programs has been used to cover up its own mishandling and poor servicing of student loans. With 100% direct student lending, there is a lack of oversight, and the DOE's self-reporting is being used to cover up gross negligence and devastating results for students. And, students no longer have a choice—we are stuck with 100% government lending for student loans.

The DOE has also used its authority to try to eliminate an entire sector of schools that serve at-risk students better than any other sector. We are well on our way to having 100% nonprofit institutions that heavily rely on federal and state funding—is this direction headed toward government run education? Are we sure that these nonprofit institutions produce quality solely based on their tax-filing status— the data examined in Injustice for All *certainly doesn't support this theory.*

Americans need to speak up for quality education—which can only be ensured by having quality metrics for all parties to education funding including the DOE and where institution quality metrics apply to all institutions. Most of all, there need to be quality metrics for those who control all of this—the DOE.

Without quality and oversight of every aspect, we risk losing one of our greatest freedoms—the opportunity for higher education that promotes a healthy nation.

Is there an agenda that has nothing to do with educating America?

Consistencies in inaccurate reporting through multiple databases, reports, and U.S. Department of Education briefings strongly yield patterns that support an agenda that appears to be twofold: *first,* to eliminate for-profit FFELP companies for federal student loans and; *second,* to eliminate for-profit institutions of higher education. The first has been accomplished. The second is well on its way. Neither has been supported by accurate information put forth by the U.S. Department of Education. Neither has anything to do with providing quality education for Americans.

III. CDR REPORTING INACCURACIES

National Cohort Default Rate

Do you find it difficult to believe that this many instances of misreported information is a simple oversight? OR are you starting to see that the manipulation may well be intentional? Let us not be so ignorant as to think that what has been uncovered thus far encompasses all the DOE's manipulation—there may be more.

Eliminating the Private Sector in Federal Student Loans

A month after President Obama was sworn into office in 2009, he released his first "President's Budget." I was sitting in a room at the U.S. Department of Education where Negotiated Rulemaking was being conducted. I was a primary negotiator for the Team II Loan Issues that were defined during the 2008 Reauthorization of the Higher Education Act of 1965. When the budget announced the intent to eliminate all Federal Family Education Loan Program (FFEL or FFELP) loans, smart phones started vibrating simultaneously and it was like we were sitting in the middle of a beehive. Half of the attendees sitting in the room were people from the FFELP community and we all knew that their jobs were on the line and the future in education might forever be changed. The DOE employees were equally shocked and that round of negotiations ended early—shortly after the announcement. *It was the start of a new America, one where prosperity was suddenly bad and should be eliminated.*

The Federal Family Education Loan Program represents those Federal Stafford, PLUS, and Consolidated Student Loans made by private loan holders (lenders, banks, credit unions, or secondary markets) and "guaranteed" by federal loan guarantee agencies. If the borrower defaults, the loan holders are "reimbursed" a percent of the student loan by the guaranty agency who is then reimbursed a percent and the debt is, then, managed by the U.S. Department of Education, usually through a collection agency. Most FFELP entities are privately held or publicly traded companies and a few are nonprofit.

The Federal Direct Student Loans (FDSLP, FDSL or direct loans) are made by the government directly to the students and cut out the "middle men" or the lenders, secondary markets and guarantee agencies. The government contracts with the federal loan servicers to collect these loans. The larger federal servicers are known as TIVAS and several nonprofit guarantee agencies have also become federal servicers on a limited basis. Ironically, some of the companies chosen for servicing the federal direct loans *are the same FFELP companies* accused of being "greedy and unethical" and therefore eliminated with the FFELP programs. (Words from the folks who eliminated FFELP, not mine.)

On March 26, 2010, the Health Care and Education Reconciliation Act of 2010[41] abolished the FFEL Program and no subsequent loans under this program were made after June 30, 2010. President Obama promoted this decision in hundreds of speeches that began as part of his 2008 election campaign and continue to date. Little did the public know that the actual profits to the government would well exceed the collective profits of the FFELP community. For example, the government's profit on federal student loans in 2013 was $41.3 billion! Is there any wonder why the 2014 profit has not been released?

Transitioning to a 3-year Cohort Default Rate

The 2008 reauthorization changed the cohort default rate definition from a 2-year measure to a 3-year measure. The first official 3-year cohort default rate as defined in the Higher Education Opportunity Act of 2008[42] were released in September 2012 and began with the FY 2009 cohort of borrowers. This meant that the first official 3-year CDRs were released during the 2012 presidential election campaign.

---

41. http://www.gov/fdsys/pkg/PLAW-111publ152/pdf/PLAW-111publ152.pdf

42. http://www2.ed.gov/policy/highered/leg/hea08/index.html

Injustice for All Insight

What constitutes a monopoly?

The Health Care and Education Reconciliation Act of 2010 abolished the Federal Family Education Loan Program (FFELP) and no subsequent loans were permitted to be made under the program after June 30, 2010. This eliminated ALL private federal student loans and many jobs in the United States. It also ended the competitive environment for quality and standards as well as the students' choice between private and direct Federal Stafford Loans for their education funding.

mo•nop•o•ly
mə'näpəlē/
n., pl. -**lies.**

1. *exclusive control of a commodity or service that makes possible the manipulation of prices*

2. *the exclusive possession or control of something*

3. *something that is the subject of such control, as a commodity or service*

4. *a company or group that has such control*

5. *the market condition that exists when there is only one seller*

As a negotiator for Negotiated Rulemaking, I can't tell you the number of times I've heard the response, "The Department doesn't have to regulate itself." So, who does regulate the DOE?

The change came from the Grijalva-Bishop Amendment[43] that defined the 3-year CDR and passed through the House subcommittee in November 2007 before being passed in both houses. The original supporters for this amendment included traditional colleges[44] and community colleges. The intent of the amendment was to eliminate for-profit colleges so that more Pell Grant money would be available for the nonprofit schools. It was clear at the time, that little consideration was given to the fact that as for-profit schools were put out of business, the at-risk students would migrate to the community colleges and other nonprofit schools—with them would come the same high default rates that for-profit schools had ALWAYS encountered because they cater primarily to at-risk students.

I worked tirelessly to fight against the Grijalva-Bishop Amendment[45] that would limit education opportunities for at-risk students. The original statutory language increased the default rates to a 4-year definition. Since the original intent was to define a 3-year CDR, I worked closely with Congressional members and legal representatives to clean up the language. Over a weekend in January 2008, I was among three people who crafted a gentler, kinder version[46] of this amendment that allowed an increase from 25% to 30% for the 3-consecutive-years' threshold for loss of Title IV Eligibility and an option for continued participation when "measureable objectives" had been met in the school's approved cohort default rate management plan.

This transition period to the new 3-year CDR definition created an opportunity for inaccurate reporting of cohort default rates because there was no historic data for comparative analysis.

---

43. http://www.congress.gov/amendment/110th-congress/house-amendment/939/text

44. http://www.aau.edu/WorkArea/DownloadAsset.aspx?id=1818

45. http://championcollegeservices.com/wp-content/uploads/2015/07/2008_01_16_PRESS_RELEASE_-_Increased_Cohort_Default_Rate_Definition_Has_Negative_Implications.pdf

46. http://www.insidehighered.com/news/2008/02/06/hea

Injustice for All Insight

What motivates the U.S. Department of Education and certain lawmakers to push the "successes" of the FDSLP?

The U.S. Department of Education and certain lawmakers may also have significant incentives to make their "direct loan program" (FDSLP) successful in the public eye. In addition to putting private companies out of business and citizens out of work, the decision to transition to 100% direct lending for student loans also put the burden of financing 100% of all federal student loans on the backs of unknowing taxpayers. This student loan financing burden is a large part of the national deficit because private banks no longer finance student loans— taxpayers do. If taxes don't bring in enough money to finance education, we borrow the money.

**Then, there is the profit to the federal government...
2013 Government Profit from Federal Student Loans:
$41.3 Billion!**

What does all of this REALLY mean to American citizens?

1. *Taxpayers finance federal student loans.*
2. *The Federal Government profits from the student loans—and the profits go into the general fund, NOT back into educating America!*

Overpromised, Under-Delivered and Now Lying about It

The FY 2009 3-year cohort default rates for the FFEL and FDSL loan programs appear to have been manipulated by the Department to justify the decision to get rid of private for-profit lenders for federal student loans and to cover up the shortcomings of its management of the student loan program since the transition to 100% direct lending began in 2010.

Public institutions represented the majority of schools participating in the FDSL Program prior to the elimination of the FFEL Program.

President Obama and the U.S. Department of Education had a vested interest in the performance of direct loans that escalated default rates with the transition to 100% direct lending for federal student loans.

Is it a coincidence that the number of defaults *missing* in the FDSLP Briefing is almost the same as the number of defaults *added to* the FFELP Briefing?[47]

Table 15: Comparison of 2012 Official FY 2009 3YR Loan Program DOE Briefings to 2014 Official Data Facts

		2012 Official FY 2009 3-year CDR	DOE BRIEFINGS for FDSLP & FFELP 2012 Official FY 2009 3-year CDR	OFFICIAL LOAN DATA 2012 Official FY 2009 3-year CDR	
FDSLP	Borrowers in Default	66,028	What the Public Saw 8.6% FDSLP CDR	195,884	What the Public SHOULD Have Seen 23.9% FDSLP CDR
FDSLP	Borrowers Entered Repayment	764,662	129,856 FEWER defaults than the data shows	819,322	What the Public SHOULD Have Seen 23.9% FDSLP CDR
FFELP	Borrowers in Default	425,651	What the Public Saw 14.6% FDSLP CDR	295,355	What the Public SHOULD Have Seen 10.6% FDSLP CDR
FFELP	Borrowers Entered Repayment	2,912,027	130,296 MORE defaults than the data shows	2,785,365	What the Public SHOULD Have Seen 10.6% FDSLP CDR

47. These two resource files are no longer available:

   a. http://www2.ed.gov/offices/OSFAP/defaultmanagement/3yrffelrates.pdf
   b. http://www2.ed.gov/offices/OSFAP/defaultmanagement/3yerdlrates.pdf

The total numbers of defaulted borrowers and borrowers entered repayment are strikingly similar when the loan program information is added together.

Table 16: 2012 Comparison of FY 2009 3YR Totals of Loan Program Briefings vs 2014 Total Loan Holder Data Facts

INFORMATION SOURCE	Total Borrowers in Default	Total Borrowers Entered Repayment
2012 DOE Briefings for FDSL & FFEL	491,679	3,676,689
2014 Official Loan Holder Data	491,239	3,604,687

There is _only a 440 defaulted borrowers' difference_ between what was subtracted from the 2012 Official FY 2009 3-year FDSLP CDR than were added to the 2012 Official FY 2009 3-year FFELP CDR.

In 2012, the Department did not release a full set of data for loan holders. Without the comprehensive data, there was no way to validate the default rate data contained in the Official Briefings posted for the FDSLP and FFELP FY 2009 3-year Cohort Default Rates. The DOE did, however, release a PDF file with a list of the "Top 100 Loan Holders" that represented very similar numbers to the September 2014 Official FY 2009 3-year Lender Data.

The 2013 release of FY 2010 3-year cohort default rate for the FDSL loan program appears to have also been manipulated by the Department and **is no longer available on the IFAP website.** We do not have a 2013 file on record for FFELP and cannot verify if this was an oversight or if it was never published. To my knowledge, 2013 was the last year any loan program level default rates were publicly released in DOE Briefings.

Is it a coincidence that the same pattern emerged for underreporting the FDSLP default rate for the FY 2010 3-year CDR released the following year?

Everything looks normal...until the DOE Briefings are compared to the available data.

Table 17: 2012 DOE Briefing for FDSLP FY 2009 3YR CDR (DOE PowerPoint)

FY 2009 3-Year FDSLP Cohort Default Rates
Calculated August 5, 2012

	Number of Schools (3-Year)	Borrower Default Rate (%) (3-Year)	Number of Borrowers Defaulted (3-Year)	Number of Borrowers Entered Repayment (3-Year)
Public	**497**	**7.3%**	**40,205**	**543,634**
Less than 2 yrs	10	11.3%	46	405
2-3 yrs	193	15.9%	12373	77676
4yrs(+)	294	5.9%	27786	465553
Private	**363**	**6.6%**	**7,344**	**110,058**
Less than 2 yrs	13	23.0%	606	2,627
2-3 yrs	26	14.5%	194	1,333
4yrs(+)	324	6.1%	6,544	106,098
Proprietary	**1,114**	**16.6%**	**18,479**	**110,969**
Less than 2 yrs	617	17.4%	8,303	47,550
2-3 yrs	368	16.4%	6,086	37,053
4 yrs(+)	129	15.5%	4,090	26,366
Foreign	**1**	**0.0%**	**0**	**1**
Unclassified	**0**	**0.0%**	**0**	**0**
Total	**1,975**	**8.6%**	**66,028**	**764,662**

Table 18: 2012 DOE Briefing for FFELP FY 2009 3YR CDR (DOE PowerPoint)

FY 2009 3-Year FFEL Cohort Default Rates
Calculated August 5, 2012

	Number of Schools (3-Year)	Borrower Default Rate (%) (3-Year)	Number of Borrowers Defaulted (3-Year)	Number of Borrowers Entered Repayment (3-Year)
Public	**1,505**	**12.4%**	**157,321**	**1,265,146**
Less than 2 yrs	137	16.5%	1,157	7,004
2-3 yrs	794	18.6%	82,971	444,077
4yrs(+)	574	8.9%	73,193	814,065
Private	**1,616**	**7.6%**	**56,249**	**736,484**
Less than 2 yrs	32	23.2%	345	1,485
2-3 yrs	163	14.4%	2,167	14,952
4yrs(+)	1,421	7.4%	53,737	720,047
Proprietary	**1,556**	**23.4%**	**211,435**	**901,616**
Less than 2 yrs	689	23.5%	19,634	83,320
2-3 yrs	589	23.8%	58,321	244,749
4 yrs(+)	278	23.2%	133,480	573,547
Foreign	**427**	**7.3%**	**646**	**8,776**
Unclassified	**1**	**0.0%**	**0**	**5**
Total	**5,105**	**14.6%**	**425,651**	**2,912,027**

Missing: The original files for the FY 2009 FDSLP 3-year CDR (3yrdlrates) and FY 2009 FFELP 3-year CDR (3yrffelrates) are no longer available on the U.S. Department of Education website.

Table 19: Comparison of 2013 Official FY 2010 Loan Program DOE Briefing to 2014 Official Data Facts

	2012 Official FY 2010 3-year CDR	DOE BRIEFINGS for FDSLP & FFELP 2012 Official FY 2010 3-year CDR		OFFICIAL LOAN DATA 2012 Official FY 2010 3-year CDR	
FDSLP	Borrowers in Default	137,977	What the Public Saw 12.8% FDSLP CDR	404,525	What the Public SHOULD Have Seen 16.5% FDSLP CDR
	Borrowers Entered Repayment	1,069,612	266,548 FEWER defaults and 1,382,780 FEWER borrowers than the data show	2,451,392	
FFELP	Borrowers in Default		What the Public DIDN'T See *To my knowledge, the DOE did not publish a Briefing for the FFEL Program in 2013.*	295,355	What the Public SHOULD Have Seen 9.6% FDSLP CDR
	Borrowers Entered Repayment			2,785,365	

Missing: The original file name (3yrdlrates) for the FY 2010 FDSLP 3-year CDR was the same as the FY 2009 FDSLP 3-year CDR and is no longer available on the U.S. Department of Education website.

Table 20: 2013 DOE Briefing for FDSLP FY 2010 3YR CDR (DOE PowerPoint)

	Fiscal Year 2009 Official				Fiscal Year 2010 Official			
	# of Schools	Borrower Default Rate (%)	# of Borrowers Defaulted	# of Borrowers Entered Repayment	# of Schools	Borrower Default Rate (%)	# of Borrowers Defaulted	# of Borrowers Entered Repayment
Public	497	7.3%	40,205	543,634	805	11.0%	76,520	689,727
Less than 2 yrs	10	11.3%	46	405	22	17.0%	118	692
2-3 yrs	193	15.9%	12,373	77,676	339	23.1%	28,937	125,196
4yrs(+)	294	5.9%	27,786	465,553	444	8.4%	47,465	563,839
Private	363	6.6%	7,344	110,058	700	8.8%	13,149	149,270
Less than 2 yrs	13	23.0%	606	2,627	21	22.5%	821	3,637
2-3 yrs	26	14.5%	194	1,333	40	15.5%	287	1,842
4yrs(+)	324	6.1%	6,544	106,098	639	8.3%	12,041	143,791
Proprietary	1,114	16.6%	18,479	110,969	1,502	20.9%	48,308	230,598
Less than 2 yrs	617	17.4%	8,303	47,550	759	21.1%	17,815	84,065
2-3 yrs	368	16.4%	6,086	37,053	501	20.9%	15,463	73,739
4 yrs(+)	129	15.5%	4,090	26,366	242	20.6%	15,030	72,794
Foreign	1	0.0%	0	1	15	0.0%	0	17
Unclassified	0	0.0%	0	0	0	0.0%	0	0
TOTAL	1,975	8.6%	66,028	764,662	3,922	12.8%	137,977	1,069,612

Comparison of FY 2010 3-Year Official "FDSLP" Cohort Default Rates to Prior Official "FDSLP" Calculations Calculated July 28, 2013

March 2015: The 2012 Official FY 2009 3-year CDR Briefings for FDSLP and FFELP, and the 2013 Official FY 2010 3-year CDR Briefing for FDSLP posted by the U.S. Department of Education cannot be located by the original file names and are *no longer available* on the IFAP website.

What Else Does the Actual Loan Holder Data Show?

The U.S. Department of Education publicly released comprehensive data for student loan holders in September 2014 that included FY 2009, FY 2010 and FY 2011 3-year cohort default rate data. The information should include data for each lender ID with borrowers in the defined CDR. This data were used for our analysis.

The lender data released in September 2014 matched the available information, highlighted below in gray, in the "Top 100 Loan Holders" published in 2012 for the lender ID (LID) information for U.S. Department of Education loans.

Table 21: 2014 Official FY 2009 3YR DOE-controlled Loan Data
("Top 100 Loan Holder" information is highlighted in gray)
DOE Data File Name: FY 2009 3-year Lender Official CDR

LENDER NAME (# Placement in Top 100 Loan Holders)	Current Rate	Current Default	Current Repayment
U.S. DEPT OF ED/2008-2009 LPCP (#1)	21.2%	148,171	697,298
US DEPT OF ED/2007-2008 STPP (#9)	27.1%	19,598	72,201
US DEPT OF ED/ABCP CONDUIT 09-10 (#14)	**59.8%**	**26,774**	**44,769**
US DEPT OF ED/ABCP CONDUIT 09-10	**54.3%**	**1,294**	**2,381**
US DEPT OF ED/REHABS	0.9%	24	2,499
US DEPT OF ED/COND DISB DSCHRGS	13.2%	23	174
US DEPT OF ED TOTAL	**23.9%**	**195,884**	**819,322**

Total DOE Loan Volume: $3,959,732,959

The CDRs for the DOE conduit portfolios were extremely high with both conduit portfolios pushing 60%.

When the comprehensive loan holder data was compared to two other sets of available data and the DOE's Official National FY 2009 3-year CDR Briefing for Institutions, there was less than a 1% variance in the percent of Borrowers Entered Repayment (approximately 22.7%) and less than a 2% variance in the percent of Borrowers in Default (approximately 40%). (see Table 22)

Table 22: Comparison of FY 2009 3YR DOE iCDR Briefings, iCDR Data, & Loan Holder Data

Compared to Institution (PEPS300) Data & DOE Briefings

DESCRIPTION	CDR%	Borrowers in Default	Borrowers Entered Repayment
2014 Official Lender Data	13.6%	491,239	3,604,687
Total Loan Holder Dollars in Repayment: $33,891,209,987			
2014 Official iCDR PEPS300 Data	13.2%	476,744	3,612,320
2014 Official 3-yr CDRs Briefing	13.4%	489,040	3,629,109
Comparison of USDOE Portfolio to Available Information			
US Dept of Ed Portfolio	23.9%	195,884	819,322
% of Official Lender Data	n/a	39.9%	22.7%
USDOE represents 11.7% of total Loan Holder Volume: $3,959,732,595			
This dollar volume *represents about half* of the reported percentage of Borrowers Entered Repayment volume.			
% of Official PEPS300 Data	n/a	41.1%	22.7%
% of Official 3-yr CDR Briefing	n/a	40.1%	22.6%

There is less than 2% variance among available information for the percentage of Borrowers in Default and the percentage of Borrowers Entered Repayment.

The percent of total dollar volume (approximately 11.7%) *was not* consistent with the percent of Borrowers Entered Repayment (approximately 22.7%). The unlikely situation where the DOE's dollar volume is approximately half of the percent of Borrowers Entered Repayment brings into question the possible underreporting of dollar volume for DOE LID portfolios.

The percent of Borrowers in Default (approximately 40%) *was almost twice as high* as the percentage of Borrowers Entered Repayment (approximately 22.7%).

The FY 2010 Loan Holder Data *showed a significant drop* in USDOE portfolio default rate; however, the current rate for the CDRs for the conduit portfolio remained extremely high and is still pushing 60%.

Table 23: 2014 Official FY 2010 3YR DOE-controlled Loan Data
DOE Data File Name: FY 2010 3-YR GA and Lender Rates

LENDER NAME	Current Rate	Current Default	Current Repayment
U.S. DEPT OF ED/2008-2009 LPCP	14.5%	226,621	1,558,484
U.S. DEPT OF ED/2009-2010 LPCP	18.2%	148,636	815,265
US DEPT OF ED/ABCP CONDUIT 09-10	**56.6%**	**25,433**	**44,872**
US DEPT OF ED/2007-2008 STPP	11.8%	3,831	32,411
US DEPT OF ED/COND DISB DSCHRGS	0.6%	2	331
US DEPT OF ED/REHABS	6.8 %	2	29
US DEPT OF ED TOTAL	**16.5%**	**404,525**	**2,451,392**

Total DOE Loan Volume: $8,107,367,310

When this comprehensive Loan Holder data was compared to two other available data sources, the USDOE's percent of Borrowers Entered Repayment (approximately 60%) and Borrowers in Default (approximately 69%) are both within 3% variance of all available data and information. (see Table 24)

Table 24: Comparison of FY 2010 3YR DOE iCDR Briefing, iCDR Data & Loan Holder Data

DESCRIPTION	CDR%	Borrowers in Default	Borrowers Entered Repayment
2014 Official Lender Data	13.5%	577,997	4,266,682
Total Loan Holder Dollars in Repayment: $28,333,184,664			
2014 Official iCDR PEPS300 Data	14.5%	587,703	4,059,740
2014 Official 3-yr CDRs Briefing	14.7%	600,545	4,082,570
Comparison of USDOE Portfolio to Other Available Information			
US Dept of Ed Portfolio	16.5%	404,525	2,451,392
% of Official Lender Data	n/a	70.0%	57.5%
USDOE represents 28.6% of total Loan Holder Volume: $8,107,367,310			
This dollar volume **represents about half** of the reported percentage of Borrowers Entered Repayment volume.			
% of Official PEPS300 Data	n/a	68.8%	60.4%
% of Official 3-yr CDR Briefing	n/a	67.4%	60.0%

There is less than 3% variance among available information for the percentage of Borrowers in Default and the percentage of Borrowers Entered Repayment.

The DOE's percent of Borrowers Entered Repayment is approximately 57.5%, yet the total loan dollar volume reported was only 28.6% of total. The unlikely scenario of having half the dollar volume compared to percent of Borrowers Entered Repayment solicits questions about under-reporting of dollar volume associated with the DOE LID portfolios.

The USDOE's percent of Borrowers in Default is significantly higher than the percent of Borrowers Entered Repayment.

The DOE's percent of Borrowers Entered Repayment is 71.1% but the percent of total dollar volume is only 56.6%. Again, especially with the transition to 100% direct lending that began in July 2010, this percentage is unlikely and points to possible unreported dollar volume.

The USDOE's percent of Borrowers Entered Repayment in the 2014 Official FY 2011 3-year CDR Lender Data appeared to be low based on estimates for transitioning to 100% direct lending; however, the USDOE's percent of Borrowers Entered Repayment in both of the other available data are not. The lower volume in the lender data also showed the Borrowers in Default slightly higher than the Borrowers Entered Repayment which is a significant decrease from the historic pattern of defaults being significantly higher but moderately declining each year.

Table 25: 2014 Official FY 2011 DOE-controlled Loan Data
DOE Data File Name: Webposting for Brian Schelling FY 2011 3-Year GA and LENDER 091014

LENDER NAME	Current Rate	Current Default	Current Repayment
U.S. DEPT OF EDUCATION/2009-2010 LPCP	11.9%	217,165	1,819,928
U.S. DEPT OF ED/2008-2009 LPCP	7.3%	71,900	983,430
US DEPT OF ED/ABCP CONDUIT 09-10	**58.6%**	**14,455**	**24,666**
US DEPT OF ED/2007-2008 STPP	8.2%	1,326	16,046
US DEPT OF ED/COND DISB DSCHRGS	1.6%	2	118
US DEPT OF ED/REHABS	0.0%	0	22
US DEPT OF ED TOTAL	**10.7%**	**304,848**	**2,844,210**

Total DOE Loan Volume: $16,208,622,744

It is not likely that the Department's percent of institutional (PEPS300) volume decreased from 60.4% in FY 2010 to 59.4% in FY 2011 or that the volume remained *virtually* the same when compared to the DOE's Official Briefings of 60.0% in FY 2010 to 60.1% in FY 2011 when the government eliminated private lenders for student loans in 2010. This percent would most likely increase fairly dramatically with the full transition to direct lending.

Table 26: Comparison of FY 2011 3YR DOE iCDR Briefing, iCDR Data and Loan Holder Data

Description	CDR%	Borrowers in Default	Borrowers Entered Repayment
2014 Official Lender Data	10.3%	410,463	4,002,351
Total Loan Holder Dollars in Repayment: $28,882,758,718			
2014 Official iCDR PEPS300 Data	13.6%	649,275	4,787,729
2014 Official 3-yr CDRs Briefing	13.7%	650,727	4,732,793
Comparison of USDOE Portfolio to Other Available Information			
US Dept of Ed LIDs Portfolio	10.7%	304,848	2,844,210
% of Official iCDR Lender Data	n/a	74.3%	71.1%
USDOE represents 56.1% of total Loan Holder Volume: $16,208,622,744 This dollar volume represents less than 80% of the percentage of Borrowers Entered Repayment volume.			
% of Official PEPS300 Data	n/a	47.0%	59.4%
% of Official 3-yr CDR Briefing	n/a	46.8%	60.1%

It is unlikely that the DOE's percent of total PEPS300 Data and Briefings *would stay virtually the same as the prior year when all new loans* in the FY 2011 CDR would have been 100% direct lending.

With Table 26, the 2014 Official Lender Data was compared to the 2014 Official PEPS300 Data, and there was a significant volume of unreported data. We subtracted the total Lender Data from the total PEP300 Data to determine the approximate missing data.

Where Did the Direct Loan Volume Go?

When the loan holder volume was increased to be consistent with the institution (PEPS300) data, the USDOE's percent of Borrowers Entered

Repayment increased from 57.5% in FY 2010 to approximately 75.8% in FY 2011 and was more consistent with a transition to 100% direct lending that began in July 2010.

With the addition of the unreported data, the DOE volume increased to 75.8% of the portfolio and the variance in comparison of loan holder data to the institutional data and DOE Briefing was less than 1%. These percentages are consistent with the transition to 100% direct loans.

There is no way to calculate the USDOE's percent of total dollar volume because we have no data for the dollar amount associated with the unreported loans. With the addition of the unreported direct loan volume, the percent of Borrowers in Default is more consistent with historical data and remains significantly higher than the percent of Borrowers Entered Repayment.

Table 27: Adjusted FY 2011 3YR DOE-controlled CDR Loan Data
Compared to DOE Briefings & Institution (PEPS300) Data

Adjusted with Unreported Data	FY 2011 3-year CDR		
Description	CDR%	Borrowers in Default	Borrowers Entered Repayment
LENDER DATA SHORTAGE COMPARED TO FY 2011 PEPS	**30.4%**	**238,812**	**785,378**
(Adjusted) 2014 Official Lender Data	13.6%	649,275	4,787,729
(Adjusted) US Dept of Ed LIDs Portfolio	16.5%	543,660	3,629,588
% of Official Lender Data	n/a	83.7%	75.8%
% of Official PEPS300 Data	n/a	83.7%	75.8%
% of Official 3-yr CDR Briefing	n/a	83.5%	76.7%

When the loan volume was increased to be consistent with the PEPS300 Data, the percent of Borrowers in Default and percent of Borrowers Entered Repayment became consistent with other available data and briefings.

Conclusion for Loan Program CDR Manipulation: The consistent theme is that data and reporting were falsely given to the American people to drive an agenda that made people think the U.S. Department of Education was performing better than it was and the FFELP community was performing worse than it was. None of this reporting was based on data facts.

The elimination of the FFELP community has created a monopoly for student loans where competition is not available to drive appropriate quality servicing of student loans. Generally, competition keeps product offerings and servicing at a higher quality.

From the 2008 election campaign to date, many of President Obama's speeches have touted the savings to Americans that have come from eliminating the FFEL Program and moving to 100% direct loans. With a $41.3 billion dollar *profit* to the U.S. government in 2013 from the FDSL Program, *the savings is—exactly where?* From all of the research that I have done, I could not find a collective profit in the FFELP community that came anywhere near that profit margin.

In the federal student loan program, students have suffered under mismanagement of the program, high interest payments incurred with Pay-As-You-Earn, IBR and ICR repayment schedules, and declining quality standards—and they don't have a choice to make it better because there is only one choice and it is one where private people, Americans, have no control.

Injustice for All Insight

Were the DOE's massive reporting errors for loan program CDRs intentional?

Is it possible that the approximately 130,000 defaulters were moved from the FDSLP CDR to the FFELP CDR in the 2012 DOE Briefings to solicit support from voters, taxpayers, and lawmakers who were led to believe that the U.S. Department of Education was managing the direct loans better than the private lenders that had been eliminated from the student loan program in 2010?

2012 was a presidential election year, and eliminating private lenders from the student loan program was the first big financial decision that Obama made in his President's Budget released in February 2009, only one month after he was sworn in.

Are the proprietary school sector and third-party servicers being blamed for manipulating cohort default rates as a diversion while the U.S. Department of Education is manipulating the rates?

Why Wouldn't Databases Used to Determine Title IV Eligibility Be Consistent?

The FY 2009 3-year Cohort Default Rate data has changed each year from the original data released in 2012. Some of this can be explained with changes in data from CDR data corrections and Erroneous Data Appeals. The lender or loan holder data for the FY 2009 3-year CDR was not available until September 2014. Through these years, the FY 2009 3-year CDR reported to the public has remained *exactly* the same as when it was originally published in September 2012.

Institution Cohort Default Rate Manipulation

The September 2014 Official National Cohort Default Rate (CDR) release was like no other in the history of the country. While Congress was in recess, the U.S. Department of Education released "adjusted" CDRs that were not authorized by Congress. Since the definition of Cohort Default Rates is statutory, the DOE knowingly and purposely overstepped its authority.

While most people believed that these "adjustments" were an effort to save certain nonprofit institutions from losing Title IV Eligibility for education funding, I have uncovered substantial evidence that supports another more devious and self-serving agenda. Bear with me, I start with the easier issues and work up to those that are, simply put, abhorrent.

September 23, 2014 DOE Electronic Announcement[48]

Subject: Adjustment of Calculation of Official Three Year Cohort Default Rates for Institutions Subject to Potential Loss of Eligibility

> *The ADJUSTMENT was made for borrowers who had a loan(s) in default and who also had one or more loan(s) that did not default and were in good standing for at least 60 consecutive days during the cohort period.*

September 23, 2014 DOE Electronic Announcement[49]

Subject: Erroneous Data Appeal—Incorrect Borrower Enrollment

---

48. http://ifap.ed.gov/eannouncements/092314AdjustmentofCalculationofOfc3Yr CDRforInstitutSubtoPotentialLossofElig.html

49. http://ifap.ed.gov/eannouncements/092314ErronousDataAppealIncorrectBorro werEnroll.html

Appeals procedures are defined in statute—I know because I helped write them. Enrollment reporting is clearly defined and late reporting of the "last date of attendance" or "less than half-time status" has never been acceptable for an Erroneous Data Appeal.

September 24, 2014 DOE 2014 National 2011 3-year CDR Briefing & Data Files (PEPS) Became Available[50]

Table 28: 2014 Official National FY 2011 3YR iCDR Briefing (DOE PowerPoint)

	Fiscal Year 2009 Official				Fiscal Year 2010 Official				Fiscal Year 2011 Official			
	# of Schools	Borrower Default Rate (%)	# of Borrowers Defaulted	# of Borrowers Entered Repayment	# of Schools	Borrower Default Rate (%)	# of Borrowers Defaulted	# of Borrowers Entered Repayment	# of Schools	Borrower Default Rate (%)	# of Borrowers Defaulted	# of Borrowers Entered Repayment
Public	1,628	11.0%	196,032	1,778,645	1,619	13.0%	250,661	1,922,773	1,637	12.9%	292,012	2,252,334
Less than 2 yrs	141	16.2%	1,202	7,401	139	16.5%	1,315	7,963	146	13.6%	1,196	8,750
2-3 yrs	851	18.3%	94,945	518,299	840	20.9%	125,764	599,467	841	20.6%	158,104	767,073
4yrs(+)	636	7.9%	99,885	1,252,945	640	9.3%	123,582	1,315,343	650	8.9%	132,712	1,476,511
Private	1,710	7.5%	63,047	835,492	1,712	8.2%	72,347	879,269	1,712	7.2%	70,186	969,156
Less than 2 yrs	42	23.1%	950	4,106	41	21.8%	1,097	5,020	43	25.0%	1,644	6,567
2-3 yrs	174	14.5%	2,357	16,244	168	14.2%	2,305	16,217	161	12.0%	2,026	16,861
4yrs(+)	1,494	7.3%	59,740	815,142	1,503	8.0%	68,945	858,032	1,508	7.0%	66,516	945,728
Proprietary	2,142	22.7%	229,315	1,006,190	2,187	21.8%	277,088	1,270,965	2,277	19.1%	288,126	1,500,812
Less than 2 yrs	1,100	21.5%	27,788	129,235	1,117	20.9%	34,811	165,921	1,177	20.6%	38,686	187,209
2-3 yrs	731	22.9%	64,146	279,713	743	21.4%	71,853	334,459	762	19.8%	77,441	390,649
4 yrs(+)	311	23.0%	137,381	597,242	327	22.1%	170,424	770,585	338	18.6%	171,999	922,954
Foreign	427	7.3%	646	8,777	432	4.6%	449	9,562	428	3.8%	403	10,488
Unclassified	1	0.0%	0	5	1	0.0%	0	1	1	0.0%	0	3
TOTAL	5,908	13.4%	489,040	3,629,109	5,951	14.7%	600,545	4,082,570	6,055	13.7%	650,727	4,732,793

Exactly WHAT Was Adjusted?

When the U.S. Department of Education announced that there would be an adjustment to the cohort default rates and provided exceptions to Errone-ous Data Appeals, most people believe that these were a type of carve-out for the community colleges and other minority-serving institutions. The DOE also refused to provide a list of those institutions that received adjustments to Congress.

The adjustments were focused on schools in jeopardy of losing Title IV funding. Based on available data and trending from schools that had FY 2009 and FY 2010 3-year rates above the 30% allowable threshold, we conducted an analysis for potential adjustments. The schools that were analyzed had two consecutive 3-year CDRs over the 30% threshold prior to the 2014 Official FY 2011 3-year CDRs:

---

50. http://ifap.ed.gov/eannouncements/092414CDRNationalBriefings3YR.html

302 Schools	FY 2009 3-year CDRs over 30%
117 Schools	FY 2009 3-year and FY 2010 3-year CDRs over 30%
-14 Schools	Schools with 2 years over 30% and showing either zero (0) borrowers or no longer reported in the FY 2011 3-year CDR data
103 Schools	*Total number of schools analyzed for adjustments*

The following is based upon our educated estimate of schools affected:

39 schools had rate adjustments	• 35 schools had adjustments for both the FY 2009 and FY 2010 3-year CDRs • 1 schools had adjustment for FY 2009 3-year CDR only • 3 schools had adjustments for FY 2010 3-year CDR only
27 schools remain eligible with adjustments	• 20 schools are now under 30% for FY 2011 with adjustment • 5 schools now have only 2 years over 30% • 2 schools now have only 1 year over 30%
12 schools face loss of Title IV Eligibility even with adjustments	• 7 schools remain over 40% for FY 2011 with adjustments • 5 schools remain over 30% even with adjustments
12 schools have no apparent rate adjustments and _now have 3 years over 30%_	• 1 Public School • 1 Private School • 10 Proprietary Schools
52 schools have no apparent rate adjustments but have come under 30% for FY 2011	• 11 Public Schools • 7 Private Schools • 34 Proprietary Schools

Injustice for All Insight

Does the U.S. Department of Education have the authority to make CDR adjustments or change CDR appeal criteria?

The DOE does not have the authority to change the definitions. The cohort default rate is defined by law. The intent of the law is to define minimum standards of institutional quality based on those borrowers who do not pay their student loans. Schools may face loss of Title IV Eligibility for both student loans and Pell Grants when their three most recent rates exceed the following thresholds:

- *One CDR over 40%*
- *Three consecutive CDRs over 30%*

The Erroneous Data Appeals criteria are defined by law. Standards for timely reporting the last date of attendance have been established as criteria for inclusion or exclusion in this appeal. The standard for reporting changes in the student's last date of at-least-half-time attendance is that schools must report changes in regular reporting to the government that occurs every sixty (60) days.

Note of Interest: The DOE waited until Congress was in recess to publish these announcements.

Was There Another Reason for the ADJUSTMENT?

When the government passed the law to transition to 100% direct lending, the FFELP lenders, servicers, and guarantee agencies started dropping like flies —they exited the loan program rapidly by the hundreds. In an attempt to slow this process and keep some companies financially stable through the transition, lawmakers agreed to purchase FFELP loans disbursed on or after October 1, 2007 from the FFELP community to provide money to those who became financially unstable as a result of the decision. These are called "conduit loans" or, more commonly, "PUT Loans."

Everything happened much quicker than lawmakers and the Department of Education anticipated, and extremely large loan transfers occurred. The process had many problems including loss of deferment, forbearance, and payment arrangements that were applied during the transfer period, which took up to 10 months in the beginning.

The students who had properly applied for and been approved for these options did nothing wrong yet because the current status was "lost" during the transfer, they went into default. It was a tragedy.

I went to the Department and met with David Bergeron, Deputy Assistant Secretary for Postsecondary Education, to discuss this situation and ask for help. I believe that because everything was happening in such rapid succession and the top priority was getting the loans on a servicing system, that the correction to this issue was overlooked, lost or impossible to complete at the time.

These unfortunate students have been paying the consequences of these defaulted loans ever since. Additionally, the schools these students attended have paid consequences of their default rates based on these poorly handled loans.

The 2014 Loan Holder Data for certain US DEPT OF ED Lender IDs show extremely high default rates:

For the FY 2009 3-year Cohort Default Rate

- The National Official FY 2009 3-year CDR was **13.4%**
- FY 2009 3-Year CDR for USDOE ABCP Conduit 09-10 (PUT Loans): **59.8%**
- FY 2009 3-Year CDR for USDOE 2009-2010 LPCP (PUT Loans): **54.3%**

For the FY 2010 3-year Cohort Default Rate	• The National Official FY 2010 3-year CDR was **14.7%** • FY 2010 3-Year CDR for USDOE ABCP Conduit 09-10 (PUT Loans): **56.6%**
For the FY 2011 3-year Cohort Default Rate	• The National Official FY 2011 3-year CDR was **13.7%** • FY 2011 3-Year CDR for USDOE ABCP Conduit 09-10 (PUT Loans): **58.6%** • FY 2011 3-Year CDR Unreported* and Assumed USDOE Direct Loans: **30.4%**

Compared to FY 2011 3-year PEPS300 National CDR Data

There is reason to believe that the 2014 cohort default rate adjustments were made so that fewer institutions would perform loan servicing appeals and other extensive auditing that would uncover inappropriate and unacceptable loan servicing associated with these high default rates for direct student loans.

Institution Cohort Default Rates

Beginning in 2012, numerous databases used to determine institutional performance show grossly inaccurate reporting which supports an agenda for eliminating for-profit institutions and promoting community colleges. In September 2012, 2013, and then 2014, the sector-level reporting for the FY 2009, FY 2010 and FY 2011 Cohort Default Rates were released. The data discrepancy patterns for all three reports are consistent and include:

Inaccurate low rates, defaults and borrowers entered repayment were reported for the public institution sector while inaccurate high rates, defaults and borrowers entered repayment were reported for the proprietary sector. The private nonprofit sector was always within 1% of accuracy.

Issues with the DOE iCDR Briefings

The 2014 National Briefing for FY 2011 3-year Rates[51] had numerous errors.

The U.S. Department of Education made _15 errors in 45 rate calculations_ in the 2014 DOE Briefing. The sector level default rates reported in the U.S.

---

51. https://ifap.ed.gov/eannouncements/092414CDRNationalBriefings3YR.html

Department of Education National Briefings does not match the national cohort default rate database (PEPS300). The inaccurate reporting consistently favored public institutions while making proprietary rates worse than they actually were. The private nonprofit rates were consistently within 1% of accuracy.

Table 29: Summary of Incorrectly Calculated 2014 Official iCDRs
as published by the U.S. Department of Education

CATEGORY OF INSTITUTION CDR WITH ERRORS	Correct CDR Calculation	2014 Official FY 2011 3-YR Briefing	DOE Briefing Borrowers in Default	DOE Briefing Borrowers Entered Repayment
FY 2009 3-year CDR				
Public 4 yrs (+)	8.0%	7.9%	99,885	1,252,945
Proprietary Totals	22.8%	22.7%	229,315	1,006,190
Foreign Totals	7.4%	7.3%	646	8,777
TOTAL OF ALL CDRs	13.5%	13.4%	489,040	3,629,109
FY 2010 3-year CDR				
Public 2–3 yrs	21.0%	20.9%	125,764	599,467
Public 4 yrs (+)	9.4%	9.3%	123,582	1,315,343
Private Less than 2 yrs	21.9%	21.8%	1,097	5,020
Proprietary Less than 2 yrs	21.0%	20.9%	34,811	165,921
Proprietary 2–3 yrs	21.5%	21.4%	71,853	334,459
Foreign Totals	4.7%	4.6%	449	9,562
FY 2011 3-year CDR				
Public Totals	13.0%	12.9%	292,012	2,252,334
Public Less than 2 yrs	13.7%	13.6%	1,196	8,750
Public 4 yrs (+)	9.0%	8.9%	132,712	1,476,511
Proprietary Totals	19.2%	19.1%	288,126	1,500,812
Proprietary Less than 2 yrs	20.7%	20.6%	38,686	187,209

Table 30: Comparison of 2014 Official FY 2009-2011 iCDR Percentages in DOE Briefing vs Data Reality by Sector

CDR RATES COMPARISON	PUBLIC			PRIVATE			PROPRIETARY		
	FY 2009	FY 2010	FY 2011	FY 2009	FY 2010	FY 2011	FY 2009	FY 2010	FY 2011
iCDR PEPS300	11.1%	13.1%	13.0%	7.5%	8.2%	7.2%	22.6%	21.6%	18.9%
DOE Briefing	11.0%	13.0%	12.9%	7.5%	8.2%	7.2%	22.7%	21.8%	19.1%
Variable	-0.1%	-0.1%	-0.1%	n/a	n/a	n/a	+ 0.1%	+ 0.2%	+ 0.2%
Effect	Public rates LOWER			Private rates SAME			Proprietary rates HIGHER		

The overall reporting by the Department portrays proprietary schools in a negative light while making public schools look like they were performing better than they actually are. **There's a pattern to the CDR reporting discrepancies that supports the stories that have been pushed to the public—where proprietary schools represent half of the defaults in the country and proprietary default rates keep escalating.** This is a spin, not the truth. The actual CDR data does not support these stories. In each of the last three (3) years, the discrepancy in the number of defaults was about 30,000 borrowers.

Table 31: Comparison of 2014 Official FY 2009-2011 iCDR #Defaults in DOE Briefing vs Data Reality by Sector

2014 CDR OFFICIAL	DOE Briefing Information		PEPS300 Data Facts	
	# BORR IN DEFAULT	What the Public Saw - SPIN -	# BORR IN DEFAULT	What the Public Should Have Seen - TRUTH -
PUBLIC FY 2009 CDR	196,032	PUBLIC SECTOR **Much Lower Than**	204,732	PUBLIC SECTOR **About The Same**
PROP FY 2009 CDR	229,315	FOR-PROFIT! -33,283	208,962	As FOR-PROFIT! -4,230
PUBLIC FY 2010 CDR	250,661	PUBLIC SECTOR **Lower Than**	259,692	PUBLIC SECTOR **Actually Higher Than**
PROP FY 2010 CDR	277,088	FOR-PROFIT! -26,427	255,811	FOR-PROFIT! +3,881
PUBLIC FY 2011 CDR	292,012	PUBLIC SECTOR **About The Same**	303,288	PUBLIC SECTOR **Actually Much Higher**
PROP FY 2011 CDR	288,126	As FOR-PROFIT! +3,886	275,794	Than FOR-PROFIT! +27,494

There is a pattern for how the numbers were changed to present this "spin" that consistently lowered public sector defaults and borrowers entered repayment by the same percentage.

There is also a pattern for how the numbers were changed to present this "spin" that consistently increased proprietary sector defaults and borrowers entered repayment by several percentage points with the default percentage always 1% higher than the borrowers entered repayment percentage.

For the private sector, the numbers were always within 1% of accuracy.

I have chosen to withhold the exact pattern of the cohort default rate manipulation until those in charge of the investigation feel that it is appropriate to share publicly.

This analysis was based upon sector totals and did not go into a credential level analysis. Based on my knowledge that the Gainful Employment data released in June 2012 and March 2014 had been manipulated, I knew already that this was not about programs or credential level evidence. I knew that it was about annihilating the for-profit sector even if they were throwing out very good, high performing schools along with those who deserved high levels of scrutiny.

Conclusion for iCDR Manipulation: The following chart depicts the story of all of the iCDR manipulation evidence put together. The consistent theme is that data and reporting were falsely given to the American people to drive an agenda that made people think public institutions were performing better than they were and proprietary institutions were performing worse than they were. None of this reporting was based on data facts.

This manipulation has ruined the reputations of hundreds of for-profit schools, has put many out of business, and has fed an agenda for singling out this sector for over-regulation and measures that the public and private sectors could not pass if they would be held to the same standards. This agenda has nothing to do with successfully educating Americans.

Table 32: Summary of DOE's FY 2009–2011 iCDR Manipulation (Public vs Proprietary)

DOE Briefing - SPIN -		PEPS Data - TRUTH -	Cohort Year	PEPS Data - TRUTH -	DOE Briefing - SPIN -	
PUBLIC SECTOR 3YR CDRs			FY 2009 3YR CDR		**PROPRIETARY SECTOR 3YR CDRs**	
		204,732 Correct		208,962 Correct		
Falsely Reported 4% LOWER than data	196,032 Falsely Reported Borrowers in Default	**TRUTH** For FY 2009 Public CDRs only had 4,230 FEWER defaults than Proprietary CDRs.			229,315 Falsely Reported Borrowers in Default	Falsely Reported 10% HIGHER than data

FALSE REPORTING

The DOE reported that the Public Sector had 33,283 fewer defaults than the Proprietary Sector. The DOE Briefing is NOT backed by any available data and is NOT the truth.

PUBLIC SECTOR 3YR CDRs			FY 2010 3YR CDR		**PROPRIETARY SECTOR 3YR CDRs**	
		259,692 Correct		255,811 Correct		
Falsely Reported 3% LOWER than data	250,661 Falsely Reported Borrowers in Default	**TRUTH** For FY 2010 Public CDRs have 3,881 MORE defaults than Proprietary CDRs.			277,088 Falsely Reported Borrowers in Default	Falsely Reported 8% HIGHER than data

FALSE REPORTING

The DOE reported that the Public Sector had 26,427 fewer defaults than the Proprietary Sector. The DOE Briefing is NOT backed by any available data and is NOT the truth.

PUBLIC SECTOR 3YR CDRs			FY 2011 3YR CDR		**PROPRIETARY SECTOR 3YR CDRs**	
		303,288 Correct		275,794 Correct		
Falsely Reported 4% LOWER than data	292,012 Falsely Reported Borrowers in Default	**TRUTH** For FY 2011 Public CDRs have 27,494 MORE defaults than Proprietary CDRs.			288,126 Falsely Reported Borrowers in Default	Falsely Reported 4% HIGHER than data

FALSE REPORTING

The DOE reported that the Public Sector had only 3,886 more defaults than the Proprietary Sector. The DOE Briefing is NOT backed by any available data and is NOT the truth.

Injustice for All Insight

 Is the inaccurate reporting by the U.S. Department of Education designed to eliminate for-profit schools or to cover up its own mismanagement of the FDSL Program? Or, is something more sinister going on?

Here are some questions we should all be asking about institution CDR manipulation:

- *Were the data manipulated to cover up the poor quality of public nonprofit education?*

- *Were the data manipulated to divert attention from the unacceptable results of the DOE's management of the FDSL Program?*

- *Were the data manipulated to hide the defaults that occurred from the abhorrent mistakes made when conduit loans were transferred from FFELP to the DOE's management?*

- *Why haven't the students been helped if the "mistakes" are so bad that they warrant adjustments to certain institutions' CDRs?*

- *Have proprietary schools been targeted and publicized as unethical, greedy, and predatory to divert attention from what is really going on at the U.S. Department of Education?*

Let us not be ignorant in believing this encompasses all the DOE's manipulation—there may be more.

Notes: http://www2.ed.gov/offices/OSFAPdefaultmanagement/3yrffe lrates.pdf (no longer available), http://www2.ed.gov/offices/OSFAP/ defaultmanagement/3yerdlrates.pdf (no longer available), this original file name was the same as the FY 2009 FDSLP 3-year CDR and is no longer available on the U.S. Department of Education website.

GOVERNMENT GREED

IN GOD WE TRUST

Big Profit Government?

When government morphs into big business with big profits, it can be lured into unethical practices as easily as any other for-profit business.

IV. CDR MANIPULATION

Who Is Really Responsible?

With student loan debt rising over $1.47 trillion, will you continue to believe that for-profit institutions are the only players that should have oversight? Follow my lead and I will show you where that yellow brick road truly leads.

Consistent Inaccuracies

The more I have dug, the more public information reports on the U.S. Department of Education websites mysteriously disappear. And DOE information is, I believe, intentionally misrepresented—skewed, spun then sent out to media outlets that are ignorant of the law and true issues; media outlets that simply regurgitate the misinformation because they do not have the capability to verify the data. The media moan about the horrible acts of for-profit institutions and lauds the unjustified successes of nonprofit institutions. The spin is part of the diabolical agenda to brand a scarlet letter on for-profit institutions by swaying and training the opinions of American citizens to suit the larger agenda. Stick with me and I will show you how complicated numbers will shine the light on this grave injustice.

Information and data readily available on the U.S. Department of Education's websites show that there are numerous parties who gain by manipulating the cohort default rates. Many would like the public to believe that for-profit institutions and their third-party servicers are manipulating default rates to maintain eligibility in the Title IV Federal Student Loan and Grant Programs. Since a school's eligibility is based upon its official cohort default rates, schools definitely have a vested interest in the outcome. Most of these institutions, however, are educating their borrowers in a manner consistent with the mandates for them to do so.

To make sense out of the morass that the DOE has made out of the student loan program, we will review a series of reports and the related data provided by the DOE that do not accurately match or calculate what the actual data show. The inaccuracies in reporting follow a consistent theme that supports the Obama Administration's agenda with no regard for those affected by these inaccuracies, including companies, schools, and the employees of such, and most importantly the students who pay the ultimate consequence of these games. The reports I analyzed include those outlined in Table 33.

Table 33: Quick Reference of DOE's CDR Briefings, Publications & Data Analyzed

Reference Document	Reference Description	Report Matches Related Database	Available on DOE website?
2012 DOE Briefing for FDSLP FY 2009 3YR CDR	2012 Official Default Rates for Direct Loans	**NO** *Does Not Match the Data*	**NO**
2012 DOE Briefing for FFELP FY 2009 3YR CDR	2012 Official Default Rates for Private Lenders	**NO** *Does Not Match the Data*	**NO**
2012 DOE Briefing for FDSLP & FFELP Rates	2012 Official Chart for FDSL and FFELP CDRs	**NO** *Does Not Match the Data*	**NO**
2012 "Top 100 Loan Holders" Information for FY 2009 3YR	List of Top 100 Loan Holders by Volume Ranking	**YES**	**NO**
2013 DOE Briefing for FDSLP FY 2010 3YR CDR	2013 Official Default Rates for Direct Loans	**NO** *Does Not Match the Data*	**NO**
2014 DOE Briefing for FY 2011 3YR CDR	2014 Official Default Rates for All Sectors & Credential Levels	**NO** *Does Not Match the Data*	**YES**
2014 Official 3YR PEPS300 Data (FY 2009, 2010 & 2011)	Comprehensive Data for Institutional CDRs	**N/A**	**YES**
2014 Official FY 2009 Lender Data	FY 2009 3-year CDR data for loan holders	**NO** *Does Not Match the Data*	**YES**
2014 Official FY 2010 Lender Data	FY 2010 3-year CDR data for loan holders	**NO** *Does Not Match the Data*	**YES**
2014 Official FY 2011 Lender Data	FY 2011 3-year CDR Data for Loan Holders	**NO** *Does Not Match the Data*	**YES**
2014 "Top 100 Loan Holders" Information for FY 2011 3YR	FY 2011 3-year CDR Information for Loan Holders	**INCONCLUSIVE** *Data Is Incomplete*	**YES**

The more I cross-referenced information in DOE reports and data files, the more shocking discrepancies I found. The Quick Reference CDR Analysis Chart provides a record of the reports and data that I analyzed, which ones were accurate and, since I started sharing my findings, which ones have magically disappeared from the DOE website.

Incentives for federal student loan servicing contractors who service millions of student loans are also based, in part, upon default rate results. The value of the federal servicer contracts outweighs any individual or group of for-profit education institutions.

Federal Student Loan Servicer Allocations Have Been Based in Part upon Default Rates

Customer Service Performance Measure Metrics for the Department of Education's (the Department's) federal loan servicers are measured on a quarterly basis. The metrics used herein represent those in effect until August 2014 and have documented results.

Budget constraints and metrics criteria contained in the federal loan servicing contracts limited what servicers could do with borrowers in order to stay profitable. Generally speaking, people at the federal servicers want to do what is best for the students but are driven in other directions based on "top agenda" priorities from the Administration and on hitting numbers for the metrics that keep them in business. If the federal servicers' contracts were in alignment with what truly drives long-term success for students, these circumstances of moving away from students as the priority would not happen. Student loan servicing isn't a "one size fits all" business—every borrower should be looked at individually to determine what is best in his or her situation. The criteria for servicing allocations changed in August 2014.[52] The data provided herein is based on the original federal direct loan servicer criteria provided in detail at the end of this chapter.

The quarterly rankings[53] for defaulted borrower counts change regularly as follows:

---

52. http://www.ed.gov/news/press-releases/us-department-education-strengthens-federal-student-loan-servicing

53. The June 30, 2011, Quarterly Allocation Report was not available at http://ifap.ed.gov.

Table 34: TIVAS Quarterly Report Results

Quarterly Report	FedLoan Servicing (PHEAA)	Great Lakes	Nelnet	Sallie Mae
Sep 30, 2010	(3) 1.95%	(1) 1.57%	(4) 2.48%	(2) 1.88%
Dec 31, 2010	(2/3) 1.74%	(2/3) 1.74%	(4) 1.78%	(1) 1.05%
Mar 31, 2011	(2) 1.30%	(3) 1.38%	(4) 1.66%	(1) 1.21%
Sep 30, 2011	(3) 1.12%	(2) 1.09%	(4) 1.33%	(1) 0.97%
Dec 31, 2011	(2) 1.50%	(4) 1.89%	(1) 1.18%	(3) 1.81%
Mar 31, 2012	(2) 1.21%	(3) 1.41%	(1) 0.73%	(4) 1.55%
Jun 30, 2012	(3) 1.31%	(4) 1.33%	(1) 0.66%	(2) 1.08%
Sep 30, 2012	(3) 1.21%	(4) 1.46%	(1) 0.66%	(2) 0.91%
Dec 31, 2012	(3) 1.42%	(4) 1.70%	(1) 0.76%	(2) 0.83%
Mar 31, 2013	(3) 0.98%	(4) 1.03%	(1) 0.58%	(2) 0.64%
Jun 30, 2013	(3) 0.91%	(4) 1.11%	(2) 0.59%	(1) 0.54%
Sep 30, 2013	(4) 1.68%	(3) 1.27%	(1) 0.58%	(2) 0.90%
Dec 31, 2013	(4) 1.79%	(3) 1.41%	(1) 0.58%	(2) 0.79%
Mar 31, 2014	(4) 1.35%	(3) 1.07%	(2) 0.97%	(1) 0.73%
Jun 30, 2014	(4) 1.58%	(3) 1.57%	(2) 0.91%	(1) 0.67%

The servicing allocation[54] changed annually as shown in Table 35.

---

54. Information for "Allocation Year" chart was found at http://ifap.ed.gov.

Table 35: TIVAS YOY Allocation Analysis

Allocation Year	FedLoan Servicing (PHEAA)	Great Lakes	Nelnet	Sallie Mae
2nd Year Final Allocation Calculation (Source: September 2010 Electronic Announcement Attachment)				
Total Score	(2) 15.0	(1) 16.0	(4) 8.0	(3) 11.0
Est Defaulted Borr	0.250%	0.270%	0.550%	0.460%
Allocation	30.0%	32.0%	16.0%	22.0%
Est # Borrowers	1,800,000	1,920,000	960,000	1,320,000
3rd Year Final Allocation Calculation (Source: August 2011 Electronic Announcement Attachment)				
(Ranking) /Total Score	(2/3) 13.0	(1) 16.0	(4) 8.0	(2/3) 13.0
Est Defaulted Borr	1.54%	1.44%	1.89%	1.29%
Allocation	26.0%	32.0%	16.0%	26.0%
Est # Borrowers	1,066,000	1,312,000	656,000	1,066,000
4th Year Final Allocation Calculation (August 2012 Determination Announcement Attachment)				
(Ranking) /Total Score	(3) 13.5	(2) 14.0	(1) 15.0	(4) 7.5
Est Defaulted Borr	1.29%	1.43%	0.98%	1.35%
Allocation	27.0%	28.0%	30.0%	15.0%
Est # Borrowers	972,000	1,008,000	1,080,000	540,000
5th Year Final Allocation Calculation (Source: August 2013 Determination Announcement Attachment)				
(Ranking) /Total Score	(2/3) 13.0	(2/3) 13.0	(1) 15.0	(4) 9.0
Est Defaulted Borr	1.13%	1.33%	0.65%	0.73%
Allocation	26.0%	26.0%	30.0%	18.0%
Est # Borrowers	806,000	806,000	930,000	558,000
6th Year Final Allocation Calculation (Source: September 2014 Determination Announcement Attachment)				
(Ranking) /Total Score	(4) 10.0	(1) 30.0	(2) 13.0	(3) 12.0
Est Defaulted Borr	1.6%	1.33%	0.54%	0.43%
Allocation	20.0%	30.0%	26.0%	24.0%
Est # Borrowers	No longer provided			
Est # Borr Based on 5th Year Allocation	620,000	930,000	806,000	744,000
Diff 5th to 6th in Volume	-186,000	+124,000	-124,000	+186,000

As demonstrated in Table 35, federal loan servicers (TIVAS) have very large numbers of borrowers to gain and lose in each year's allocation based upon their ranking within the allocation methodology.

Consider the motivations for federal loan servicers. Here are the two federal servicers most affected from the 3rd to the 4th allocation years.

Table 36: Allocation Changes for Nelnet & Sallie Mae from 3rd to 4th Year

3rd to 4th Year Allocations		3rd Year Allocation	4th Year Allocation	Change
Nelnet	Est Defaulted Borrowers	1.89%	0.98%	**+ 424,000**
	Est # Allocated Loans	656,000	1,080,000	
Sallie Mae	Est Defaulted Borrowers	1.29%	1.35%	**- 526,000**
	Est # Allocated Loans	1,066,000	540,000	

Historically, when millions of students are involved, a default rate takes YEARS to change yet, the servicer who was historically in last place moved to first place in one year. In over 28 years of default management experience, I have never seen a default rate cut in half in one year. High volume would make this even more difficult. Certain proprietary schools are being blamed for reducing their own default rates in some unethical method that somehow has nothing to do with all of the laws and regulations the schools have to follow to educate borrowers about their rights and responsibilities. Yet, BIG numbers of default reductions have rapidly occurred with federal servicers who have millions of dollars to gain or lose while these servicers often have questionable servicing and practices that may not serve the students' best interest.

There is minimal change in allocation numbers from the 4th to the 5th year. The quarterly servicing results, however, are showing aggressive strategies by Sallie Mae to recapture a larger piece of the servicing. In a year-over-year comparison of June 2013 to June 2012 quarterly results, Sallie Mae reduced its default rate by half. In June 2012, Sallie Mae's results were 1.08% compared to June 2013 when they were 0.54%. This resulted in movement from 4th to 3rd place in the 6th year allocation for an estimated 744,000 borrowers this year—that is 186,000 more borrowers than Sallie Mae received in the 5th year allocation.

Authority for Deferment and Forbearance Eligibility

The federal servicers are solely responsible for determining eligibility and collecting proper documentation for deferments and forbearances that greatly affect these loan portfolios and directly contribute the measures and metrics upon which the DOE relies to determine the percent of the federal student loan portfolio that each of the servicers is awarded each year.

PART 682—FEDERAL FAMILY EDUCATION LOAN (FFEL) PROGRAM

34 CFR § 682.210 Deferment. Federal regulations clearly define all deferments available for FFEL student loan borrowers and the criteria they need to fulfill for being approved for these deferment options. The required eligibility documentation is audited by and "determination" is made by the federal student loan servicers and interpreted within the regulatory language as "the Secretary grants" and "approved by the Secretary." Nowhere within the regulatory language is there any reference to an institution of higher education or its third-party servicer making any determination for approving or not approving a deferment for a FFEL loan.

34 CFR § 682.211 Forbearance. Federal regulations clearly define all discretionary and mandatory forbearance options available for FFEL student loan borrowers and the criteria they need to fulfill for being approved for these forbearance options. The required eligibility documentation is audited and "determination" is made by the federal student loan servicers and interpreted within the regulatory language as "the Secretary grants" and "approved by the Secretary." Nowhere within the regulatory language is there any reference to an institution of higher education or its third-party servicer making any determination for approving or not approving a deferment for a FFEL loan.

PART 685—WILLIAM D. FORD FEDERAL DIRECT LOAN (Direct loan) PROGRAM

34 CFR § 685.204 Deferment. Federal regulations clearly define all deferments available to borrowers and the criteria they need to fulfill for being approved for these deferment options. The required eligibility documentation is audited by and "determination" is made by the federal student loan servicers and interpreted within the regulatory language as "the Secretary grants" and "approved by the Secretary." Nowhere within the regulatory language is there any reference to an institution of higher education or its third-party servicer making any determination for approving or not approving a deferment for a direct loan.

34 CFR § 685.205 Forbearance. Federal regulations clearly define all discretionary and mandatory forbearance options available for direct loan borrowers and the criteria they need to fulfill to be approved for these forbearance options. The required eligibility documentation is audited by and "determination" is made by the federal student loan servicers and interpreted within the regulatory language as "the Secretary grants" and "approved by the Secretary." Nowhere within the regulatory language is there any reference to an institution of higher education or its third-party servicer making any determination for approving or not approving a deferment for a direct loan.

Schools Are Mandated to Perform Borrower Counseling

The institutions are mandated to perform borrower education (counseling) with student borrowers and are somehow seen as manipulative when students understand and exercise the very rights and responsibilities that the schools are tasked with teaching them.

In a memo dated August 21, 2012, The Institute for College Access & Success (TICAS) wrote a memo[55] to Interested Parties regarding the "Steps the Education Department Should Immediately Take to Curb Default Rate Manipulation." TICAS accused schools of manipulating their CDRs by appealing the rates based on "Improper Servicing" of loans. The schools have the right to file "Improper Loan Servicing Appeals" and this is an appropriate method of auditing the quality of the servicing of these loans. The first terms of the "Improper Loan Servicing Appeal" were defined in the Higher Education Amendments of 1992 and there have been several amended laws since then. Instructions for

---

55. http://www.ticas.org/files/pub/TICAS_memo_on_CDR_evasion_082112. pdf

appeals are outlined in the DOE's "Cohort Default Rate Guide."[56] Implications by TICAS that schools are somehow doing something wrong when exercising their rights by law are outrageous.

TICAS accused schools of manipulating their CDRs by helping students obtain deferments and forbearances. Schools are mandated to educate borrowers on their rights and responsibilities including their rights for delayed or reduced payments when they cannot make timely payments. The authority for granting these options called deferments and forbearances is solely under the Secretary and those servicers who collect loans on behalf of the Secretary. Schools do not have authority to grant these benefits that the students are entitled to have under law. Insinuating that there is something wrong when schools are properly educating borrowers about their options to avoid default and assisting them in exercising the options that they qualify for is also misguided.

INJUSTICE FOR ALL INSIGHT

More Interest = More Government Profits

In 2013, the actual profit on federal student loans was estimated at $41.3 BILLION! This is largely based on repayment plans that put students into situations where minimal or no principal is being paid—not really CDR manipulation, just manipulation. More interest is more profit to the government and it goes into the federal general fund to pay the national debt, not into educating America.

NOTE: Find additional information at http://www.usatoday.com/story/news/nation/2013/11/25/federal-student-loan- profit/3696009/ and https://www.tuition.io/blog/2013/11/federal-government-profits-from-student-loans-outdo-apple-revenues/

The fact that my company has produced lower-than-average default rates with significantly higher-than-average repayment rates is testimony to the fact that when borrower education and default prevention are properly managed,

---

56. http://ifap.ed.gov/DefaultManagement/guide/attachments/CDRMasterFile.pdf

everyone wins—especially the students. These results are provided in detail at the end of this chapter in a *Career Education Review* article dated September 2012 that highlights my response letter to TICAS dated August 21, 2012.

INJUSTICE FOR ALL INSIGHT

Violation of Ethics Laws?

Robert Shireman was the founder of TICAS and left in 2009 to join the Obama Administration. During his tenure with the U.S. Department of Education, the FFEL Program was eliminated, and he helped execute the broad and damaging federal regulations that targeted proprietary schools known as Gainful Employment. Immediately prior to joining the Administration, Shireman hosted public forums for eliminating the FFELP community. Mr. Shireman is the focus of an ongoing ethics investigation related to his actions while employed by the US-DOE. On March 20, 2014, Inside Higher Ed *published an article titled "Judge Compels TICAS Emails" because:*

> *...A federal judge on Wednesday ordered a college access advocacy group to turn over emails and other documents to government investigators, who are probing whether a former Education Department official violated ethics laws during the Obama administration's first push to more tightly regulate for-profit colleges...*

> *...TICAS is not the subject of the inspector general's investigation, but it has aggressively fought the subpoena for its documents..."*

NOTE: https://www.insidehighered.com/news/2014/03/20/federal-judge-orders-ticas-supply-emails-probe-former-education-department-official

School Requirements for Borrower Education

PART 685—WILLIAM D. FORD FEDERAL DIRECT LOAN (Direct loan) PROGRAM

34 CFR § 685.304 Counseling borrowers. Institutions of higher education are mandated to provide relevant information to direct loan borrowers during entrance and exit counseling. This includes explaining information in the Master Promissory Note (MPN) and providing links to federal websites designed to assist and educate student loan borrowers.

- Information provided on http://studentaid.ed.gov/repay-loans/defer-ment-forbearance for students describes deferment and forbearance eligibility.

- Information provided on http://www.direct.ed.gov/postpone.html for students describes deferment and forbearance eligibility.

What Does the Government Stand to Gain?

In an article titled "Government Profits To Soar More Than $700 Million With New Student Loan Rates" by David Jesse and published by the *Detroit Free Press* on August 25, 2013, substantial financial gains are documented that would motivate the government to make certain changes in higher education funding. Here are some highlights of the monetary impact named in the article.[57]

> A law touted by politicians as their way of keeping money in the pockets of the nation's college students will instead funnel more than $700 million in additional profit into the federal government's wallet over the next 10 years, a new analysis shows.

> The law, regulating interest rates for federal student loans, was passed by Congress and signed by President Barack Obama this summer. It was hailed by politicians on both sides of the aisle as a win in the campaign to combat a rising tide of student loan indebtedness.

> In total, the CBO projects the government to clear $175 billion in profit over the next decade on student loans.

---

57. http://www.freep.com/article/20130825/NEWS05/308250092/federal-government-student-loan-profits-going-up

Injustice for All Insight

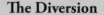

The Diversion

Are proprietary schools being blamed for CDR manipulation as a DIVERSION for what is REALLY going on? While federal student loan servicers quickly lower CDRs that determine their next year's allocation for federal student loans which represent BILLIONS, small mom-and-pop schools with an average of 500–1,000 students per year are being blamed for manipulating cohort default rates.

Does the current rationale make any sense at all?

1. *Federal loan servicers represent the Secretary of Education and have the ONLY authority to approve deferments, forbearances and repayment options for student loans.*

2. *When federal loan servicers successfully educate student loan borrowers about their rights and responsibilities and help them exercise the options, the servicers are "doing their jobs well."*

3. *Schools do NOT have the authority to approve deferments, forbearances, or repayment options for federal student loans.*

4. *Schools are mandated to educate borrowers about their federal student loan rights and responsibilities including options for deferments, forbearances, and repayment schedules.*

5. *When nonprofit institutions successfully educate student loan borrowers about their rights and responsibilities and help them exercise their options, nonprofit institutions are "doing their jobs well."*

6. *When for-profit institutions successfully educate student loan borrowers about their rights and responsibilities and help them exercise their options, for-profit institutions are "manipulating their cohort default rates."*

Taking a Look at Who Has the Most to Gain from CDR Manipulation

Let's take a look at the parties to the loan in summary:

Proprietary Schools: An institution's ability to get Title IV federal loan and grant funds is dependent upon its cohort default rates. Some states, like California, also use these rates for state aid eligibility. While there are some large chains of schools that own numerous schools, the vast majority of proprietary school owners are individuals who love their businesses and know every student by name.

The average proprietary school has 500 to 1,000 students with federal student loans each year and the school owners pay the highest tax rate on their profits. The taxes paid are the return on investment (ROI) for the taxpayers who are funding 100% of all new student loans. That's right, normal people (taxpayers) are the lenders for every student loan funded since June 30, 2010.

The taxes paid by for-profit institutions make proprietary education the *least expensive option for taxpayers* who are now lending the money for 100% of every student loan funded because there is an ROI. Additionally, schools are mandated to educate borrowers about options like deferments, forbearances, and alternate repayment schedules when they can't make timely payments on their student loans. Yet, the proprietary school sector and its third-party servicers are blamed for manipulating their CDRs when their borrowers understand their rights and exercise them.

More unemployment deferments were approved by federal loan servicers on behalf of the Secretary of Education over the last few years because unemployment rates were at record-high levels during the great recession that began in 2008.

More forbearances were approved by federal loan servicers (*obo* the Secretary) because there was an increase in extenuating financial circumstances during this same time. For example, if an employed borrower had a spouse who lost a job, the family income decreased but the borrower did not qualify for an unemployment deferment. In this case, forbearance was a viable option for financial relief to the family during a very difficult time for many Americans.

Why does the current belief system support thinking that proprietary schools and third-party servicers are unethical when successfully educating borrowers about their student loan rights and responsibilities as these entities are mandated to do? Isn't borrower understanding of deferment and forbearance options one of the goals of financial literacy and borrower education?

The difference between schools and their third-party servicers (TPS) and the federal loan servicers is that schools and their TPS don't have authority to grant deferments and forbearances but federal loan servicers do. Schools and their TPS can only educate borrowers about options and help them fill out forms or exercise their options. The ultimate approval is under the authority of the Secretary and those federal loan servicers that represent the Secretary.

Institutions serving at-risk populations definitely want to maintain eligibility for federal student loans and grants. As community colleges enroll more of these students in the wake of bad publicity largely caused by inaccurate reporting from the U.S. Department of Education for the proprietary sector, the community colleges will have to become more vested in the outcomes of their climbing cohort default rates.

Limiting the focus of CDR manipulation to for-profit institutions does not appropriately serve the students, the taxpayers, or the federal fiscal interest.

Federal Student Loan Servicers: Large federal loan servicing companies manipulating default rates to gain hundreds of thousands of borrower accounts that represent billions of dollars in profits is a more likely reality than some negative interpretation of effective borrower education by for-profit institutions.

People will behave the way in which they are rewarded. Until federal loan servicing contracts are truly in alignment with the students' best interest, there will continue to be a conflict when choosing between the students' best interest and staying in business.

I believe that most federal loan servicers would be thrilled if their rating system were based on metrics tied to the long-term success of the students instead of temporary measures that will most likely cause certain borrowers to fail down the road. For example, borrowers are at higher risk when payments go up, interest rates increase, or "balloon payments" rise for taxes when loans are forgiven in the IBR, PAYE, REPAYE repayment plans.

Some questionable decisions, however, involving large federal loan servicing contracts have been made and I'm not the only one who feels leery.[58]

In an article[59] titled "Keep a Wary Eye on Sallie Mae" that was posted on *Nonprofit Quarterly* on June 11, 2014, the following was expressed:

> Sallie Mae has long been the subject of numerous investigations for its less than salutary practices. The latest was last month when the Justice Department fined Sallie Mae and the new Navient $97 million for having inappropriately charged active-duty members of the military high interest rates and late fees on their loans in violation of the Service members Civil Relief Act. For the last decade or so, Sallie Mae has been reviewed, critiqued, investigated, and fined for alleged deceptive lending practices, discrimination against black and Latino loan applicants, maintaining inadequate reserves, and questionable debt collection practices.
>
> On the heels of the settlement agreement with Justice regarding overcharging members of the military, Navient is somehow one of four bidders shortlisted by Arne Duncan's Department of Education for a contract worth close to $900 million. The contract would enable the firm, if selected, to originate and disburse loans and grants in furtherance of Education's "Funding America's Future, One Student at a Time" mission.

The following profit information has been posted for Sallie Mae and Navient:

2014 reports for Sallie Mae:[60]

- Full-year private education loan originations: $4.1 billion

- Private education loan portfolio: $8.2 billion, up 27% over 2013 (year-over-year or YOY)

- Net interest income up 25% YOY

- Net profit: $578 million or 7%

- Closed purchase for a $750 million asset-backed commercial paper facility

58. Reference articles can be found at http://educatedrisk.org/reviews/navient and http://www.studentloanborrowerassistance.org/sallie-mae-saga-government-created-student-debt-fueled-profit-machine/

59. https://nonprofitquarterly.org/policysocial-context/24341-keep-a-wary-eye-on-sallie-mae.html

60. https://www.salliemae.com/assets/about/investors/shareholder/earnings-info/2014/Fourth-Quarter%202014%20Earnings%20Release.pdf

2014 reports for Navient,[61] a subsidiary of Sallie Mae until the Fall of 2014

- Acquired $13 billion in student loans during the year

- Charge-off rates on private education loan portfolio improved to lowest levels since 2008

- $1 billion authorized for common share repurchases, effective January 1, 2015

- Gaap net income: $1.1 billion, down from $1.4 billion in 2013

- On February 25, 2015, Navient announced[62] the purchase of a leading asset recovery firm that is expected to add another $70 million in revenue in 2015

In a year when the Consumer Financial Protection Bureau ordered Sallie Mae (also known as Sallie Mae Bank and Navient Solutions) to pay $96.6 million in restitution and penalties[63] for "systematically violating the legal rights of U.S. service members," the combined net profit for these companies was still close to $1.7 BILLION.

On June 18, 2014, Navient issued a statement on the extension of their U.S. Department of Education Loan Servicing Contract[64] and failed to mention the value of the contract. Based on publicly available information, the USDOE awarded Navient with a contract extension that also included this year's allocation for 25% of the federal student loan portfolio—an additional estimated revenue value of over $200 million.

The Administration and Federal Government: Before President Obama was elected in 2008, he was touting community colleges and his goal of educating America by 2020. He also made it clear that he did not like entrepreneurs in general with private lending and proprietary education being no exception. He got rid of private lenders for federal student loans by saying that the U.S. Department of Education would better manage the loans at a lower cost to

61. http://news.navient.com/releasedetail.cfm?ReleaseID=892351

62. http://news.navient.com/releasedetail.cfm?ReleaseID=883336 and http://news.navient.com/releasedetail.cfm?ReleaseID=898276

63. http://www.consumerfinance.gov/newsroom/statement-by-cfpbs-holly-petraeus-on-doj-fdic-enforcement-actions-against-sallie-mae/

64. http://news.navient.com/releasedetail.cfm?ReleaseID=855446

the government. The default rates for the direct (FDSL) loans and the private (FFEL) loans were not accurate when they were last released by loan program in September 2012, right before Obama's re-election. They were not accurate because USDOE Briefing reported the direct loan default rates as 8.6% when they were really 23.9%. Additionally, the USDOE reported private lender default rates as 14.6% when they were really 10.6%. To get these inaccurate numbers, approximately 129,000 defaults were subtracted from the FDSLP rate and added to the FFELP rate in the 2012 Official FY 2009 3-year Default Rate Briefings.

The inaccuracy of both the direct and private loan program default rates swayed public opinion to believe that the direct loan program was more successful than it actually was and that Obama had made a good decision for our country. Was this deception to justify eliminating the private lenders or to look good in the 2012 Presidential Election—or both?

Barack Obama has made it very clear that he does not like for-profit businesses and his actions have supported either getting rid of these businesses or placing the lion's share of the country's financial burdens on the backs of those who have been blessed by success—which comes with hard work, perseverance, and personal risk to get there and stay there.

Why is public perception negative about entrepreneurs making a profit when they took the risk and achieved success, in this case with student loans, while it is acceptable for Obama's government to make tremendous profits from those same students? **In fact, if the federal student loan "business" had been a stand-alone company in 2013, it would have ranked #3 in profits, only exceeded by Exxon and Apple.**

While students entering the workforce after graduating enjoy the benefits of low- to middle-income taxpayers, Obama's government is making profits on federal student loans that, in many cases, outweigh the benefits of the low-to middle-income tax benefits. Where in this situation does this help the students?

The article titled "The Federal Student Loan Racket," on MyGovCost.org on November 14th, 2014,[65] has eloquently stated:

---

65. http://www.mygovcost.org/2014/11/14/the-federal-student-loan-racket/

Since 2008, roughly $1 out of every $10 new dollars borrowed by the U.S. government through the end of its 2014 fiscal year has gone to fund the Federal Direct Student Loan program, which lends the money borrowed by Uncle Sam to college students at over double the interest rate that the U.S. government is charged by its lenders.

Later in the article, Suze Orman, personal finance guru, is quoted,

... Do you know that from 2007 to 2012, the government made $66 billion in profit on federal student loans? We can all debate how our government, should generate revenue to support federal spending programs, but doing it on the backs of young adults who need an education to compete in the increasingly competitive global workforce is just appalling.

Lawmakers are also questioning the practices of the U.S. Department of Education and their relationship with Sallie Mae. In a March 2014 Senate hearing, James Runcie, Federal Student Aid Chief Operating Officer for the USDOE, sited the DOE's concern about dislocating borrowers if they didn't continue the TIVAS contracts as the reason for their continued relationship. In response, Chairman Tom Harkin stated, *"It sounded like your answer, Mr. Runcie, was that they're too big to fail."* Senator Elizabeth Warren asserted, *"We know that there are problems with Sallie Mae, it has become public; and the actions you are taking and the oversight you are exercising has obviously not been enough to correct the problem; and I'm very concerned about re-upping a multimillion-dollar contract with Sallie Mae when Sallie Mae has demonstrated time and time again that it's not following the rules."*

In an article titled "Education Department Finds Numerous Problems At Sallie Mae, Levies No Fines" posted in the *Huffington Post* on December 11, 2013,[66] the questionable relationship between the DOE and its TIVAS is highlighted:

The allegations, detailed in a Dec. 9 letter from the Education Department to Sen. Elizabeth Warren (D-Mass.), for the first time provide a glimpse into the extent of problems plaguing the $1 trillion federal student loan portfolio, and the apparently lackluster department response to faulty behavior by companies that interact

---

66. http://www.huffingtonpost.com/2013/12/11/education-sallie-mae_n_4428048.html

with borrowers on its behalf and collect payments on government-backed student debt. The letter was obtained by The Huffington Post.

The findings come as Education Secretary Arne Duncan battles accusations that his department tolerates wrongdoing by companies it pays to service federal student loans, most notably Sallie Mae. The nation's largest handler of student debt, Sallie Mae is under investigation by at least three federal agencies for allegedly violating borrowers' rights. At least one of them—the Federal Deposit Insurance Corporation—has told Sallie Mae it intends to publicly accuse the company of harming borrowers.

But the pending investigations and likely enforcement action didn't stop the Education Department from telling Sallie Mae in October that it intends to renew its lucrative contract to service federal student loans. The department told Warren that it was "not aware" of any issues or findings that would warrant any fines or termination of its existing contract with the company. Poor servicing of federal student loans has contributed to some policymakers' fears that the nation's $1.2 trillion in unpaid student debt risks curtailing economic growth in the coming years....

...Over the last 10 years, according to its letter to Warren, the Education Department and its inspector general have concluded that Sallie Mae incorrectly billed the department for its services, failed to report certain fees, failed to pay other parties rightful fees, filed untimely claims when borrowers defaulted on their debts, and reported incorrect repayment terms. More broadly, the Education Department wrote, it has found "general management and reporting deficiencies" as well as "due diligence" errors.

But the Education Department didn't seem too concerned. James Runcie, Office of Federal Student Aid chief operating officer, described the various findings as "compliance issues" in the letter. He told Warren, who had asked whether the department would terminate its Sallie Mae contract or fine the company as punishment for wrongdoing, that the issues had not risen to the level where these penalties were considered appropriate, and they were resolved through the implementation of corrective action plans.

The Education Department doesn't know how many borrowers were harmed by the destructive practices, it conceded in its letter to Warren....

...The Education Department told Warren that it has fined 11 companies that participate in the Federal Family Education Loan program, the bank-based lending initiative that Congress and the Obama administration ended in 2010, and collected $747,500 in penalties.

Sallie Mae is not among them. In fact, the Education Department has not publicly reprimanded Sallie Mae for any of the alleged failings it has documented in its roughly two dozen reviews of the company over the past 10 years....

...In its letter, the Education Department said that as part of its reviews of Sallie Mae, it "ensures that appropriate corrective action has been taken by Sallie Mae, including any necessary restitution of funds to the department." The department added that it generally recoups funds by reducing what it pays companies when they submit invoices.

The Education Department didn't specify whether any such funds were recovered from Sallie Mae. However, the department determined Sept. 25 [2013] that it was time to recoup some $22 million in improper payments made to Sallie Mae several years ago, following a 2009 recommendation by the department's inspector general that it recover the money.

From a related article titled "Department of Education Laughs Off Questions From Congress" posed by *Jobs with Justice* on April 3, 2014:[67]

Much of the questioning focused on the Department of Education's seeming reluctance to discipline student loan servicers and debt collectors that are in breach of their contracts (Sallie Mae, for example), and the failure of the Department of Education as a whole to help struggling student borrowers. As evidence, Senator Tom Harkin (D-Iowa) pointed out that the department effectively pays its debt collectors more than $1 billion per year for as little as "writing one letter" to a struggling borrower.

A large portion of the Senate HELP committee hearing was spent discussing the Department of Education's profits made off student debt, a reported $41.3 billion in 2013. Senator Elizabeth Warren (D-Mass.) noted that for the government to "break even" on student loans, they'd only need to charge an interest rate of about two and a half percent, yet currently, interest rates on federal

---

67. http://www.jwj.org/department-of-education-laughs-off-complaints

student loans are set to be twice that for undergraduates and up to triple that for graduate students. When asked if the profits from these loans went back toward helping struggling borrowers or investing further in grants for students, Runcie admitted that, "They do not—they're used to fund the government generally, they do not come back specifically into the program [for students]."

In response, Senator Warren said simply, "I think this is obscene, we are taxing students for the privilege of borrowing money…"

…Senator Warren asked why the department planned to renew its contract with Sallie Mae, which made more than $100 million in profits from this contract between 2007 and 2011, citing that the publicly traded corporation is under investigation by the Federal Deposit Insurance Corporation (FDIC), the Department of Justice and the Consumer Financial Protection Bureau (CFPB) for dozens of contract and rule violations, including misreporting loan balances to students and failing to remove students from default status even after their loans were rehabilitated. Runcie actually admitted that the Department could do more—like add stricter language to Sallie Mae's existing contract—but he said it would be difficult to move the existing student loans to a new servicer…

…The larger question, ultimately, and the one that didn't come up during the hearings is this: Why is the Department of Education (led by Secretary Arne Duncan, James Runcie and the rest of their gang) making billions of dollars in profits and going out of its way to protect its big bank friends while doing very little to actually help and protect borrowers? When government agencies act like corporations, it's time for something to change.

INJUSTICE FOR ALL INSIGHT

Rewarding Unethical and Illegal Business Practices

The practice of rewarding unethical and illegal behavior with new contracts makes me wonder if this TIVA servicer knows about the data manipulation or other seedy information and remains silent in exchange for continued contracts with the DOE that feed billions into the Sallie Mae-Navient coffer.

In recent testimony before a House Committee on Education and the Workforce subcommittee, Kathleen Tighe, Inspector General for the U.S. Department of Education, stated, *"Through its [DOE] Federal Student Aid office (FSA), the Department disburses approximately $140 BILLION in student aid annually and manages an outstanding loan portfolio of $1.47 TRILLION. This makes it one of the largest financial institutions in the country. As such, effective oversight and monitoring of its operations are critical."*

More interesting facts can be found in "The Student Debt Crisis and the U.S. Department of Education: How a Government agency Shirks Oversight Responsibility and Operates Like a Big Bank" on *Jobs with Justice*.[68]

Summary: CDR Manipulation Based on Fact

There are tremendous numbers of borrowers with student loan debt totaling over $1.47 trillion. Here's one last look at the players:

1. The average privately-held proprietary school that serves between 500 and 1,000 students a year. Many for-profit schools also have higher overhead and reduced profits because they serve at-risk students who need more one-on-one attention than traditional students. For those who are really

---

68. http://www.jwj.org/wp-content/uploads/2014/03/Student-Debt-and-ED-Fact-Sheet_final.pdf

blessed, net profits may be a few million dollars upon which they pay taxes in the highest tax bracket.

2. Profits for large federal servicers (TIVAS) are measured in hundreds of millions for each company every year. According to a report issued in September 2014 by the National Consumer Law Center[69] titled "Pounding Student Loan Borrowers: The Heavy Costs of the Government's Partnership with Debt Collection Agencies," over $1 BILLION in fees were paid to private student loan collectors in 2014 and this is estimated to climb to $2 BILLION in 2016.

3. The Department of Education's profits in 2013 were $41.3 BILLION. When deferments, forbearances, and repayment schedules that don't adequately pay down the principal are approved for students, a large portion if not all of the student's payments are applied to interest (profit). Or worse, when this accrued interest remains unpaid, it is capitalized and interest is charged on the capitalized interest (increased loan balance) which increases profit for the DOE. The DOE can take extraordinary actions like seizing tax refunds and wage garnishment if the students go into default because this is a federal debt.

Is it any wonder that this "big business" is implementing federal regulations to expand repayment programs that put borrowers into circumstances where the loan period extends to 20–25 years and payments are dropped to interest only or negative amortization? Fraud and abuse in student loans should be stopped at all levels including for-profit and nonprofit institutions, third-party servicers that handle federal funds, federal loan servicing companies, and within the federal government itself.

And I ask again,
"CDR Manipulation:
Who is REALLY responsible?"

The 2013 collective profit of the DOE and four TIVAS for
student loans that can be verified is:
OVER $43 BILLION!

---

69. http://www.nclc.org/images/pdf/pr-reports/report-sl-debt-collectors.pdf

Facts about Student Loans and Interested Parties to the Loans

- U.S. Department of Education realized $41.3 BILLION in untaxed profit in 2013. It has not announced its 2014 profit.

- Sallie Mae enjoyed a 2013 profit of $1.7 BILLION and 28% taxes were assessed. Their loan portfolio exceeds $310 BILLION in student loans.

- NelNet[70] had a 2013 profit of $303 MILLION and has a current federal student loan portfolio of over $29 BILLION.

- FedLoan Servicing (PHEAA) is nonprofit ($0 taxes assessed).

- Great Lakes Higher Education Corporation is nonprofit ($0 taxes assessed).

- The total federal student loan debt is over $1.2 TRILLION.

- The total fees paid for collecting student loan debt was over $1 BILLION.

- Total fees for collection are expected to reach $2 BILLION in 2016.

- The four TIVAS service over 26 million borrowers.

- The PAYE program increases the loan repayment period from ten (10) to twenty (20) years and the IBR and other various options can increase it to 25–30 years, substantially increasing the interest (DOE profit) paid by the borrowers.

- Until Congress decides otherwise, any principal left unpaid at the end of the extended PAYE, REPAY, or IBR repayment period is "forgiven" although the borrower will pay taxes on the amount forgiven in a "balloon payment."

- The DOE started negotiating language in 2015 at the request of President Obama to expand the income-driven repayment programs, and we anticipate the structure to mirror that of the PAYE program—the program is already being called REPAY.

- Over 40 million citizens or over 13% of all Americans have student loan debt.

---

70. http://www.omaha.com/money/nelnet-posts-record-profits-for/article_7d4d8231-dc7e-530a-996c-ba5685018ea7.html

- As of June 30, 2014, there were approximately 7 million federal student loan borrowers in default.[71]

- While the DOE won't publish delinquent information for the FFEL portfolio, as of June 30, 2014, there were nearly 1.7 million direct loan borrowers over 90 days delinquent.

In comparison, the average proprietary school is:

- Owned by an entrepreneur

- Has personal guarantees on business financial obligations

- Serves 500–1,000 student annually

- Has annual net profits of several hundred thousand to several million dollars on which they have few to no personal deductions and pay the highest tax bracket

EXAMPLE OF FOR-PROFIT COLLEGE IN ARIZONA for Single Self-employed Owner with $1 MILLION in Net Profit (AGI):

Tax Description	Tax Rate	Tax Amount
Federal	$119,996 + 39.6% of income in excess of $415,500	$516,030
State	4.54%	$45,400
FICA (Social Security)	12.4% Maximum Earnings of $118,500	$14,694
FICA (Medicare)	2.9% + 0.9% additional self-employed > $200,000	$29,000 plus $7,200
This Income Loses Personal Deductions for Standard Deductions, Child Tax Credit, and Charitable Contributions among others		
TOTAL TAXES (61.2%)		$612,324
NET INCOME with high personal risk		$387,676

Federal Direct Loan Servicer Allocation Methodology

The DOE's allocation metrics that were in effect until August 2014 are defined beginning on the following page.

---

71. http://www.treasury.gov/press-center/press-releases/Pages/JL2689.aspx

Allocation Methodology

The Department has provided its federal loan servicers broad latitude to determine how best to service their assigned loans in order to yield high performing portfolios and high levels of customer satisfaction. We use metrics to measure the performance of each federal loan servicer.

There are two sets of performance metrics that we use to allocate new loan volume. One set of performance metrics applies to FedLoan Servicing (PHEAA), Great Lakes Educational Loan Services, Inc., Nelnet, and Sallie Mae. The other set of metrics applies to the NFP Members of the federal loan servicer team.

FedLoan Servicing (PHEAA), Great Lakes Educational Loan Services, Inc., Nelnet, and Sallie Mae

The five performance metrics the Department uses to allocate new loan volume among FedLoan Servicing (PHEAA), Great Lakes Educational Loan Services, Inc., Nelnet, and Sallie Mae are as follows:

- Three metrics measure the satisfaction among separate customer groups, including borrowers, financial aid personnel at postsecondary schools participating in the federal student loan programs, and Federal Student Aid and other federal agency personnel who work with the servicers.

- Two metrics measure the success of default prevention efforts as reflected by the percentage of borrowers and percentage of dollars in each servicer's portfolio that go into default.

The Department compiles quarterly customer satisfaction survey scores and default prevention statistics for FedLoan Servicing (PHEAA), Great Lakes Educational Loan Services, Inc., Nelnet, and Sallie Mae into annual measures to determine each servicer's allocation of loan volume. Annual allocations are determined as described in each servicer's contract under Attachment A-4, Ongoing Allocation Methodology.

- The Department factors the servicers' scores on all five of the performance measures into the allocation formula in the same way. The servicer with the best score (highest ACSI score or lowest default statistic) is awarded four points on that dimension. The servicer with the next best score is given three points. Third and fourth place are allocated two points and one point, respectively. Thus, ten points (4 + 3 + 2 + 1= 10) are allocated among the servicers for each of the five performance measures.

- To determine an individual servicer's allocation of new loans, the Department first sums the points that servicer earns across the five performance measures. The Department then divides this total by 50. The result of this division is the servicer's proportion of new work. The Department divides the servicer's total by 50 because that is the total number of points allocated to all servicers across the five performance measures (10 total points per measure x 5 performance measures = 50).

NFP Members of the Federal Loan Servicer Team

The five performance metrics the Department uses for the NFP members of the federal loan servicer team are as follows:

- Two metrics measure the satisfaction among separate customer groups, including borrowers and Federal Student Aid and other federal agency personnel who work with the servicers.

- Three metrics measure the success of default prevention efforts as reflected by the percentage of borrowers that are 30 or fewer days delinquent, percentage of borrowers that are more than 90 days delinquent, and percentage of borrowers for whom a delinquency of more than 180 days was resolved.

The Department does not guarantee that an NFP member of the federal loan servicing team will receive more than its initial allocation of borrower accounts. The first allocation of additional volume for NFP members of the federal loan servicer team will not occur before August 2013.

Performance Measure Methodology Customer Satisfaction

As applicable, the Department has segmented performance scores to ensure comparability across the federal loan servicers regardless of differences in the types of borrowers or schools serviced. We calculate separate borrower customer satisfaction scores for each loan status (borrowers in repayment, in grace, and/ or in school). We calculate school customer satisfaction scores and default prevention statistics by type of school (private, proprietary, and public). We use the average of the segment scores in our allocation methodology.

The analytical methodology used by our independent vendor, CFI Group, to evaluate customer satisfaction is consistent with that used in the American Customer Satisfaction Index (ACSI). The ACSI, established in 1994, is a uniform, cross-industry measure of satisfaction with goods and services available to U.S. consumers, including both the private and public sectors. The ACSI summarizes the responses to three uniform survey items that measure customer satisfaction with a score that has a minimum score of zero and a maximum score of 100. CFI encourages companies that measure customer satisfaction using the ACSI to strive to achieve and maintain overall customer satisfaction scores in the low 80s. The highest ACSI score ever recorded is a 91, and the national average across all economic sectors is 76.

CFI Group specializes in the application of the ACSI methodology to individual organizations. As our independent vendor, CFI Group develops the surveys and conducts the analysis.

Default Prevention

The Department generates default prevention measures with simple arithmetic and rounds all results to the hundredths place.

FedLoan Servicing (PHEAA), Great Lakes Educational Loan Services, Inc., Nelnet, and Sallie Mae

The Department divides the number of borrowers in repayment that go into default during the quarter by the number of unique borrowers in the repayment portfolio at the end of each quarter to generate each servicer's defaulted borrower "count" statistic.

The Department divides the dollar value of the loans that go into default during the quarter by the total value of the repayment portfolio at the end of the quarter to generate each servicer's defaulted borrower "amount" statistic.

NFP Members of the Federal Loan Servicer Team

The Department divides the number of borrowers in current repayment status who are less than or equal to 30 days delinquent at the end of the quarter by the number of all borrowers in both current and delinquent repayment status at end of each quarter to generate the percent of "borrowers in current repayment status" statistic.

The Department divides the number of borrowers who are greater than 90 days delinquent during the quarter by the number of borrowers in both current and delinquent repayment status at the end of each quarter to generate the percent of "borrowers greater than 90 days delinquent" statistic.

The Department divides the number of borrowers who are less than or equal to 30 days delinquent at the end of quarter and who had a delinquency of 180 days or greater at the end of the prior quarter by the number of borrowers who are 180 days or more delinquent at the end of the quarter to generate the "delinquency resolution of borrowers greater than 180 days delinquent" statistic.

....

September 2012 *Career Education Review* Article Highlighting Ms. Hammer's Response to TICAS CDR Manipulation Allegations

Response to "The Institute for College Access & Success (TICAS) Memo" Dated August 21, 2012
Career Education Review, September 2012

By Mary Lyn Hammer, President & CEO Champion College Services

In response to the recent report from the Senate Health, Education, Labor, and Pensions Committee's two-year investigation of the for-profit college industry, The Institute for College Access & Success (TICAS) issued a memo addressed to "Interested Parties" dated August 21, 2012. The intent as outlined in the memo was to discuss "...three ways companies may be manipulating their CDRs, and the steps the Department of Education should immediately take to ensure full compliance with federal law and protect taxpayers from subsidizing schools with CDRs above the permitted thresholds. The three issues discussed are: appealing CDRs based on "improper servicing" of loans; combining campuses for reporting purposes; and the abuse of forbearances."

Since I have been specializing in default prevention (cohort default rates or CDRs) since 1987, helped draft regulatory criteria for default prevention (originally "Appendix D," and now "Subpart M" and "Subpart N"), and was a negotiator for the CDR appeals processes, it became apparent very quickly that the recommendations of TICAS were based on misinformation and inaccurate facts.

1. Appealing CDRs Based on "Improper Servicing" of Loans.

a. Loan servicing appeals are one of the only ways that the public can "audit" those under contract for federal student loan servicing. It is a right given to schools that also supports proper servicing for students and ensures accurate reporting of CDRs for Title IV federal fund eligibility. In fact, this is one of the practices in place that is defined in federal regulations (34 CFR 668.193 & 668.212) that insures program integrity and protects the taxpayers' interest.

b. The transition from FFELP to direct lending caused many issues with proper servicing and quality of servicing encompassing those related to PUT Loans (those FFELP loans disbursed on our after October 1, 2010, that were transferred to the Department of Education for servicing) including but not limited to:

   i. Students with multiple loan programs, multiple servicers, and multiple payments to manage. Even students with these "multiples" within one company experienced chaos in loan servicing. For example, the FFELP Loans were on one computer system, the PUT Loans on another and the direct loans on yet another—and the systems didn't communicate! The students were very confused when their loans appeared to be with one company and they still had to submit 3 separate payments and three sets of forms to change their repayment schedules or to apply for deferments and forbearances that they were entitled to. Some students had as many as 7 or 8 different loan servicers to communicate with.

ii. Long intervals of time where proper loan servicing was interrupted during the "transfer" of the records (as much as 9–10 months when the loans were not serviced.)

iii. Lost and misapplied payments.

iv. Lost and misapplied deferment and forbearance forms that were not consistently applied to all of the students' loans. Many students had properly applied for and been approved for deferments that they were entitled to by law, yet when the loan transfers were complete, the status no longer reflected a current status but rather reflected a delinquent status. The student did nothing wrong. The schools did nothing wrong. Many of these loans went into default when they shouldn't have. It is truly a tragedy for the students and the schools who are also suffering the consequences of processes that went wrong with the federal loan servicers.

v. Servicing for FFELP loans suffered as the financial stability of these FFELP companies quickly declined. Profits are made on the interest paid on loans and as the loan balances decrease, the profits decrease. With all of the "newest" loans transferred to the Department, the profitability of the loan servicers diminished, forcing them to decrease servicing efforts to what was minimally required in "due diligence." Efforts were focused on collecting those loans with higher balances that netted higher profits. Efforts for lower balances (non-degree programs) were minimal because profits on them were minimal.

vi. Servicing for PUT and direct loans based on minimal servicing fees suffered as loan volume quickly changed. Only four primary servicers were originally chosen to service these loans. These servicers were handling literally hundreds of thousands of loans being transferred in addition to virtually all of the new loan volume. No matter how successful a company is, no company can grow at that rate and do it well. The federal student loan program is complicated and it takes time to ensure proper and quality hiring, training, and servicing.

d. Federal regulations for loan servicing appeals provide a very limited basis for inclusion in an appeal. If a loan servicer cannot fulfill the obligations under these rules, their contract for servicing should be examined for administrative capabilities.

   i. A defaulted FFEL is considered improperly serviced for cohort default rate purposes if one or more of the following occurs:

      1. The borrower never made a loan payment, and the school can document that the lender was required but failed to send at least one letter (other than the final demand letter) urging the borrower to make payments on the loan.

      2. The borrower never made a loan payment, and the school can document that the lender was required but failed to attempt at least one telephone call to the borrower.

      3. The borrower never made a loan payment, and the school can document that the lender was required but failed to submit a request for pre-claims assistance or default aversion assistance to the guaranty agency.

      4. The borrower never made a loan payment, and the school can document that the lender was required but failed to send a final demand letter to the borrower.

      5. The borrower never made a loan payment, and the school can document that the lender was required but failed to submit a certification (or other documentation) to the guaranty agency to demonstrate that the lender performed skip tracing.

   ii. A defaulted direct loan is considered improperly

serviced for cohort default rate purposes if one or more of the following occur:

1. The borrower never made a loan payment, and the school can document that the Federal Servicer was required but failed to send at least one letter (other than the final demand letter) urging the borrower to make payments on the loan.

2. The borrower never made a loan payment, and the school can document that the Federal Servicer was required but failed to attempt at least one telephone call to the borrower.

3. The borrower never made a loan payment, and the school can document that the Federal Servicer was required but failed to send a final demand letter to the borrower.

4. The borrower never made a loan payment, and the school can document that the Federal Servicer was required but failed to document that skip tracing was performed if the Federal Servicer determined it did not have the borrower's current address.

e. The "Recommended Action" by TICAS states "Before any final CDRs are released next month, the Department should carefully review all PUT loan servicing appeals to ensure that such appeals are not being used to evade CDR thresholds." Because loan servicing appeals cannot be initiated until after the official (final) CDRs are released, it is impossible for the Department to take any course of action for them prior to the release. Additionally, the Department is required to review and approve all corrections and appeals before issuing a final determination that changes a cohort default rate.

Recommended Action: Leave "Loan Servicing Appeals" in place as an audit trail for proper student loan servicing and as accurate determination consideration for Title IV Eligibility.

2. Combining Campuses for Reporting Purposes. The phrase "unintended consequences" is used quite often in Washington, D.C. Prohibiting companies to consolidate OPE ID's to insure financial stability and compliance would have many unintended consequences. Here are some considerations:

a. Certain cities and states in America have higher unemployment rates, lower standards test scores, and lower income levels than other areas of the country. These are facts that can be validated through numerous data sources. The students in these areas are at-risk students because of circumstances that are not related to colleges and these are also the people in our country who need additional training and education to become working and contributing members of our society.

b. Many institutions have closed locations for inner-city students because the risks are too high. This will continue to happen if students in these high-risk areas are not able to attend branch campuses of areas that serve lower-risk students. The United States applies this in theory with higher income people paying more in taxes than lower income people. It only makes good business sense to educate our high-risk students by offsetting risks with lower-risk students.

c. The biggest tragedy (unintended consequence) would be in disallowing businesses to make these choices, thus limiting access to education for those at-risk who need training beyond secondary education, and widening the gap between the socioeconomic sectors of our country.

Recommended Action: Data and business management is easier to successfully navigate with consolidated data. Many resources can be shared and maximized for efficiencies that drive successful outcomes and savings when businesses are allowed to pool their collective resources. Businesses should have the freedom to apply for these options to improve their business models. Remember that the changes must be approved by the Department of Education and often come with closer scrutiny for a period of time after the initial approval to ensure successful implementation of the changes. In other words, there are processes in place that ensure integrity in these areas so no action is necessary. The unintended consequences of these proposed limitations would be reduced access to education and training options for at-risk students.

3. Abuse of Forbearances. The important language in this section is the statement that "…some for-profit college corporations are abusing forbearance and deferment, using them as tools to manipulate the school's CDR regardless of the student's particular situation or whether it is in the student's best financial interest." We acknowledge that some institutions and default management companies overuse or misuse forbearances—but not all—and there should be oversight to prevent abuses. Here are the considerations:

a. Deferments are entitlements for the borrowers—if they qualify, they are entitled to have them. The criteria for qualifying are defined in statute and in federal regulations and have nothing to do with the school's integrity. In fact, helping the student learn about these options represents integrity by educating students beyond the classroom so they can have long-term financial freedom.

b. Forbearance is designed as a temporary solution when the student doesn't qualify for any other available option and cannot become current any other way. It is not intended as a long-term fix. Forbearances are granted at the lender's (servicer's) discretion. If the servicer did not approve, the student wouldn't be granted forbearance. It is often used to bridge the gap in time where a delinquency has occurred before the student qualifies for a deferment or alternate payment schedule.

c. Federal loan servicer contracts are based on portfolio successes and data that would encourage the servicers to approve forbearances and other options that may not be in the best interest of the students. These companies are given a percent of the federal loan portfolio based on performance—there are trends in data that show there is manipulation by the federal loan servicers in these areas as well. Again, the students and schools pay the consequences for actions by these companies. This is such an extensive area that details will be left for another article.

d. The TICAS memo states that an Income-Based Repayment

(IBR) plan is a good option for borrowers. In fact, this may be a worse option for many borrowers since it is a schedule that the student lives with for one year at a time, has heavy penalties if proper documentation is not submitted in a timely manner each year, and may have unpaid interest accruing similar to a forbearance if the IBR payment approved puts the student in a negative amortization schedule.

e. The memo suggests that that Department examine institutions with CDRs that spike after the CDR window closes. As a point in fact about spikes at this time, many "graduated repayment schedules" that are structured similar to those ARM mortgage loans that default at a high rate have higher payments in the years after the CDR window closes. Data demonstrates that in student loans and mortgage loans, the rate of default increases when the payments go up. The accrued and unpaid interest during the years with lower payments is also very costly to borrowers. This is a payment option that should be examined for many reasons because it sets up borrowers and taxpayers for failure.

Recommended Action: The increase from a 2-year CDR to a 3-year CDR has been implemented. This is a period beyond what was originally discussed within the Department as appropriate for making the school responsible beyond the program completion date. The Department should be encouraged to develop repayment schedules and servicing programs that promote long-term success. Bringing back the incentives for students who make timely payments would be a great start—rewarding those who do the right thing is just more effective than punishing those who do the wrong thing.

While I can only speak to the institutions and data that Champion College Services is responsible for, I can say that everyone wins when you do what is right for the students. This may sound like an advertisement and it is intended to show that, when integrity is used, the numbers will speak for long-term financial success for students, schools and taxpayers.

Champion College Services has been in business since 1989 and specializes in at-risk students. During a better economy, on average, we cut default rates in half. The climate has become more challenging with a bad economy and complications with the transition from FFELP to direct lending. We have always focused on what was in the best interest of the students and our success in teaching them good habits for long-term financial success shows in the most recently available and relevant data as follows:

- **FY 2009 Cohort Default Rates** for Champion tenured clients, on average, were *reduced by 7.1%* while the rest of the nation experienced significant increases.

FY 2009 2-YEAR OFFICIAL COHORT DEFAULT RATES	
Champion Tenured Clients	7.1% Reduction!
National Average	25.7% Increase!
Proprietary Average	29.3% Increase!

- **Gainful Employment Informational Rates** proved that Champion's tenured clients show significantly higher repayment rates for *students' successful repayment* than institutions in the same sector (proprietary) and credential levels as follows:

2011 GE REPAYMENT RATES RELEASED JUNE 2012			
Credential Level	Champion	National	Champion Difference
Undergraduate Certificate	42.43	38.36	4.07 Higher!
Associates Degree	50.97	35.22	15.75 Higher!
Bachelor's Degree	56.66	42.31	14.35 Higher!
1st Professional Degree	54.15	48.57	5.58 Higher!

In summary, the TICAS memo is based on an investigation by the Senate HELP committee and should be taken seriously. We strongly support finding solutions for schools and default management companies who are not in integrity. We also acknowledge that there are many who have integrity, who help dreams come true, and who support long-term financial success for students. The differences between those with and without integrity are worthy of separation in the minds of lawmakers and in the minds of Americans remembering that America is the land of opportunity for education and for business and we need these to rebuild our country.

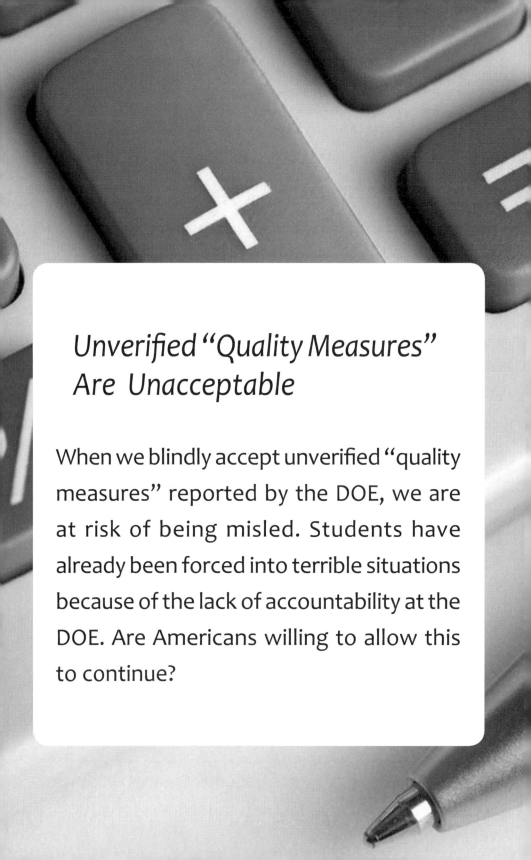

Unverified "Quality Measures" Are Unacceptable

When we blindly accept unverified "quality measures" reported by the DOE, we are at risk of being misled. Students have already been forced into terrible situations because of the lack of accountability at the DOE. Are Americans willing to allow this to continue?

V. GAINFUL EMPLOYMENT MANIPULATION

WHY DID THE GOVERNMENT RELEASE GE "STREAMLINED" RATES LACKING BACKUP DATA DETAILS TO THE PUBLIC?

When big decisions are based on data reporting not verified for accuracy by third-party auditors, the consequences from relying on the accuracy of that information can create a domino effect that harms students who are earnestly trying to make a better life through educational resources. The consequences of these decisions can be astronomical.

Sham-Filled Rates and Measures Details

On June 26, 2012, the U.S. Department of Education publicly released the FY 2011 Gainful Employment "Streamlined" Informational Rates (Streamlined) to the press, public, and Wall Street. These streamlined rates included less than a third of the programs as defined in the final GE federal regulations and *only* contained the rates, *not* the data detail behind these rates. Because of the blatant omissions, the numbers were simply a sham. And the manner in which those inaccurate numbers were released was diabolical, in that it was extraordinarily difficult for industry professionals, the public, or the media to dispute the streamlined findings without immersing oneself into a sea of numbers to fish out the facts. I was appalled and so I chose to dive in and review what I believed to be a plethora of inaccuracies that I have included in this chapter.

The FY 2011 Gainful Employment "Final" Informational Rates (Final) contained all of the programs as defined in the final GE federal regulations and also had a good portion of the data details for the rates. Most people didn't know this larger set of data existed because *it was only given out to select members of the press and Wall Street.*

I found out about this Final data when I participated in the webinar hosted by the U.S. Department of Education on June 26, 2012. Most interested parties didn't participate in this webinar because the Dear Colleague Letter (ANN-12-15) notification[72] for the webinar wasn't posted until approximately 7:56 pm ET on June 25, 2012 and the webinar took place at 8:00 am ET on June 26, 2012! Several members of my team at Champion College Services and I were participants at 5:00 am Arizona time.

For the first 20 minutes of the call, my friend in the proprietary school business in Washington, DC and I couldn't see the screen. We were also writing emails back and forth with a Wall Street analyst. The analyst could see the screen after the first few minutes and my proprietary school friend and I couldn't see it for 20 minutes. During that time, it was obvious that the people on the call were talking about a different set of data than the FY 2011 Gainful Employment Streamlined Informational Data that we had.

After 20 minutes, my proprietary school friend and I could see the screen, *and* we were looking at the host's screen. As we typed in our questions, we saw the questions scrolling up the right side of the host's screen along with questions from others on the call. The questions from others were answered and those from my friend and me were overlooked. When we heard the male's voice say something like "We've answered all of the questions so we're going to end the call early," we knew without a doubt that proprietary schools were being targeted.

The PowerPoint PDF for the webinar and the transcribed Q&A are currently available. The media link for the recording in the Gainful Employment Electronic Announcement #38[73] does not get you to a recording.

---

72. http://ifap.ed.gov/dpcletters/ANN1215.html

73. https://www.ifap.ed.gov/eannouncements/062612GEEAnnouncement38.html

Table 37: GE Announcements #37 and #38 (IFAP screenshot)

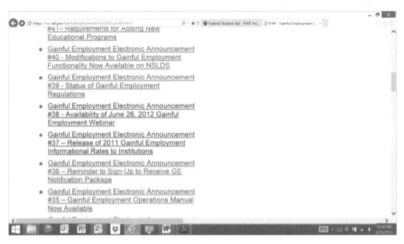

Out of fifty-two GE webinars posted in 2012, the June 26, 2012 GE Webinar #8 was the **only one** that does not have a video recording posted.

Table 38: Gainful Employment Webinar #8 (IFAP screenshot)

After the June 26, 2012 webinar ended, I searched for several hours and found the FY 2011 Gainful Employment "Final" Informational Data buried within the Department's website. The FY 2011 Gainful Employment (GE) "Streamlined" Informational Data released to the public **did not contain** the detailed data that the FY 2011 GE "Final" Data had so, for those who didn't look at the Final data, assumptions were made that the streamlined data were accurate.

Some of the following information is repeated from my Manifesto chapter. I believe having the relevant data in one section makes analyzing the GE information less complicated. All data analysis, statistics, and payment schedules used in this chapter have been verified for accuracy in an "Independent Accountants' Report" conducted by Kaiser & Carolin, P.C. (March 7, 2015) and concluded with "no exceptions" for all Gainful Employment data analyzed by Mary Lyn Hammer.

INJUSTICE FOR ALL INSIGHT

The Truth about the GE Data

There were two sets of data for the FY 2011 GE Informational Rates:

The "Streamlined" data: *Released to the general public included rates for 3,787 programs with no supporting data.*

The more comprehensive "Final" data: *Not released to the general public included 13,587 programs and the data details behind the GE rates.*

The "Final" data contained details about the GE rates that allowed an audit and resulted in calculations that were not consistent with the Streamlined rates released to the public, to reporters, and to Wall Street. The discrepancies yielded results in favor of public institutions and were damaging to proprietary institutions.

A disproportionate number of schools from each sector were reported in the "FY 2011 Streamlined Informational Data" that was released to the public compared to the comprehensive "FY 2011 Final GE Informational Data."

Table 39: FY 2011 GE Streamlined vs Final Data

Sector	Credential Level	# Programs in FINAL GE Data	# Programs Reported in STREAMLINED GE Data	% of Final Programs Reported in STREAMLINED
PUBLIC	Undergraduate Certificate	5,159	266	5.16%
PUBLIC	Post Baccalaureate Certificate	142	2	1.41%
PRIVATE	Undergraduate Certificate	437	95	21.74%
PRIVATE	Post Baccalaureate Certificate	179	16	8.94%
PROPRIETARY	Undergraduate Certificate	4,509	1,989	44.11%
PROPRIETARY	Associate's Degree	2,073	909	43.85%
PROPRIETARY	Bachelor's Degree	836	327	39.11%
PROPRIETARY	Post Baccalaureate Certificate	42	6	14.29%
PROPRIETARY	Master's Degree	309	138	44.66%
PROPRIETARY	Doctorate Degree	59	30	50.85%
PROPRIETARY	First Professional Degree	19	9	47.37%

The data for the "missing programs" was inconsistent:

1. Several programs had all data and weren't reported.

2. Title IV loan amounts were provided and yet repayment rate information was missing.

3. Repayment rate information and Title IV loan information were listed as blank, zero (0), or N/A when debt-to-earnings calculations were provided.

4. Debt and earnings information were provided however the debt-to-earnings rates were blank.

The following chart provides information based on the average of available information for each data point:

Table 40: FY 2011 GE "Final" Data Analysis by Sector & Credential Level

FY 2011 GAINFUL EMPLOYMENT INFORMATIONAL RATE ANALYSIS	This contained the detailed data behind the calculations. DOE FILE NAME: GE2011InformationalRates062612FINAL		
	Average Debt	Average Total Earnings	Average Discretionary Earnings
Undergraduate Certificate			
PUBLIC	$4,148	$30,476	$14,420
PRIVATE	$6,365	$22,598	$8,897
PROPRIETARY	$6,808	$17,274	$2,874
Associate Degree			
PUBLIC	*There are no gainful employment accountability metrics in place for these programs.*		
PRIVATE	*There are no gainful employment accountability metrics in place for these programs.*		
PROPRIETARY	$8,060.93	$25,329.54	$8,803.91
Bachelor's Degree			
PUBLIC	*There are no gainful employment accountability metrics in place for these programs.*		
PRIVATE	*There are no gainful employment accountability metrics in place for these programs.*		
PROPRIETARY	$10,110	$35,467	$18,740
Post Baccalaureate Certificate			
PUBLIC	$11,475	$69,299	$52,544
PRIVATE	$12,080	$67,810	$51,155
PROPRIETARY	$8,579	$65,740	$48,985
Masters Degree			
PUBLIC	*There are no gainful employment accountability metrics in place for these programs.*		
PRIVATE	*There are no gainful employment accountability metrics in place for these programs.*		
PROPRIETARY	$13,289.65	$58,804.15	$42,057.66
Doctorate Degree			
PUBLIC	*There are no gainful employment accountability metrics in place for these programs.*		
PRIVATE	*There are no gainful employment accountability metrics in place for these programs.*		
PROPRIETARY	$10,663.62	$82,270.63	$65,515.63
First Professional Degree			
PUBLIC	*There are no gainful employment accountability metrics in place for these programs.*		
PRIVATE	*There are no gainful employment accountability metrics in place for these programs.*		
PROPRIETARY	$24,413	$38,000	$23,237

The GE final data *does not* support the belief that proprietary colleges force high loan debt on their students and don't place them in jobs where they can afford their payments. In fact, the relevant proprietary school median debt is reasonable for the education credential levels and earnings when the correct payment calculations are used. For Post Baccalaureate Certificate programs, the proprietary debt is significantly lower than for public and private colleges.

The debt-to-earnings (D/E) rates were *incorrectly calculated* and based on grossly erroneous annual payments that were not calculated using the standard repayment criteria for 10-, 15-, and 20-year repayment schedules as defined in the GE final federal regulations.

The defined payment schedules for each credential level that *should have* been used are as follows:

Table 41: GE Standard Repayment Criteria for Annual Payment Calculations

10-year Standard Repayment	15-year Standard Repayment	20-year Standard Repayment
Undergraduate Certificate	Bachelor's Degree	Doctorate Degree
Associate's Degree	Master's Degree	First Professional Degree
Post Baccalaureate Certificate		

Grossly exaggerated annual payments for proprietary programs misrepresented debt-to-earnings ratios for proprietary programs including 193 supposed "failing programs" at proprietary colleges. To the best of my knowledge, the DOE never printed a rescission or publicly corrected the inaccurate GE rates upon which many conclusions and opinions were based *including significant drops in enrollment and EDU stock values.*

Indictments related to the original GE process and for leaking (incorrect) information to Wall Street short sellers and other unethical behaviors have been buried more than once for Robert Shireman, former Deputy Undersecretary at the U.S. Department of Education, who was the driving force behind Gainful Employment 1.0. Shireman was also one of the Obama Administration's appointees who had lobbied within two years prior to his appointment—in fact, he lobbied for most if not ALL of the two years prior to his appointment and there were certain activities that he continued even after his appointment that might be interpreted as lobbying and, as such, were completely unethical.

In the comprehensive "Final" FY 2011 GE Informational Rate data, the payment calculations for programs where *all sectors* are compared were the most accurately reported ratios:

- The UNDERGRADUATE program payments were consistent with the average debt amount and the defined length of repayment period.

- The POST BACCALEAUREATE program payments were similar to the payments calculated for the average debt amount and defined length of repayment period. The payments for the proprietary programs had the biggest discrepancy.

The payment calculations for credential levels where the proprietary schools had the only applicable programs (foreign programs excepted), were inaccurately calculated too high. This had negative influences, inflating the debt-to-earnings, which fed the public's misguided belief system that for-profit schools are predatory and leave students buried in high debt and with low paying jobs.

These miscalculated payments were significantly higher for proprietary schools in credential levels where public and private institutions didn't report. (see Table 42)

Table 42: Summary of Average Corrections to FY 2011 GE "Final" Annual Payments by Sector & Credential Level

Corrected GE2011INFORMATIONALRATES062512FINAL

Credential Level School Type	Average INCORRECT Annual Payment Reported to Public	Average CORRECT Annual Payment	Annual Payment Adjustment for Correct Payment (+/-)	% of Adjustment Needed for Correct Payment	Difference in Monthly Payment
Undergraduate Certificate					
PUBLIC	$600	$573	**($27)**	**-5%**	($2)
PRIVATE	$977	$879	**($97)**	**-11%**	($8)
PROPRIETARY	$954	$940	**($14)**	**-2%**	($1)
Associate's Degree					
PROPRIETARY	$2,055	$1,113	**($942)**	**-85%**	($79)
Bachelor's Degree					
PROPRIETARY	$2,825	$1,086	**($1,739)**	**-160%**	($145)
Post Baccalaureate Certificate					
PUBLIC	$1,372	$1,585	**$212**	**13%**	$18
PRIVATE	$1,647	$1,668	**$21**	**1%**	$2
PROPRIETARY	$762	$1,185	**$422**	**36%**	$35
Master's Degree					
PROPRIETARY	$2,050.72	$1,416	**($635)**	**-45%**	($53)
Doctorate Degree					
PROPRIETARY	$2,431	$977	**($1,454)**	**-149%**	($121)
First Professional Degree					
PROPRIETARY	$3,947	$2,236	**($1,711)**	**-77%**	($143)

NOTE: There are **no quality measures in place for public and private institution programs** in the following credential levels:

Associate's Degree	Bachelor's Degree	Master's Degree	Doctorate Degree

When the correct annual payments were applied, the following changes occurred:

Table 43: Corrected FY 2011 "Final" Debt-to-Earnings (D/E) Rates by Sector & Credential Level

Corrected GE2011INFORMATIONALRATES062512FINAL

School Sector Corrected D/E Outcomes	Repayment Rates (Unchanged)	Debt-to-Earnings Ratios Reported Using INCORRECT Payments		Debt-to-Earnings Ratios Using CORRECT Payments	
		Annual D/E Ratio	Discretionary D/E Ratio	Annual D/E Ratio	Discretionary D/E Ratio
Undergraduate Certificate					
PUBLIC	51.87	1.99	16.50	1.88%	3.97%
	PASS	PASS	PASS	PASS	PASS
PRIVATE Correct D/E Passes 3/3	43.71	3.91	69.74	3.89%	**9.88%**
	PASS	PASS	FAIL	PASS	**PASS**
PROPRIETARY Correct D/E Passes 2/3	38.36	5.52	85.40	5.44%	32.71%
	PASS	PASS	FAIL	PASS	FAIL
Associate's Degree					
PROPRIETARY Correct D/E Passes 3/3	35.23	8.81	68.60	4.40%	**12.64%**
	PASS	PASS	FAIL	PASS	**PASS**
Bachelor's Degree					
PROPRIETARY Correct D/E Pass 3/3	42.31	9.86	40.19	3.06%	**5.79%**
	PASS	PASS	FAIL	PASS	**PASS**
Post Baccalaureate Certificate					
PUBLIC	60.18	2.99	4.76	2.29%	3.02%
	PASS	PASS	PASS	PASS	PASS
PRIVATE Correct D/E Passes 3/3	72.63	3.04	46.06	2.46%	**3.26%**
	PASS	PASS	FAIL	PASS	**PASS**
PROPRIETARY	44.63	1.30	1.90	1.80%	2.42%
	PASS	PASS	PASS	PASS	PASS
Master's Degree					
PROPRIETARY	48.92	4.76	18.87	2.41%	3.37%
	PASS	PASS	PASS	PASS	PASS
Doctorate Degree					
PROPRIETARY	45.58	3.40	4.81	1.19%	1.49%
	PASS	PASS	PASS	PASS	PASS
First Professional Degree					
PROPRIETARY Correct D/E Passes 3/3	48.57	13.60	62.72	**5.88%**	**9.62%**
	PASS	FAIL	FAIL	**PASS**	**PASS**

The U.S. Department of Education NEVER publicly corrected or rescinded these grossly inflated debt-to-earnings rates, which ruined the reputations and diminished the value of all proprietary schools based on the assumed accuracy of the DOE information that incorrectly labeled the for-profit sector as predatory.

Table 44 identifies the thresholds in both the original GE regulations (gray column) and those in the GE 2.0 regulations. We did this to show the effects of the correct payments for both sets of thresholds. References to "PASS/ZONE" include rates that pass the thresholds of GE 1.0 and are in the "ZONE" for GE 2.0.

Table 44: Gainful Employment DTE (D/E) Rate Definitions for Original & GE 2.0 Regulations

	GE 1.0	GE 2.0
Repayment Rates		
Passing	Over 35%	Moved from being an eligibility measure to disclosure requirement.
Failing	Under 35%	
Annual Debt-to-Earnings Rates		
Passing	12% or Less	8% or Less
Zone	n/a	Over 8% and Under 12%
Failing	Over 12%	Over 12%
Discretionary Debt-to-Earnings Rates		
Passing	30% or Less	20% or Less
Zone	n/a	Over 20% and Under 30%
Failing	Over 30%	Over 30%

The payment corrections for those schools identified as "failing all 3 rates" was most telling. For programs identified in the FY 2011 Streamlined Data as "Failed 3 rates"[74] (193 proprietary programs), payments were not calculated properly and in compliance with the original regulatory definitions for 10-, 15-, and 20-year repayment schedules. We could not identify a pattern except that they were grossly inaccurate (see Table 45).

Table 45: Corrections to FY 2011 "Streamlined" Failing Programs Annual Payment

Corrected FY2011StreamlinedFailed3Rates

Proprietary Schools Credential Level	Total Programs Reported as Failing All 3 Rates	Average INCORRECT Annual Payment Used by DOE	Average CORRECT Annual Payment	% of Difference
Undergraduate Certificate	31	$1,692	$1,281	**32%**
Associate's Degree	125	$2,874	$1,195	**178%**
Bachelor's Degree	36	$4,125	$1,078	**311%**
First Professional Degree	1	$8,747	$2,167	**304%**
Average of Reported Programs	**193**	**$2,948**	**$1,191**	**184%**

After correct payments were applied, these 193 failing programs (Failed 3 Rates) scored as follows for the GE measures:

- 103 programs passed the annual rate measure

- 54 programs passed both the annual and discretionary rate measures

- 30 programs had rates but were missing pertinent data so calculations couldn't be verified

- **Only 6 programs remained failing all 3 metrics**

- 56 of these programs fall within the "zone" for GE 2.0

---

74. DOE file name: FY2011StreamlinedFailed3Rates

Based on correct payment calculations, the following information emerged from the data facts (see Tables 46 and 47).

Table 46: Corrected FY 2011 Failing Program Annual Payment Calculations (Actually Failing and GE 2.0 Zone)

Corrected FY2011StreamlinedFailed3Rates

Proprietary Schools Credential Level	Total Programs Reported as Failing All 3 Rates	# Passing GE 1.0 Programs with Rates in the GE 2.0 ZONE Definition (PASS/ZONE)	# Programs Failing ALL 3 Metrics AFTER CORRECTIONS
Undergraduate Certificate	31	**17**	5
Associate's Degree	125	**33**	1
Bachelor's Degree	36	**5**	0
First Professional Degree	1	**1**	0
Totals	**193**	**56**	**6**

Table 47: Corrected FY 2011 Failing Program Annual Payment Calculations (Actually Passing & Missing Information)

Corrected Fy2011StreamlinedFailed3Rates

Proprietary Schools Credential Level	# Pass BOTH Annual & Discretionary Rates	# Passing Annual Rate	# Programs with Data Missing (N/A) Could NOT Be Fully Verified
Undergraduate Certificate	0	22	**4**
Associate's Degree	28	72	**24**
Bachelor's Degree	26	8	**2**
First Professional Degree	0	1	**0**
Totals	**54**	**103**	**30**

Based upon patterns in several sets of data that support the targeting of proprietary schools, **I believe the "zone" metric was defined to achieve the desired number of failing programs the DOE wanted** even though it was not consistent with its own rationale as explained in several hundred pages of the Preamble for the original Gainful Employment rules published on October 29, 2010. This inconsistancy makes these criteria arbitrary and capricious because they are based on eliminating schools, NOT ensuring quality. The miscalculations for payments had a significant effect on the debt-to-earnings ratios for the 193 programs identified as failing all 3 metrics (see Table 48).

Table 48: Summary of Corrections for FY 2011 Failing Programs DTE (D/E) Rates

Corrected FY2011StreamlinedFailed3Rates (Streamlined Failing Programs)

Total Programs (All Proprietary) Reported as Failing All 3 Rates	Repayment Rates Unchanged	Reported Debt-to-Earnings Ratios Reported Using INCORRECT Payments		CORRECT Debt-to-Earnings Ratios Using CORRECT Payments	
		Annual D/E Ratio	Discretionary D/E Ratio	Annual D/E Ratio	Discretionary D/E Ratio
Undergraduate Certificate *NOTE: The Streamlined Ratios did NOT match the Final Data and Ratios for several programs					
31	19.87	**14.85***	**124.60***	**10.59%**	76.65%
	FAIL	FAIL	FAIL	**PASS/ ZONE**	FAIL
Associate's Degree					
125	21.33	14.89	128.54	**6.46%**	44.24%
	FAIL	FAIL	FAIL	**PASS**	FAIL
Bachelor's Degree					
36	25.08	17.69	81.06	**4.57%**	**22.51%**
	FAIL	FAIL	FAIL	**PASS**	**PASS/ZONE**
First Professional Degree					
1	30.66	55.74	100	13.81%	100%
	FAIL	FAIL	FAIL	FAIL	FAIL
AVERAGE OF REPORTED PROGRAMS					
193	21.84	15.57	114.87	**6.80%**	64.79%
	FAIL	FAIL	FAIL	**PASS**	FAIL

PASS/ZONE = PASS for GE 1.0 and in the ZONE for GE 2.0

When correct payments were applied to the FY 2011 "Streamlined" Informational Data, only 6 or less than 1% of proprietary programs failed all 3 measures defined in the original Gainful Employment regulations. The data shows that reasonable loan debt and annual payments in relation to earnings are the common standard at proprietary colleges. The belief that unreasonable debt, high payments and low relative earnings for most for-profit institutions is unsubstantiated and, in fact, is completely false.

Out of the 193 proprietary school programs that were reported as failing all 3 rates, the corrected payments yielded ONLY 6 programs that failed all 3 metrics.

These are real questions that we should all be asking the DOE:

- What is the truth in the FY 2011 missing data for over 95% of the public programs and over 80% of private nonprofit programs included in "gainful employment" definitions?

- Are public and private schools submitting the required data?

- If public and private schools *aren't* submitting data, why aren't they held to the same standards and deadlines that proprietary schools are?

- If public and private schools *are* submitting the required data, why is the data missing or unreported?

- Why isn't the data and rate information being released for certain proprietary schools when they have submitted their data as required?

- Why were only 7,934 programs included in the FY 2012 GE Informational Rates released during the GE NPRM process in March 2014? Compared to 13,587 programs in the FY 2011 GE Final Data, have 5,653 programs already been eliminated?

- Why wasn't the "median debt" included in the FY 2012 GE Information Rates when it is a critical data point for verifying the accuracy of the rates? I believe this exclusion was not an oversight but rather another diversion from the truth.

Table 49: Inconsistent # Programs in FY 2011 & FY 2012 GE Informational Data [75]

FY 2011 Final Data	FY 2011 Streamlined Data	FY 2012 Informational Data
13,587	3,787	7,934

75. Although the author was not able to complete an audited comparison of all 3 sets of data in time for inclusion in this book, additional information will be posted on her website after publication.

INJUSTICE FOR ALL INSIGHT

Gainful Employment

Misguided beliefs that are fueling over-regulation and "predatory" labeling of ALL for-profit institutions are based upon a misguided belief driven by inaccurate and manipulated data facts. The manipulation of facts has been customized to support the agenda of the Obama Administration and certain former and current members of Congress to eliminate proprietary schools as a whole because of a tax-filing status.

The FACT that this agenda can only be supported by blatant manipulation of data reveals that the intent of these actions has NOTHING to do with the best interest of the students. The costs to students and taxpayers for the U.S. Department of Education to execute this agenda go way beyond the balance sheet. The ultimate injustices we are now reaping have NOT given our children opportunities. The truth is that opportunities for our children to pursue their dreams and desires through education are vanishing and will crush the very foundational belief of our nation that every citizen has the right to pursue prosperity.

Accurate FACTS that are consistent in numerous data sources prove that, as a whole, the for-profit institutions ARE delivering a quality education to a lion's share of at-risk students with reasonable and affordable student loan debt. These students should continue to have the freedom to choose what they want to do and where they go to college.

There is no doubt that schools out of compliance with laws and regulations should be held accountable. But these non-compliant schools exist in ALL sectors of education and, to protect ALL students, ALL sectors of higher education must to be held to the same high standards.

Default Rates ARE Influenced by At-risk Students

YOY Difference of Public and Proprietary Sectors				
SECTOR AVERAGE	**FY2009 iCDR%**	**FY2010 iCDR%**	**FY2011 iCDR%**	**FY 2012 iCDR%**
PUBLIC	14.3%	16.1%	15.0%	13.9%
PROPRIETARY	17.8%	18.0%	16.4%	13.9%
PUBLIC DIFFERENCE	-3.5%	-1.9%	-1.4%	**NO DIFFERENCE**

Translation: As the reputations of all for-profit schools are ruined through false reporting and publicity about certain bad players, the at-risk students are increasing in the public sector and the public sector will inherit all of the same problems that the proprietary sector has had for many years. The difference is the public sector, primarily community colleges, are not prepared to handle the problems and we will have an even larger population of uneducated Americans who do not have entry-level training for those jobs that do not require a degree.

VI. SECTOR–LEVEL PERFORMANCE DATA

Examining All the Facts to Determine What the Data Really Shows

I invite you to examine all of the facts. Your current belief about sector-level education may or may not be accurate and the accuracy of law makers' and public opinion will determine the future of at-risk citizens and, ultimately, the stability of America.

An Objective, Spin-free Review of Sector Data Facts

Default Rates have been published since 1987. Originally, these rates were defined as an indicator for the quality of education at every institution providing federal student loans under Title IV of the Higher Education Act of 1965. A two-year cohort default rare measuring period was used to determine the rates from 1990 until 2008. Beginning with the FY 2009 cohort default rate, a three-year cohort default rate measuring period was calculated and is currently used for determining Title IV eligibility for federal student loans and grants.

To date, socio-economics have not been considered for schools other than historically black colleges and universities (HBCUs) and tribal colleges even though there are thousands of schools, primarily for-profit colleges, that cater to the low-income students. These low-income students were the reason that the Higher Education Act was written. Training and education allowed these students to transition from poverty to happy working-class citizens—which is critical to our nation's health. Somehow, the schools catering to these "at-risk" students are only recognized if that school is designated as serving black or tribal students—and there are many at-risk students who don't fall into these two categories.

The following analysis of ALL institutions includes both good and bad indicators for cohort default rates, graduation rates and costs to students showing a broad big-picture view of sector performance based on actual data facts that are not published or promoted with the public.

Good Quality CDR Indicators

Institutions are rewarded for having low default rates defined as 3 consecutive years UNDER 15%. Benefits include the following:

- Waiver of 30-day delayed certification for first-time student loan borrowers
- Allowed to pull down federal funding in a single (1) disbursement instead of multiple disbursements throughout the academic year

For all 3 years reported in 2014, the following trends emerged:

1. PROPRIETARY had similar data to PUBLIC for schools with loans and CDR rates under 15%.

2. PROPRIETARY outperformed PUBLIC for schools with loans and CDR rates of 0%.

3. PROPRIETARY outperformed COMMUNITY COLLEGES[76] for schools with loans and CDR rates under 15%.

4. PROPRIETARY outperformed COMMUNITY COLLEGES for schools with loans and CDR rates of 0%.

---

76. "Known Community Colleges" — are those believed to be in this subsector and may not contain all colleges that fall within this definition.

GOOD QUALITY INDICATORS

Table 50: FY 2009 3YR iCDRs Good Quality Indicators by Sector

	# with Loans in Data Provided by ED	# with CDR's Less Than 15%	% with CDR's Less Than 15%	# with CDR's of 0%	% with CDR's of 0%	Notes
PUBLIC	1,567	**831**	**53.0%**	40	**2.6%**	PROPRIETARY outperforms PUBLIC for schools with 0% and have good data for schools under 15%.
PRIVATE	1,528	1,333	87.2%	144	9.4%	
PROPRIETARY	1,488	**649**	**43.6%**	91	**6.1%**	
KNOWN COMMUNITY COLLEGES	938	**319**	**34.0%**	36	**3.8%**	PROPRIETARY outperforms COMMUNITY COLLEGES across the board.

Table 51: FY 2010 3YR iCDRs Good Quality Indicators by Sector

	# with Loans in Data Provided by ED	# with CDR's Less Than 15%	% with CDR's Less Than 15%	# with CDR's of 0%	% with CDR's of 0%	Notes
PUBLIC	1,567	**714**	**45.6%**	32	**2.0%**	PROPRIETARY outperforms PUBLIC for schools with 0% and have good data for schools under 15%.
PRIVATE	1,546	1,340	86.7%	116	7.5%	
PROPRIETARY	1,590	**661**	**41.6%**	76	**4.8%**	
KNOWN COMMUNITY COLLEGES	938	**226**	**24.9%**	29	**3.1%**	PROPRIETARY outperforms COMMUNITY COLLEGES across the board.

Table 52: FY 2011 3YR iCDRs Good Quality Indicators by Sector

	# with Loans in Data Provided by ED	# with CDR's Less Than 15%	% with CDR's Less Than 15%	# with CDR's of 0%	% with CDR's of 0%	Notes
PUBLIC	1,581	**799**	**50.5%**	28	**1.8%**	PROPRIETARY outperforms PUBLIC for schools with 0% and have similar data for schools under 15%.
PRIVATE	1,557	1,391	89.3%	104	6.7%	
PROPRIETARY	1,714	**828**	**48.3%**	77	**4.5%**	
KNOWN COMMUNITY COLLEGES	952	**289**	**30.4%**	25	**2.6%**	PROPRIETARY outperforms COMMUNITY COLLEGES across the board.

Conclusion: PROPRIETARY schools represent large numbers and percentages of schools with CDR rates UNDER 15% and the highest percent with 0% CDRs that are indicative of good quality indicators. In fact, PROPRIETARY had similar or better results than public institutions and known community colleges.

This analysis is based upon the 2014 PEPS300 data file for FY 2009, FY 2010, and FY 2011 also available on ED's website. The analysis includes all schools with 30 (thirty) or more borrowers in the denominator.

Bad Quality CDR Indicators

As part of the Budget Reconciliation Act of 1990, Congress and the U.S. Department of Education decided that Cohort Default Rates (CDR) were a measure of quality education. The definition was a 2-year window where the denominator was based on the number of students who enter repayment within one federal fiscal year (FFY1) and the numerator was based on the number of borrowers included in FFY1 who also defaulted before the end of the second federal fiscal year (FFY2).

As part of the Higher Education Act of 2008, Congress decided that CDR's should be based upon an additional year of defaults. The definition was a 3-year window where the denominator was based on the number of students who enter repayment within one federal fiscal year (FFY1) and the numerator was based on the number of borrowers included in FFY1 who also defaulted before the end of the third federal fiscal year (FFY3). In September 2014, CDR rates were released for the first time where 3 consecutive years under the new 3-year CDR definition were available to determine eligibility. Institutions lose federal grand and loan eligibility under Title IV of the Higher Education Act when they have 1 CDR over 40% or 3 consecutive CDR's over 30% for the 3 most recent years of data available.

For all 3 years reported in 2014, the following trends emerged:

1. PROPRIETARY has the highest percent of low borrower schools serving fewer than 30 borrowers. For FY 2011, this represented 9.7% of all proprietary institutions. Schools with fewer than 30 borrowers are not subject to sanctions.

2. PROPRIETARY schools with 30 or more borrowers and facing loss of eligibility or "Limit, Suspend & Termination"(LS&T) represent only 0.8% of all proprietary institutions. This does not represent the outrageous numbers of for-profit schools with absurdly high default rates that has been presented by media and opponents of for-profit schools.

3. PROPRIETARY schools with 30 or more borrowers and FY 2011 over 40% represent 1.1% of all proprietary institutions. This percent is consistent with public and private Institutions.

4. PROPRIETARY schools with 30 or more borrowers and FY 2011 over 30% represent only 6% of all proprietary institutions.

5. PROPRIETARY schools DO NOT represent large numbers for bad quality indicators. In fact, the opposite is true.

NOTE: Schools face sanctions up to and including loss of eligibility for Title IV funding include those schools with three consecutive CDRs over 30% or one CDR over 40%. The information in the PEPS300 data released on September 24, 2014 does not include information about appeals or adjustments that have not been made in the database and, therefore was not considered. This analysis is based upon the PEPS300 data file for FY 2009, FY 2010, and FY 2011 available on the DOE's website. The analysis includes all schools with 30 (thirty) or more borrowers in the denominator.

Table 53: FY 2009 3YR iCDR Bad Quality Indicators by Sector

Institution Type	Number of Institutions with Loans in Data Provided by ED	Low Borrower Institutions with Less Than 30 Borrowers		Institutions with CDR Rates OVER 40% Low Borrower Institutions (less than 30 borrowers)	
		Number of Low Borrower Institutions	Percent of Low Borrower Institutions	Number of Institutions with CDR's Over 40%	Percent of Institutions with CDR's Over 40%
PUBLIC	1,567	88	5.6%	6	0.4%
PRIVATE	1,528	192	12.6%	6	0.4%
PROPRIETARY	1,488	298	20%	20	1.3%
KNOWN COMMUNITY COLLEGES	938	85	9.1%	6	0.6%

| Institutions with CDR Rates OVER 40% | | Institutions with CDR Rates OVER 30% | | | |
| Institutions with 30 or More Borrowers | | Low Borrower Institutions (less than 30 borrowers) | | Institutions with 30 or More Borrowers | |
Number of Institutions with CDR's Over 40%	Percent of Institutions with CDR's Over 40%	Number of Institutions with CDR's Over 30%	Percent of Institutions with CDR's Over 30%	Number of Institutions with CDR's Over 30%	Percent of Institutions with CDR's Over 30%
2	0.1%	12	0.8%	31	2.0%
3	0.2%	9	0.6%	18	1.2%
20	1.3%	54	3.6%	128	8.6%
2	0.2%	12	1.3%	30	3.2%

Table 54: FY 2010 3YR iCDR Bad Quality Indicators by Sector

| Institution Type | Number of Institutions with Loans in Data Provided by ED | Low Borrower Institutions with Less Than 30 Borrowers | | Institutions with CDR Rates OVER 40% | |
| | | | | Low Borrower Institutions (less than 30 borrowers) | |
		Number of Low Borrower Institutions	Percent of Low Borrower Institutions	Number of Institutions with CDR's Over 40%	Percent of Institutions with CDR's Over 40%
PUBLIC	1567	80	5.1%	5	0.3%
PRIVATE	1546	194	12.5%	6	0.4%
PROPRIETARY	1590	306	19.2%	33	2.1%
KNOWN COMMUNITY COLLEGES	938	78	8.3%	5	0.5%

| Institutions with CDR Rates OVER 40% | | Institutions with CDR Rates OVER 30% | | | |
| Institutions with 30 or More Borrowers | | Low Borrower Institutions (less than 30 borrowers) | | Institutions with 30 or More Borrowers | |
Number of Institutions with CDR's Over 40%	Percent of Institutions with CDR's Over 40%	Number of Institutions with CDR's Over 30%	Percent of Institutions with CDR's Over 30%	Number of Institutions with CDR's Over 30%	Percent of Institutions with CDR's Over 30%
3	0.2%	13	0.8%	56	3.6%
0	0%	13	0.8%	16	1.0%
11	0.7%	57	3.6%	115	7.2%
3	0.3%	13	1.4%	53	5.7%

Table 55: FY 2011 3YR iCDR Bad Quality Indicators by Sector

Institution Type	Number of Institutions with Loans in Data Provided by ED	Low Borrower Institutions with Less Than 30 Borrowers (percentages are less reliable when low numbers are used)		Over Threshold 1 over 40% or 3 over 30% (30 or more borrowers)		Institutions with CDR Rates OVER 40% / Low Borrower Institutions (less than 30 borrowers)	
		Number of Low Borrower Institutions	Percent of Low Borrower Institutions	Number of Institutions Over Threshold	Percent of Institutions Over Threshold	Number of Institutions with CDR's Over 40%	Percent of Institutions with CDR's Over 40%
PUBLIC	1,581	41	2.6%	2	0.1%	1	0.1%
PRIVATE	1,557	91	5.8%	0	0.0%	1	0.1%
PROPRIETARY	1,714	166	9.7%	14	0.8%	12	0.7%
KNOWN COMMUNITY COLLEGES	952	41	4.3%	2	0.2%	1	0.1%

| Institutions with CDR Rates OVER 40% | | Institutions with CDR Rates OVER 30% | | | |
| Institutions with 30 or More Borrowers | | Low Borrower Institutions (less than 30 borrowers) | | Institutions with 30 or More Borrowers | |
Number of Institutions with CDR's Over 40%	Percent of Institutions with CDR's Over 40%	Number of Institutions with CDR's Over 30%	Percent of Institutions with CDR's Over 30%	Number of Institutions with CDR's Over 30%	Percent of Institutions with CDR's Over 30%
1	0.1%	3	0.2%	46	2.9%
2	0.1%	2	0.1%	17	1.1%
18	1.1%	25	1.5%	103	6.0%
1	0.1%	3	0.3%	44	4.6%

As you can see, there are not an outrageous number of proprietary schools facing loss of Title IV eligibility *especially considering that 10 of these schools received no adjustments for their CDRs.*

Conclusion: The quality measures for education among higher education institutions in the United States is very similar between the public, private, and proprietary college sectors based on available data for cohort default rates.

The most prominent factor that determines the default rate outcomes is the populations served. Those institutions serving traditional students with medium- to high-income levels enjoy lower default rates than those institutions serving low-income at-risk student populations.

The College Navigator Database

The College Navigator appears to be the most comprehensive database available from the U.S. Department of Education and contains extensive quality indicator and financial information plus many pertinent data points. Some of the information provided is not clearly defined and assumptions are made that may not be accurate.

For example, the average student loan debt is provided in any sector of education and does not come close to the reported 2014 national average student loan debt of $28,400. Because, the student loan debt amounts are significantly lower than the national average, they appear to represent an academic year amount, not a cumulative total student loan debt amount. If cumulative debt amounts are unavailable proper labeling for "annual" debt would be helpful for making decisions for students and lawmakers.

Most of the information is not readily available. A comprehensive report of all schools or even by sector cannot be generated. The reports must be pulled in batches and do not contain any financial information that is pertinent to decision making. To conduct our analysis of the data, we pulled batches of information for all sectors and added the financial information manually.

From the College Navigator FY 2010 data available at the time of our analysis, we can see the following pertinent facts:

- Proprietary schools serve the largest population of Pell Grant recipients (62.6% at-risk students). When you couple this with the FY 2011 3-year CDR sector average rate of 18.9%, you can see that the proprietary schools and their third party servicers did a great job of helping students make timely payments or exercise their rights of deferment and forbearance during the worst economic times since the Great Depression.

- Community colleges serve a lower percent of at-risk students with 42.7% in Pell Grant recipients, yet they have a higher FY 2011 3-year CDR sector average rate of 20.4%. This indicates that students aren't learning to make payments or exercise their rights of deferment and forbearance as efficiently as the proprietary sector. The most likely reason is stronger relationships between students and school staff when the number of students in attendance at an institution is lower—the student to financial aid counselor or TPS ratios is better and the proprietary school students receive a higher level of borrower education and financial literacy training. This doesn't make the community colleges bad—it just shows that they lack the budget needed to provide staffing at the same level of other schools serving at risk students.

- The graduation rate for proprietary schools is the highest of all sectors at 60.4% while the graduation rate at public schools is 45.7%. As a group, the community colleges have the lowest overall graduation rate of 26.6%.

- When looking at the cost of Pell Grant and Federal Student Loan funding by sector, an apples-to-apples comparison uses the sector total amount divided by the graduation rate. In other words, how much taxpayers' money does it typically take for the average graduate. Since community colleges are often compared to proprietary schools, here are these comparisons:

Community College Pell Grant Cost: $13,954 is the highest;

Community College Student Loan Cost: $20,310 is the highest;

When you look at these costs in combination with the lowest graduation rate average of 26.6%, data shows that community colleges are in need of training and investments to drive efficiencies and increase success for ALL parties involved—especially students and taxpayers.

Proprietary School Pell Grant Cost: $6,436 is the lowest;

Proprietary School Student Loan Cost: $12,679 is the lowest;

When you reduce these costs for proprietary schools by the income taxes paid (ROI) because they are for-profit, the cost to taxpayers for students attending proprietary institutions is minimal. This fact combined with the highest graduation rate by sector of 60.4% supports the fact that proprietary education is an important part of educating America.

NOTE: Cost equals total aid divide by (number recipients multiplied by grad percentage). The College Navigator data contains many pertinent data facts not limited to and including the following:

Table 56: College Navigator Financial Data by Sector

COLLEGE NAVIGATOR INFORMATION	TRADITIONAL PUBLICS (NOT COMMUNITY COLLEGES)	PRIVATE NON-PROFIT SECTOR	PROPRIETARY SECTOR	COMMUNITY COLLEGES
FY 2010 3-year CDR Schools with Loans	629	1,546	1,590	938
Total Navigator Pell & Student Loans	$ 31,290,762,428	$ 15,586,149,147	$ 16,376,829,454	$ 19,626,087,899
Average Federal Funds per School	$ 49,746,840	$ 10,081,597	$ 10,299,893	$ 20,923,335
Total Navigator Pell Grant $	$ 9,672,248,296	$ 3,677,539,878	$ 5,252,199,565	$ 11,043,823,539
Ave % of Students with Pell Grants	**38.9%**	**41.1%**	**62.6%**	**42.7%**
Total # Students with Pell Grants	2,396,203	930,037	1,351,111	2,975,387
Average Pell Grant per Recipient	$ 4,019	$ 3,917	$ 3,813	$ 3,739

College Navigator Financial Data by Sector (continued)

COLLEGE NAVIGATOR INFORMATION	TRADITIONAL PUBLICS (NOT COMMUNITY COLLEGES)	PRIVATE NON-PROFIT SECTOR	PROPRIETARY SECTOR	COMMUNITY COLLEGES
Total Pell divided by (# recipients x grad %)	$ 8,861	$ 7,108	$ 6,438	$ 13,932
Total Navigator Fed Student Loans	$ 21,598,514,131	$ 11,908,609,269	$ 11,124,629,889	$ 8,582,264,350
Ave % Students with Student Loans	51.3%	97.5%	65.8%	30.1%
Total # Students with Student Loans	3,111,949	1,581,829	1,452,628	1,588,608
Average Federal Student Loan Debt	$ 6,857	$ 10,506	$ 7,088	$ 5,182
Student Loan Cost total loans divided by (# recipients x grad %)	$ 15,204	$ 13,534	$ 12,683	$ 20,278
Navigator Average FY 2010 CDR	10.7%	8.4%	18.0%	19.6%
Estimated Dollars in Default *	$ 2,283,197,475	$1,395,986,961	$1,853,325,341	$1,613,575,246
Average Graduation Rate	45.7%	55.6%	60.4%	26.6%

* Estimated dollars in default provided only includes FY 2010 funding (1 year) and are not a cohort default rate (3 year) calculation.

Conclusion: Data provided on the College Navigator is extremely valuable because it is extensive and provided for ALL schools. The report availabilities need to be improved so that auditing and verification of data can be completed.

INJUSTICE FOR ALL INSIGHT

If recovering defaulted dollars serves the federal fiscal interest, why aren't the cohort default rates reported in dollars?

FY 2010 ESTIMATED DOLLARS IN DEFAULT:

Public Nonprofit Colleges $7,102,703,002

Private Nonprofit Colleges $4,892,833,543

Proprietary Colleges $6,495,724,413

NOTES: Using the College Navigator FY 2010 data and the 2014 Official National Briefing for the FY 2010 3-year Cohort Default Rates (CDRs), the author estimated the dollars in default by sector that resulted in a national student loan debt average of $25,214 compared to the DOE's actual published national student loan debt average of $25,250 for the same period. The average annual sector-level student loan debt for FY 2010 was determined using College Navigator data and by totaling the "Average Amount of Aid Received" for Federal Student Loans divided by the total number of campuses in the database. Because the College Navigator provides annual loan data, not cumulative data, the estimated number of loans was determined for each credential level until the national average cumulative loan amount was very similar to the average cumulative loan amount used in this model as described above. Program length and completion rates were also take into consideration.

Less than 2 years: The average annual sector-level average debt was multiplied by 0.75.

2-3 years: The average annual sector-level average debt was multiplied by 1.85.

4 years(+): The average annual sector-level average debt was multiplied by 3.75.

The "Sector Credential-level Average Debt" was determined by multiplying each sector's average debt by the credential-level loan factor described above. This was completed for each sector and each credential-level within each sector. Using the 2014 Official National Briefing for the FY 2010 3-year CDRs, the "Sector Credential-level Dollars in Default" was determined by multiplying that sector credential-level's number of "Borrowers in Default" by its "Sector Credential-level Average Debt." The "Sector's Total Dollars in Default" is the total of its "Sector Credential-level Dollars in Default."

The information provided proves that the Proprietary Sector outperforms all other sectors in terms of the highest graduation rates and the lowest cost to student loan borrowers. Not every student wants to or is prepared to go to a public college. Low-income at-risk students in particular need more attention and guidance that is provided on a regular basis at for-profit institutions.

If the reporting and data availability and analysis were structured where this information was readily available, the misinformation could be mitigated. Decisions by lawmakers, regulators, parents, and students should be based upon the truth in the data and not in manipulated facts to drive a misguided agenda. A tax-filing status should not be a determining factor in measuring the quality of education. Let the data facts speak for the quality. The data is available—Americans just need access to it.

The College Scorecard Did Not Equally or Accurately Represent All Schools

The College Scorecard, hosted on www.whitehouse.gov, was also included in our research.

According to the Federal Student Aid website[77], "In February 2013, the Administration released the College Scorecard, a new planning tool to help students and their families make more educated decisions about college" and "…students and their families can look up the cost and assess the value of colleges…" This statement is only true if the student is interested in a college selected as worthy of including in this site.

Because there were no report formats available, we collected information for all schools listed in the PEPS300 data file. The available information was limited to Net Price, Graduation Rate, Default Rate, and Median Borrowing and, in numerous cases, was inconsistently populated for the institutions included on the site.

There were several issues with the College Scorecard information as follows:

⊙ The College Scorecard does not contain a full database of colleges and, in fact, has a disproportionate representation of the different sectors of higher education as follows:

---

77. http://studentaid.ed.gov/about/announcements/college-scorecard

Table 57: FY 2010 College Scorecard vs iCDR Data by Sector

ANALYSIS	COMMUNITY COLLEGES	TRADITIONAL PUBLICS	PRIVATE	PROPRIETARY
Total # Schools in iCDR PEPS300 Data	1,241	639	1,721	2,144
# Schools with Scorecard	904	606	1,188	308
% Schools in iCDR PEPS300 with Scorecard	72.8%	94.8%	69.0%	14.4%
# Schools with Scorecard & No iCDR	133	12	70	5
# Schools without Scorecard	337	33	533	1,835

- There were NO schools in the College Scorecard site that contain the following key search words: *Law, Legal, Cosmetology, Salon, Beauty, Barber, Hair or Massage*

- I'd like to note that many of these same schools are those with missing data in the GE Informational Rates.

- The information in the College Scorecards that did exist was often incomplete. Numerous schools on the site showed "no data" when there should have been data reported—there was data for the school on the College Navigator site. For example, numerous schools were missing the median borrowing information even though the school had a default rate with a significant number of borrowers.

Table 58: FY 2010 College Scorecard Missing Information

ANALYSIS	COMMUNITY COLLEGES	TRADITIONAL PUBLIC	PRIVATE	PROPRIETARY
# Schools with Scorecard	904	606	1,188	308
# Missing Net Price	1	6	15	8
# Missing Grad %	2	9	16	14
# Missing Median Borrower	97	13	79	1
# Missing Median Borrower & Has iCDR	11	1	13	1
Average # Borrower in Missing iCDR	242	437	18	13

⊙ Many schools had false and misleading information posted. For example, certain schools that didn't have FY 2010 CDRs had "0%" instead of "No Data" in their College Scorecards. This implies a high quality for the institution and gives a false impression to students and others who are led to believe that students are so satisfied with their education that everyone pays their student loans on time.

Table 59: College Scorecard Proper vs Improper Reporting Synopsis
Analysis of FY 2010 Information In The College Scorecards

	# Schools with NO FY 2010 CDR & Properly Reported "No Data" in College Scorecard for CDR Rate	# Schools with NO FY 2010 CDR & IMPROPERLY Reported CDR Showing 0% as the CDR Rate
COMMUNITY COLLEGES	25	108
ALL OTHER PUBLIC	6	6
PRIVATE	44	26
PROPRIETARY	1	4

Table 60: FY 2010 College Scorecard Average Financial Information by Sector
Analysis of FY 2010 Information In The College Scorecards

ANALYSIS	COMMUNITY COLLEGES	TRADITIONAL PUBLICS	PRIVATE	PROPRIETARY
# Schools with Scorecards	904	606	1,188	308
Average Net Price	$7,167.50	$11,607.77	$20,486.85	$21,155.05
Average Median Debt	$6,353.22	$15,237.63	$19,448.40	$15,308.03
Average Grad %	22.5%	44.9%	56.2%	51.3%
Cost of Average Median Debt per % Grad	$282.37	$339.37	$346.06	$298.40
Average FY 2010 CDR %	19.6%	10.7%	8.4%	18.0%

⊙ The information in the College Scorecard does not support a story where Proprietary schools have worse outcomes that public institutions and leave students with high loan debt. On the contrary, the Proprietary schools included had a reasonable average median debt for the average graduate percentage. When you divide the median debt by the graduation percent, these Proprietary schools have an average cost of median debt per graduation percentage of $298 compared to Community Colleges cost of $282. The Proprietary cost is lower than both the public (other) and private college costs. The Proprietary schools also have a higher graduation rate than all public schools and a lower FY 2010 CDR Rate than Community Colleges.

After I began to speak about this information in January 2015 with DOE employees present, the data from the College Scorecard website was removed.

We attempted to determine the exact date that the database had been removed using several companies that periodically archive snapshots of websites. Two sites shut down when the College Scorecard URL was entered and wouldn't show us anything for the College Scorecard URL. These were http://screenshotmachine.com/ and http://snapito.com/index.html.

The Wayback Machine website last archived the College Scorecard site on February 13th. The information is available at the following link: https://web.archive.org/web/20150213214414/http://www.whitehouse.gov/issues/education/higher-education/college-score-card.

Table 61: "This page can't be displayed." (whitehouse.gov screenshot)

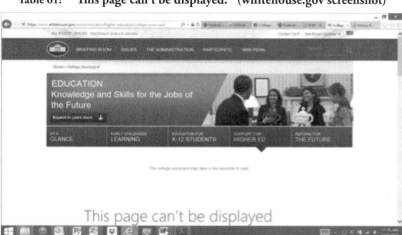

At this time, we can only verify that the College Scorecard data was available on February 13, 2015 and was no longer available on March 18, 2015. Approximately twenty DOE employees were present during my last speech on February 23, 2015.

The "New" College Scorecard: Different Format, Still Inaccurate and Misleading

Fast forward to September 5, 2015, when the "new" College Scorecard was released by the U.S. Department of Education and hosted on the Whitehouse. gov website.

While the format looks better and is easier to read, the information is still skewed to favor certain institutions. By eliminating certain subsets of students in the reporting, the statistics were changed to support an agenda that makes public institutions look like they are performing better than they are. These data manipulations coupled with derogatory statements that are unsupported by actual data reveal an agenda—again—that has nothing to do with ensuring quality education for American citizens.

- The "Average Annual Cost" used an average of $16.8K or $16,800. The information icon reveals, "Average Annual Cost. The average annual net price for federal financial aid recipients, after aid from the school, state, or federal government. For public schools, this is only the average cost for in-state students."

Table 62: College Scorecard "Average Annual Cost" (DOE screenshot)

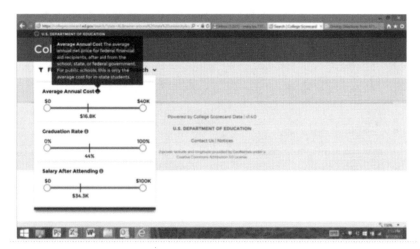

Translation: The DOE eliminated the costs for all out-of-state students who attended public schools. This is the higher cost of attending public institutions so the DOE eliminated all information that would have made the average accurately higher than what was reported. Private non-profit and for-profit institutions have out-of-state costs included in their calculations so the information provided is not equitable or accurate because it does not compare apples-to-apples but rather compares apples-to-oranges.

- The "Graduation Rate" used an average of 44%. The information icon reveals, "Graduation Rate. The graduation rate after six years for schools that award predominantly four-year degrees and after four years for all other schools. These rates are only for full-time students enrolled for the first time."

Table 63: College Scorecard "Graduation Rate" (DOE screenshot)

Translation: The DOE used six years as a measurement for reporting graduation rates for 4-year schools which is consistent with mandatory reporting criteria that defines "on-time" graduation for students that complete the course of study within 150% of the original course length. However, the DOE's use of four years for all other schools gives a longer period of time to include graduates for two-year institutions and shorter programs. For example, 150% of the course length at a two-year institution is three years, not four years.

The DOE data only includes full-time students and those who are enrolled for the first time. Part-time students are an important part of every college so why would they be eliminated from the calculation?

The DOE data also only includes students "enrolled for the first time." What exactly does that mean? Does it only include first time at the original institution? Does it include first time students at any institution eliminating transfer students from the calculations? Why would students who attended school more than once be eliminated? For example, if a student attended a community college and then transferred to a four-year college be counted?

Again, the DOE's information is not equitable or accurate. Furthermore, it must have taken DOE data managers and programmers many tax-paid hours to develop coding for eliminating all of these subgroups of students. Why was it so important to eliminate these numbers? Could it be to improve statistics for public institutions?

- The "Salary After Attending" used an average of $34.3K ($34,300). The information icon reveals, "Salary After Attending." The median earnings of former students who received federal financial aid, at 10 years after entering the school.

Table 64: College Scorecard "Salary After Attending" (DOE screenshot)

Translation: Income information is only provided for federal financial aid recipients because it is currently against the law for the DOE to collect the information for non-recipients of financial aid.

And yes, the Department sends the social security numbers over to the IRS to obtain "median earnings" information. For most public schools, many consider this overstepping authority into private personal information. For all proprietary schools, this is called "Gainful Employment."

○ The opening page for "Data Insights" states with bold highlighting, "While there is variation in the amount of debt and fraction of students borrowing by sector, on average, **students at private for-profit two-year and four-year institutions have high rates of borrowing and their graduates often have large amounts off debt.** While debt per se may not be problematic where students are able to repay their loans, it should be paired with other data, such as completion rates and post-school earnings, to provide a more comprehensive picture of student outcomes."

Table 65: College Scorecard "Data Insights" (DOE screenshot 1)

Translation: This is the DOE's attempt to direct public opinion to believe that students at private for-profit institutions are left with high debt that the student can't afford.

A high rate of borrowing is not a bad quality indicator. This simply means that most for-profit institutions cater to at-risk students with low income so they qualify for more financial aid.

Because proprietary schools have the highest graduation rates of all sectors, they have higher loan balances. This also produces the best return on investment as shown in the College Navigator audited data analysis for FY 2011. For example:

- Community Colleges' average graduation rate is 26.6% and the average loan debt is $5,182. This produces a net cost per graduation percent (average loan divided by graduation rate) of $195, the highest cost to students among all institutions.

- Proprietary Schools' average graduation rate is 60.4% and the average loan debt is $7,088. This produces a net cost per graduation percent of $117, the lowest cost to students among all institutions.

The actual data, when analyzed in total as we have done, shows that for-profit schools have high graduation rates and reasonable debt when compared to earnings primarily measured in gainful employment data between three and four years after graduation—not ten years after starting school.

We agree that other data like completion rates and post-school earnings should be used to provide a more comprehensive picture of student outcomes at all institutions, not just those that fall within the limiting definitions for Gainful Employment.

- Another page for Data Insights reveals with bold highlighting, **"The data in the National Student Loan Data System (NSLDS) on enrollment intensity and transfer status are both of poor quality for Pell-only students prior to 2012.** Because of this, the data do not support reporting completion rates disaggregated by full-time and part-time status, or first-time and not-first-time status. Moreover, since transfers can only be identified if the student receives Title IV aid at the transfer-in institution, the NSLDS cannot reliably identify all transfer students."

Table 66: College Scorecard "Data Insights" (DOE screenshot 2)

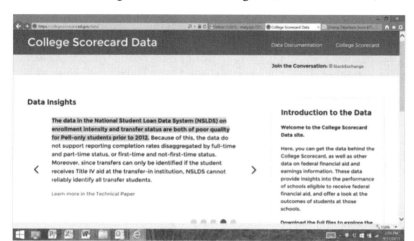

Translation: Public schools, especially Community Colleges, have been using "transfer out rates" as their excuse for low and unacceptable graduation rates. I find it interesting that the DOE is acknowledging the inaccuracy of these "transfer out rates" on the College Scorecard website.

○ During the first few days, I glanced through the information to decide where I would start my analysis. By September 17, 2015, I was unable to search for individual or groups of schools. Every search returned an error message of "Error: Forbidden." Interesting, considering that the majority of public comments focused on the missing and inaccurate data and inequitable methods of calculation used for Obama's new "College Scorecard."

Is it a coincidence that the "new" College Scorecard data is no longer available within two weeks of its unveiling and after the media has promoted it? Is it a coincidence that the information has disappeared after the majority of bloggers and analysts have pointed out the inconsistencies and inaccuracies of the information? Could this happen twice in one year? Is it a coincidence that the site went down when I was downloading the data zip file?

Table 67: College Scorecard "Error Forbidden" (DOE screenshot)

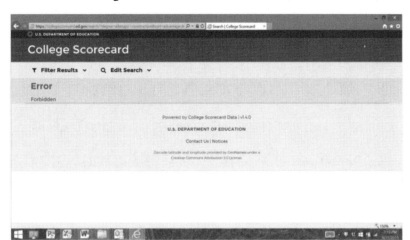

Can Parents and Students Make Wise Decisions with College Scorecard?

The College Scorecard was touted as the "go to" site for obtaining valuable information so that parents and students could make sound decisions about college choices.

Data provided did not provide a freedom of information. In fact, the limitation of available information for all schools in addition to incorrect and missing information for certain schools shows that the site was more probably set up to drive an agenda that has nothing to do with quality education.

If the information that was available on this site hosted as part of whitehouse. gov was in integrity, why has all the information removed, keeping Americans uninformed?

Are These Standards Acceptable?

When the one consistent point in the DOE's reporting is manipulation that falsely gives the American public the belief that a specific sector is bad, wouldn't it be a logical leap to assume a reason exists?

VII. 2015 iCDR SHOWS ONE POINT OF CONSISTENCY

WILL THE DOE AND THE ADMINISTRATION CONTINUE THIS ASSAULT ON EDUCATION?

Passing the blame onto a specific school sector won't solve American education challenges. Data manipulation may temporarily hide the truth from Americans, but the relevant question is: Will American citizens see the truth in time to avoid the catastrophic impact on our country?

With the release of the FY 2012 Official Cohort Default Rates scheduled for September 21, 2015, and my book so close to completion, I decided that I would not release *Injustice for All* without including the 2015 CDR release and analyzing the information provided. Part of me was hoping that the information was going to be corrected. The other part of me knew that the Administration's agendas would move forward no matter what anyone says or does to stop it. We've seen these injustices happen in so many ways since 2008. This year is no different.

Are there reasons why education is a target of the long-range agendas of our political leaders? Absolutely! **Agendas that promise "loan forgiveness"**—with a 1099 income tax; **"free" education**—only you don't get to choose where; and **government-managed student loan programs**—where the government profits from students *all* seduce you because the publicity about these "wonderful things" only focuses on the promises written in bold and not what else goes with them. These are exactly the type of promises that have swayed the opinions of Americans in ways that suit agendas that have little to do with the best interest of students, employers, and the federal fiscal interest.

2015 Official FY 2012 iCDRs

On September 15, 2015, the DOE announced that it was delaying the release of the FY 2012 CDRs to September 28, 2015 for schools to receive data and September 30, 2015 for the public to see the official briefings and have access to the available data. At this point, I lost all hope for the DOE to rectify the situation themselves.

Table 68: 2015 Official FY 2012 iCDR Briefing (DOE PowerPoint)

	Fiscal Year 2012 Official				Fiscal Year 2011 Official				Fiscal Year 2010 Official		
# of Schools	Borrower Default Rate (%)	# of Borrowers Defaulted	# of Borrowers Entered Repayment	# of Schools	Borrower Default Rate (%)	# of Borrowers Defaulted	# of Borrowers Entered Repayment	# of Schools	Borrower Default Rate (%)	# of Borrowers Defaulted	# of Borrowers Entered Repayment
Public 1,667	11.7%	301,453	2,563,157	1,637	12.9%	292,012	2,252,334	1,619	13.0%	250,661	1,922,773
Less than 2 yrs 148	12.2%	1,241	10,151	146	13.6%	1,196	8,750	139	16.5%	1,315	7,963
2-3 yrs 854	19.1%	173,628	905,058	841	20.6%	158,104	767,073	840	20.9%	125,764	599,467
4yrs(+) 665	7.6%	126,584	1,647,948	650	8.9%	132,712	1,476,511	640	9.3%	123,582	1,315,343
Private 1,727	6.8%	73,747	1,083,328	1,712	7.2%	70,186	969,156	1,712	8.2%	72,347	879,269
Less than 2 yrs 49	22.4%	2,318	10,336	43	25.0%	1,644	6,567	41	21.8%	1,097	5,020
2-3 yrs 161	14.6%	6,193	42,274	161	12.0%	2,026	16,861	168	14.2%	2,305	16,217
4yrs(+) 1,517	6.3%	65,236	1,030,718	1,508	7.0%	66,516	945,728	1,503	8.0%	68,945	858,032
Proprietary 2,294	15.8%	235,384	1,486,162	2,277	19.1%	288,126	1,500,812	2,187	21.8%	277,088	1,270,965
Less than 2 yrs 1,199	17.7%	33,393	188,549	1,177	20.6%	38,686	187,209	1117	20.9%	34,811	165,921
2-3 yrs 747	17.7%	62,650	353,777	762	19.8%	77,441	390,649	743	21.4%	71,853	334,459
4 yrs(+) 348	14.7%	139,341	943,836	338	18.6%	171,999	922,954	327	22.1%	170,424	770,585
Foreign 431	3.3%	372	11,266	428	3.8%	403	10,488	432	4.6%	449	9,562
Unclassified 2	0.0%	0	5	1	0.0%	0	3	1	0.0%	0	1
TOTAL 6,121	11.8%	610,956	5,143,918	6,055	13.7%	650,727	4,732,793	5,951	14.7%	600,545	4,082,570

This year's DOE mathematician had the same rounding issues that were present last year. The FY 2012 iCDR calculations had 6 errors in rounding the rates. This contributed to the total of all three relevant official iCDRs (FY 2010-2012) which ended up being a whopping 16 errors out of 45 total calculations—or a 35.6% error rate.

Ironically, 8 of the 16 errors or *50% of the errors were made on public sector calculations*. All of the errors calculated the rate *.1% lower* than the correct rounding shows.

Table 69: Summaries of Incorrectly Calculated Official FY 2009-2012 iCDRs

(Grey highlight indicates corrected math calculations.)				
2014 Official FY 2009 3YR iCDRs	**# of Schools**	**Borrower Default Rate (%)**	**# of Borrowers Defaulted**	**# of Borrowers Entered Repayment**
PUBLIC	**1,628**	**11.0%**	**196,032**	**1,778,645**
Less than 2 yrs	141	16.2%	1,202	7,401
2-3 yrs	851	18.3%	94,945	518,299
4yrs(+)	636	**8.0%**	**99,885**	**1,252,945**
PRIVATE	**1,710**	**7.5%**	**63,047**	**835,492**
Less than 2 yrs	42	23.1%	950	4,106
2-3 yrs	174	14.5%	2,357	16,244
4yrs(+)	1,494	7.3%	59,740	815,142
PROPRIETARY	**2,142**	**22.8%**	**229,315**	**1,006,190**
Less than 2 yrs	1,100	21.5%	27,788	129,235
2-3 yrs	731	22.9%	64,146	279,713
4yrs(+)	311	23.0%	137,381	597,242
FOREIGN	**427**	**7.4%**	**646**	**8,777**
UNCLASSIFIED	**1**	**0.0%**	**0**	**5**
TOTAL	**5,908**	**13.5%**	**489,040**	**3,629,109**

2014 & 2015 Official FY 2010 3YR iCDRs	**# of Schools**	**Borrower Default Rate (%)**	**# of Borrowers Defaulted**	**# of Borrowers Entered Repayment**
PUBLIC	**1,619**	**13.0%**	**250,661**	**1,922,773**
Less than 2 yrs	139	16.5%	1,315	7,963
2-3 yrs	840	**21.0%**	**125,764**	**599,467**
4yrs(+)	640	**9.4%**	**123,582**	**1,315,343**
PRIVATE	**1,712**	**8.2%**	**72,347**	**879,269**
Less than 2 yrs	41	**21.9%**	**1,097**	**5,020**
2-3 yrs	168	14.2%	2,305	16,217
4yrs(+)	1,503	8.0%	68,945	858,032
PROPRIETARY	**2,187**	**21.8%**	**277,088**	**1,270,965**
Less than 2 yrs	1,117	**21.0%**	**34,811**	**165,921**
2-3 yrs	743	**21.5%**	**71,853**	**334,459**
4yrs(+)	327	22.1%	170,424	770,585

2014 & 2015 Official FY 2010 3YR iCDRs (continued)	# of Schools	Borrower Default Rate (%)	# of Borrowers Defaulted	# of Borrowers Entered Repayment
FOREIGN	432	4.7%	449	9,562
UNCLASSIFIED	1	0.0%	0	1
TOTAL	5,951	14.7%	600,545	4,082,570

2014 & 2015 Official FY 2011 3YR iCDRs	# of Schools	Borrower Default Rate (%)	# of Borrowers Defaulted	# of Borrowers Entered Repayment
PUBLIC	1,637	13.0%	292,012	2,252,334
Less than 2 yrs	146	13.7%	1,196	8,750
2-3 yrs	841	20.6%	158,104	767,073
4yrs(+)	650	9.0%	132,712	1,476,511
PRIVATE	1,712	7.2%	70,186	969,156
Less than 2 yrs	43	25.0%	1,644	6,567
2-3 yrs	161	12.0%	2,026	16,861
4yrs(+)	1,508	7.0%	66,516	945,728
PROPRIETARY	2,277	19.2%	288,126	1,500,812
Less than 2 yrs	1,177	20.7%	38,686	187,209
2-3 yrs	762	19.8%	77,441	390,649
4yrs(+)	338	18.6%	171,999	922,954
FOREIGN	428	3.8%	403	10,488
UNCLASSIFIED	1	0.0%	0	3
TOTAL	6,055	13.7%	650,727	4,732,793

2015 Official FY 2012 3YR iCDRs	# of Schools	Borrower Default Rate (%)	# of Borrowers Defaulted	# of Borrowers Entered Repayment
PUBLIC	1,667	11.8%	301,453	2,563,157
Less than 2 yrs	148	12.2%	1,241	10,151
2-3 yrs	854	19.2%	173,628	905,058
4yrs(+)	665	7.7%	126,584	1,647,948
PRIVATE	1,727	6.8%	73,747	1,083,328
Less than 2 yrs	49	22.4%	2,318	10,336
2-3 yrs	161	14.6%	6,193	42,274

2015 Official FY 2012 3YR iCDRs (continued)	# of Schools	Borrower Default Rate (%)	# of Borrowers Defaulted	# of Borrowers Entered Repayment
4yrs(+)	1,517	6.3%	65,236	1,030,718
PROPRIETARY	2,294	15.8%	235,384	1,486,162
Less than 2 yrs	1,199	17.7%	33,393	188,549
2-3 yrs	747	17.7%	62,650	353,777
4yrs(+)	348	14.8%	139,341	943,836
FOREIGN	431	3.3%	372	11,266
UNCLASSIFIED	2	0.0%	0	5
TOTAL	6,121	11.9%	610,956	5,143,918

Interesting trends have also emerged as the reporting for FY 2012 was not consistent with prior 3-year iCDR trends.

PUBLIC SECTOR: Historically, the official briefing data and rates show the DOE Briefing **rate 0.1% lower than what the iCDR Data shows**. This year, the FY 2012 iCDR for the public sector reflects the same rate of 11.7% for both sources. The sector average iCDR based on the data shows a decrease YOY decrease for the last four years from 14.3% down to 13.9%, which shows **a decrease from FY 2009 to FY 2012 of 0.4%.**

PRIVATE SECTOR: Historically, the official briefing data and rates match the iCDR Data. This year, there was a significant difference where the DOE Briefing showed the private sector iCDR calculated at 6.8% when the iCDR Data shows it to be 7.2%—**the DOE reported the private sector rate 0.4% too low.** The sector average iCDR based on the data shows a YOY decrease for the last four years from 7.5% down to 7.2%, which shows **a decrease from FY 2009 to FY 2012 of 0.3%.**

PROPRIETARY SECTOR: Historically, the official briefing data and rates show the DOE Briefing rate **0.2% higher than what the iCDR Data shows.** This year, there was a more significant difference where the DOE Briefing showed the proprietary sector iCDR calculated at 15.8% when the iCDR Data shows it to be 15.4%—**the DOE reported the proprietary sector rate 0.4% too high.** The sector average iCDR based on the data shows a YOY decrease for the last four years from 17.8% to 13.9%, which **shows a decrease from FY 2009 to FY 2012 of 3.9%.**

NATIONAL AVERAGE: The DOE Briefings consistently show the National Official Average **higher than the iCDR Data shows**—this appears to say that the manipulation is more important than reporting an accurate national average.

The FY 2012 Sector Average iCDR was exactly the same for public and proprietary sectors at 13.9%!

Table 70: YOY Comparison of Official FY 2009-2012 iCDR Rates in DOE Briefings vs Data Reality by Sector

	FY2009 CDR%	FY2010 CDR%	FY2011 CDR%	FY2012 CDR%
PUBLIC				
Official Briefing	11.0%	13.0%	12.9%	11.7%
iCDR PEPS300 Data	11.1%	13.1%	13.0%	11.7%
Sector Average iCDR	14.3%	16.1%	15.0%	**13.9%**
PRIVATE				
Official Briefing	7.5%	8.2%	7.2%	**6.8%**
iCDR PEPS300 Data	7.5%	8.2%	7.2%	**7.2%**
Sector Average iCDR	7.7%	8.4%	7.3%	6.5%
PROPRIETARY				
Official Briefing	22.7%	21.8%	19.1%	**15.8%**
iCDR PEPS300 Data	22.6%	21.6%	18.9%	**15.4%**
Sector Average iCDR	17.8%	18.0%	16.4%	**13.9%**
ALL SCHOOLS				
Official Briefing	13.4%	14.7%	13.7%	11.8%
iCDR PEPS300 Data	**13.2%**	**14.5%**	**13.6%**	**11.7%**

Once again, the main contributor to the rate calculations not matching between the DOE Official Briefings and the iCDR Data, the numbers of borrowers in default and borrowers entered repayment have been drastically changed.

PUBLIC SECTOR: The same trend has held for the last four years for the public sector where DOE Briefing numbers and rates are lower than the iCDR Data actually shows. For the FY 2012 iCDR, the DOE Briefing reported Borrowers in Default at 301,453 when the iCDR Data shows it to be 306,443. The DOE Briefing showed both the public sector Borrowers in Default Borrowers Entered Repayment at **2% lower than what the iCDR Data shows**.

PRIVATE SECTOR: Although the trend for the private sector was fairly accurate from FY 2009–2011 which showed data within 1% of accuracy, the FY 2012 showed it to be grossly inaccurate. The DOE Briefing reported private sector Borrowers in Default at 73,747 when the iCDR data shows 81,781—the DOE reported the private sector Borrowers in Default **10% lower than what the iCDR Data shows**. The DOE reported the Borrowers Entered Repayment **5% lower than what the iCDR Data shows**. This gross misreporting of numbers netted a private sector default rate of 6.8% instead of the iCDR Data calculation of 7.2%.

PROPRIETARY SECTOR: The same trend has held for the last for years for the proprietary sector where DOE Briefing numbers and rates are significantly higher than the iCDR Data actually shows. For the FY 2012 iCDR, the DOE Briefing showed even more exaggerated numbers and reported Borrowers in Default at 235,384 when the iCDR shows 214,880—the DOE reported the proprietary sector Borrowers in Default **10% higher than what the iCDR Data shows**. The DOE reported the Borrowers Entered repayment **6% higher than what the iCDR Data shows**. This gross misreporting of numbers netted a proprietary sector default rate of 15.8% instead of the iCDR Data calculation of 15.4%.

The YOY trends from FY 2009–2012 that have remained consistent are that public sector information rates have always been lowered in the DOE's Official Briefings and the proprietary sector information and rates have always been grossly inflated in the DOE's Official Briefings. At first, this reporting produced information consistent with the DOE's story that the proprietary schools represented half of the defaults in the country.

Table 71: YOY Comparison of Official FY 2009-2012 iCDR Defaults in DOE Briefings vs Data Reality by Sector

	FY2009 # Borr in Default	FY2010 # Borr in Default	FY2011 # Borr in Default	FY2012 # Borr in Default
DOE BRIEFINGS TOTAL	**489,040**	**600,545**	**650,727**	**610,956**
iCDR (PEPS300) DATA TL	**476,744**	**587,703**	**649,275**	**603,659**
PUBLIC				
Official Briefing	196,032	250,661	292,012	301,453
iCDR (PEPS300) Data	204,732	259,692	303,288	306,443
Briefing Difference	**-8,700**	**-9,031**	**-11,276**	**-4,990**
Briefing % Difference	**-4%**	**-3%**	**-4%**	**-2%**
PRIVATE				
Official Briefing	63,047	72,347	70,186	73,747
iCDR (PEPS300) Data	62,729	71,784	69,577	81,781
Briefing Difference	**+318**	**+563**	**+609**	**-8,034**
Briefing % Difference	**+1%**	**+1%**	**+1%**	**-10%**
PROPRIETARY				
Official Briefing	229,315	277,088	288,126	235,384
iCDR (PEPS300) Data	208,962	255,811	275,794	214,880
Briefing Difference	**+20,353**	**+21,277**	**+12,332**	**+20,504**
Briefing % Difference	**+10%**	**+8%**	**+4%**	**+10%**
DIFFERENCE BETWEEN BORROWERS IN DEFAULT FOR PUBLIC vs PROPRIETARY				
DOE Reported Difference in # Default (Public vs Prop iCDR)	**-33,283**	**-26,427**	**+3,886**	**+66,069**
Actual Difference # Default (Public vs Prop iCDR)	**-4,230**	**+3,881**	**+27,494**	**+91,563**
Total # Borr in Default in Reporting Manipulation for Public vs Prop iCDR	29,053	30,308	23,608	25,494
Total % of Reporting Manipulation in Briefings from Data	**14.0%**	**11.8%**	**8.2%**	**11.2%**

As the public sector Borrowers in Default have drastically increased from 204,732 in FY 2009 to 306,443 in FY 2012, the DOE's attempt to cover this up has increased the need to change DOE Briefing numbers to minimize the fact that the **public sector Borrowers in Default has increased a staggering 54%.**

Table 72: Summary of DOE's Manipulation of FY 2012 iCDRs (Public vs Proprietary)

DOE Briefing - SPIN -		PEPS Data - TRUTH -	Cohort Year	PEPS Data - TRUTH -	DOE Briefing - SPIN -	
PUBLIC SECTOR 3YR CDRs			FY 2012 3YR CDR		PROPRIETARY SECTOR 3YR CDRs	
		306,443 Correct		214,880 Correct		
Falsely Reported **2% LOWER** than data	301,453 Falsely Reported Borrowers in Default	**TRUTH** For FY 2012 Public CDRs have 91,563 MORE defaults than Proprietary CDRs.			235,384 Falsely Reported Borrowers in Default	Falsely Reported **10% HIGHER** than data

FALSE REPORTING
The DOE reported that the Public Sector had 66,069 more defaults than the Proprietary Sector. The DOE Briefing is NOT backed by any available data and is NOT the truth.

INJUSTICE FOR ALL INSIGHT

The Truth about Sector Performance
Based on iCDR Data

The public sector now represents 51% of the nations' Borrowers in Default and 50% of the nations' Borrowers Entered repayment.

Based on the iCDR Data, **the public sector now has 91,563 more Borrowers in Default than the proprietary sector represents**—*not the picture the DOE wants Americans to see when asking taxpayers to foot the bill for two "free" years of education at the public community colleges that represent 96% of the increase in public sector defaults when you compare FY 2009 to FY 2015.*

At the same time, the proprietary sector Borrowers in Default have increased minimally from 208,962 to 214,880, a mere increase of 3%.

The proprietary sector now represents only 35% of the nations' defaults.

2015 Official FY 2012 Loan Holder Default Rates

The FY 2012 default rates for several of the conduit and put loan portfolios have come down; however, the FY 2012 ABCP Conduit 2009-2010 loan portfolio still has a 56.0% default rate.

Table 73: 2015 Official FY 2012 DOE-controlled Loan Data

LID	LENDER NAME	CURR RATE	CURR DEF	CURR REP	DOLLARS IN REPAY
895577	US DEPT OF ED/ABCP CONDUIT 09-10	**56.0%**	3,916	6,998	$ 68,645,140
897577	U.S. DEPT OF EDUCATION/2009-2010 LPCP	7.0%	80,706	1,145,553	$ 1,465,701,750
898577	US DEPT OF ED/2007-2008 STPP	6.8%	613	8,999	$ 55,124,401
899577	U.S. DEPT OF ED/2008-2009 LPCP	5.3%	33,063	622,932	$ 5,706,307,530
888577	US DEPT OF ED/COND DISB DSCHRGS	6.6%	9	137	$ 1,853,032
896577	US DEPT OF ED/REHABS	0.0%	0	11	$ 79,550
	US DEPT OF ED TOTAL	**6.6%**	**118,307**	**1,784,630**	**$ 7,297,711,403**
	FY2012 TOTAL LENDER DATA	7.2%	178,683	2,485,130	$13,959,645,893

Based on the FY 2012 iCDR Data, the unreported FDSL Program loans represent 424,976 Borrowers in Default and 2,678,919 Borrowers Entered Repayment which represents a 15.9% cohort default rate. This FDSLP default rate is significantly higher than the FY 2012 Official iCDR Data rate of **11.7%**.

When the reported conduit and put loan portfolio volume is added to the FDSLP volume, the U.S. Department of Education represents 543,283 Borrowers in Default and 4,463,549 Borrowers Entered Repayment which represents a DOE-managed loan portfolio default rate of **12.2%**.

2015 CDR Conclusions

As the default rates at public schools rise, the DOE has found an increasing need to manipulate numbers to cover up for the increasing volume of defaults in the public sector. When Congress begins to focus on collecting the defaulted dollars instead of all the finger-pointing games, the public sector will be in the middle of the federal fiscal target.

Proprietary schools will continue to cater to at-risk students and will continue to provide better-than-average borrower education and financial aid counseling needed by the inexperienced students.

The bottom line is that the default rates represent a low-income poor socioeconomic culture that needs more than electronic entrance and exit interviews to navigate through the complex financial aid world—and the proprietary sector helps these at-risk students get through this process better than any other sector.

Passing blame won't help the students or our country. Financial recovery will occur when the DOE stops lying and blaming others—and focuses on the appropriate management of programs that fit the individual needs of the students.

Borrower Education Is Key

When the Administration and the U.S. Department of Education dangle low payments and loan forgiveness in front of student borrowers with little to no financial credit experience, of course many of these bright-eyed kids take what appears to be the easiest path for student loan repayment. Most of these students don't consider the long-term money trap they have entered into where their payments have increased from 10 years to 20-25 years; where they may pay more in interest than they took out in loans; and where they will have a "balloon" payment for taxes when the balance of their loan is forgiven in 20-25 years, at a time when they may be sending their own children to college.

I believe most of these students would make different choices if they truly understood these consequences and if they could choose a program that rewarded them for good repayment behaviors. I urge lawmakers to consider this and keep in mind that student loan borrower education goes beyond the classroom. It is in America's best interest to foster sound financial habits that will support and strengthen our nation's economy.

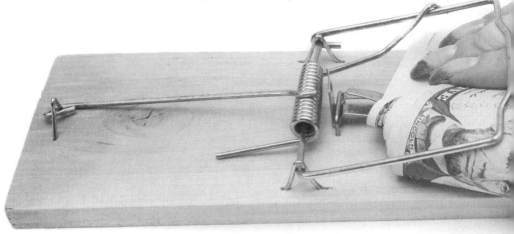

VIII. THE IMPACT

WHAT EFFECT DO REPAYMENT SCHEDULES
HAVE ON BORROWER SUCCESS?

If our goal is to provide loans to fund educational opportunities that create income sources to help people transcend poverty; we must also make wise choices by designing repayment structures that nurture the financial success of loan recipients. If we fail, generations to come will suffer the consequences of the baggage from yet another unproductive entitlement program.

Repayment plans and programs should accommodate the best interests of every type of student. For some, good credit is a habit that has been passed down through generations. For others, it is a life-changing experience. Then, we should educate borrowers to make appropriate repayment choices that support their success through the life of the loan and support long-term financial health in all areas of their lives. Different borrowers have different familial financial imprints. HOW can a student be adequately equipped to properly repay student loans if they come from a family in which the loans they receive are generally payday loans and who frequently purchases furniture from rent-to-own establishments?

The impact of repayment schedules for student loans varies and is based largely upon the socio-economic background of the student borrower. Repayment plans are not a "one size fits all." People with their level of knowledge and understanding need to be taken into consideration.

Traditional students who come from a more financially sound family structure are better able and equipped to make decisions about repayment schedules that have variable payments or escalating payments such as those offered in the Federal Direct Student Loan Program.

Nontraditional students who represent the low- to lower middle-class have completely different needs. For the sake of understanding, I will compare this type of nontraditional student to the subprime mortgage market. Behaviors are strong in any class of people and for those who have grown up using entitlement programs like food stamps, free lunch, and such, we are teaching a whole new way of thinking and being. That whole new way is one that is not embraced by the people who surround and influence these borrowers. Don't get me wrong, these are not bad people—they are just living the only way that they know. This is not just about borrower education or financial literacy; it is about a social revolution for those who want an education with the goal of bettering their lives for themselves and generations to come.

These nontraditional students are why the Higher Education Act of 1965 was written. These people still have hopes for the American Dream. I take that very seriously because this is also my story. We have been in business for 26 years and have serviced close to 3 million at-risk students over the years. We educate them to have long-term success so that they aren't dependent upon Champion to succeed, they are dependent upon the knowledge that we have imparted as a gift for a new life; a life of hope and dreams and prosperity; a life of the American Dream.

Many of our borrowers are first-generation recipients of a higher education experience. Many are first-generation recipients of ANY type of loan. Many are from families where no one has ever had a checking account and where paying bills includes a trip to Circle K for a money order. They live from paycheck to paycheck in hopes that something will change and in hopes that they will have the chance to make their dreams come true. They are a very proud and grateful bunch and they often request to speak with a manager so that they can tell us what a positive influence our staff has had on solving their concerns when they can't afford their payments. We receive thank you notes and other various items of thanks. We know that we are changing peoples' lives, one student at a time.

Our goal is to give everyone a "fighting chance" to become a Champion and to live the American Dream.

1. FREEDOM OF CHOICE

2. ACCESS TO HIGHER EDUCATION

3. SUCCESSFUL CAREER

4. FINANCIAL FREEDOM

Because the type of data used herein is not readily available for student loans, we used research and reports about mortgage loans and their history as an indicator of what we can expect and what we have seen to be consistent with federal student loans.

References to FRM or fixed rate mortgage borrowers are similar to traditional students.

References to subprime ARM loans are references to nontraditional student loan borrowers. The concerns, behaviors and solutions are not based upon the institution type (sector); they are based upon the socio-economic background of the student. We deliver the data for the repayment schedule analysis in terms of the institution type only because that is the format used by the government for reporting student loan data. **We feel strongly that this is not an institutional issue; it is a borrower-centric issue.**

The Link between At-risk Student Loan Borrowers and ARM/Subprime Mortgage Borrowers

Source: The Federal Reserve Board http://www.federalreserve.gov/pubs/feds/2011/201121/

Although the demographic and financial characteristics of ARM and FRM borrowers are quite similar, the data from the Survey of Consumer Finances (SCF) suggest that ARM borrowers differ from FRM borrowers in their uses of credit and attitudes toward it. ARM borrowers are more likely to have been turned down for credit in the past five years, hardly ever pay off their credit card balances in full, and utilize a higher share of credit card limits. Although due to data limitations we do not estimate the marginal propensity to consume vis-à-vis the disposable income changes due to ARM payment resets, using a test of borrowing constraints common in the consumption literature, we find the consumption growth of households who report having an ARM is indeed more sensitive to past income than the consumption growth of other households, indicating that perhaps they are more constrained than other households. An important caveat is that due to data limitations, we do not attempt to identify any causal relationship between choosing an ARM and being borrowing constrained. Future work should address this causality issue, as well as estimate directly the size of the effect of mortgage payment resets on consumption.

When all financial assets are included, the median ratio of financial assets to income for ARM borrowers is 7 percentage points (about 13 percent) below that of FRM borrowers.

While ARM borrowers appear to have a similar attitude towards installment credit in general, differences in attitude arise in the details. For example, a higher fraction of ARM borrowers believe it is okay to use debt when one loses income. ARM borrowers are significantly more likely to have a financial planning period of less than one year and are significantly more likely to have been turned down for credit.

We also estimated probit models of the probability that a household hardly ever pays off its credit card and the probability that the household is currently utilizing more than 80 percent of its credit limit using similar specifications. High utilization rates have been used by other authors to proxy for credit constraints (Gross and Souleles 2002). These models suggest that controlling for other household characteristics, ARM borrowers are 2.4 percentage points (or 6 percent) more likely to utilize a high proportion of their credit card limits. They are also 3.5 percentage points (more than 10 percent) more likely to hardly ever pay off their credit card balance in full each month.

Prior research on ARMs argues that, unlike households with a fixed-rate mortgage (FRM), households with an ARM are subject to a "payment shock" when the interest rate on their mortgage resets to a higher level and their monthly mortgage payment increases. This payment shock, it is hypothesized, may lead households to cut back on their consumption or to default on their mortgages. For example, Buist and Yang (2000) link higher interest rates with higher default rates through an increasing payment burden and conclude that interest rate volatility can worsen ARM default risk. Ambrose, LaCour-Little and Huszar (2005) find relatively high rates of default among ARM borrowers, which they also attribute to "the payment shock that often affects adjustable rate loans."

Translation: Variable and changing payments are a high risk for ARM/ nontraditional borrowers.

The ARM Parallel

The subprime borrower accounts for a high percentage of defaults that is not proportional to the market share. The similar pattern in federal student loans supports the theory of "the student loan bubble."

Source: The Department of Statistics and Operations Research http://stat-or.unc.edu/

In the third quarter of 2007, subprime ARMs making up only 6.8% of USA mortgages outstanding also accounted for 43% of the foreclosures which began during that quarter.

By October 2007, approximately 16% of subprime adjustable rate mortgages (ARM) were either 90-days delinquent or the lender had begun foreclosure proceedings, roughly triple the rate of 2005.By January 2008, the delinquency rate had risen to 21% and by May 2008 it was 25%.

According to RealtyTrac, the value of all outstanding residential mortgages, owed by U.S. households to purchase residences housing at most four families, was US$9.9 trillion as of year-end 2006, and US$10.6 trillion as of midyear 2008. During 2007, lenders had begun foreclosure proceedings on nearly 1.3 million properties, a 79% increase over 2006. This increased to 2.3 million in 2008, an 81% increase vs. 2007, and again to 2.8 million in 2009, a 21% increase vs. 2008.

Another example is the interest-only adjustable-rate mortgage (ARM), which allows the homeowner to pay just the interest (not principal) during an initial period. Still another is a "payment option" loan, in which the homeowner can pay a variable amount, but any interest not paid is added to the principal. Nearly one in 10 mortgage borrowers in 2005 and 2006 took out these "option ARM" loans, which meant they could choose to make payments so low that their mortgage balances rose every month. An estimated one-third of ARMs originated between 2004 and 2006 had "teaser" rates below 4%, which then increased significantly after some initial period, as much as doubling the monthly payment.

The Financial Crisis Inquiry Commission reported in January 2011 that many mortgage lenders took eager borrowers' qualifications on faith, often with a "willful disregard" for a borrower's ability to pay. Nearly 25% of all mortgages made in the first half of 2005 were "interest-only" loans. During the same year, 68% of "option ARM" loans originated by Countrywide Financial and Washington Mutual had low- or no-documentation requirements.

The Financial Crisis Inquiry Commission reported in January 2011 that many mortgage lenders took eager borrowers' qualifications on faith, often with a "willful disregard" for a borrower's ability to pay. Nearly 25% of all mortgages made in the first half of 2005 were "interest-only" loans. During the same year, 68% of "option ARM" loans originated by Countrywide Financial and Washington Mutual had low- or no-documentation requirements.

Translation: Give schools the ability to "say no" and limit borrowing to those students whom they know will not pay.

The Fed then raised the Fed funds rate significantly between July 2004 and July 2006. This contributed to an increase in 1-year and 5-year ARM rates, making ARM interest rate resets more expensive for homeowners. This may have also contributed to the deflating of the housing bubble, as asset prices generally move inversely to interest rates and it became riskier to speculate in housing.

The Interest Rate Impact

Increases in interest rates found in variable rate loans have a direct impact on delinquent and default rates.

Source: The Rise in Mortgage Defaults
Christopher J. Mayer, Karen M. Pence, and Shane M. Sherlund (2008)

The fall in nonprime originations coincided with a sharp rise in delinquency rates. The share of subprime mortgages that were seriously delinquent increased from about 5.6 percent in mid-2005 to over 21 percent in July 2008. Alt-A mortgages saw an even greater proportional increase from a low of 0.6 to over 9 percent over the same time period. This dramatic rise in delinquency rates has spurred widespread concerns about the effects on borrowers, lenders, investors, local communities, and the overall economy.

Within subprime and Alt-A mortgages, delinquencies have been particularly pronounced for loans that include an adjustable interest rate component—floating-rate mortgages, short-term hybrids, and long-term hybrids. For example, looking at subprime mortgages, the serious delinquency rates for both adjustable-rate and fixed-rate loans were about 5.6 percent in mid- 2005. But by July 2008, serious delinquencies on adjustable-rate mortgages had risen to over 29 percent, while the similar rate for fixed-rate mortgages rose to 9 percent. Similarly, serious delinquency rates for both adjustable-rate and fixed-rate Alt-A mortgages were about 0.6 percent in mid-2005. But by July 2008, the delinquency rate on adjustable-rate Alt-A mortgages had risen past 13 percent, while the delinquency rate on fixed-rate mortgages had risen over 5 percent.

The vast majority of borrowers with option adjustable-rate mortgages appear to have exercised the option to make small "minimum" payments on their mortgages. By making payments less than the accrued interest due, these borrowers increased, rather than decreased, their mortgage balances over time. Figure 1 shows the share of borrowers with option adjustable- rate mortgages in the 2004, 2005, 2006, and 2007 vintages whose mortgage balances in a given number of months were larger than at origination. Most borrowers in the 2004 vintage paid off at least the interest in the first months of their mortgages, but by month 18, over 50 percent of these borrowers had balances that exceeded their size at origination.

Translation: Subprime ARM loans default at the highest rate.

Eliminating the One-Size-Fits-All Repayments

In most years where data is reported, the subprime ARM borrower represents a relatively small percent of the people borrowing. For those same years, these people represent the largest percent of defaults.

Percent of Foreclosures Started[78]:

Prime Fixed	*17.6%*
Prime ARM	*18.7%*
Subprime Fixed	*12.0%*
Subprime ARM	*43.0%*

The following information for student loan repayment schedules shows why there shouldn't be a "one size fits all" plan. The best advice to borrowers is not consistent between the different sectors because the average loan balances and average incomes vary.

The Graduated Repayment Plan consistently showed that it was not in the best interest of the students because they pay more interest, and because only the savvy borrowers with significantly increasing income will successfully navigate the significant increases in the loan payments at intervals during the repayment cycle.

In most cases, the choice of repayment plans will be made as the borrower decides if the lower payments justify additional interest and number of payments. In our 25 years of experience, we have found that a significant number of students will pay the higher payments to save money and, more importantly, get the payments completed earlier. It is a mental, emotional and financial burden to have student loan payments for 20-30 years.

For those who do decide the lower payments are worth the higher cost and number of payments, the plan that is in his/her best interest depends upon the loan balance and income of the borrower. The answer, as you will see herein, is not the same for every borrower.

We would also like to point out that borrowers who choose the Pay As You Earn (PAYE) and IBR options may have to pay income taxes on the dollar amount of loans forgiven at 20 or 25 years respectively into the repayment. In most of these cases, the time for repaying at least doubles. If the payments are low enough to lead to loan forgiveness, the borrowers do not have the money to make the income tax (balloon) payment at 20 or 25 years. At that point, the

---

78. Source: Mortgage Bankers Association http://www.mba.org/NewsandMedia/PressCenter/58758.htm

debt is with the IRS who charges interest and penalties and who is much more aggressive in their collections. We fail to see why these would be good options for the borrowers. It is very much like the Subprime ARM loans with balloon payments that borrowers historically have defaulted upon.

Methodology for Example Calculations

We have used examples from data that are readily available on various federal websites.

- The average loan debt and payment calculator used can be found at: https://studentloans.gov/myDirectLoan/mobile/repayment/repaymentEstimator.action

- Income data used is from the 2012 Information Gainful Employment Final Data

For those examples where loan forgiveness was involved:

1. We calculated a 3% cost of living increase per year for the earnings for 20 or 25 year, whichever is applicable, to get a projected income at the time the loan(s) are forgiven.

2. We added the loan forgiveness provided on the government website to get the total income in the year in which the loan is forgiven.

3. We calculated the federal and Arizona state tax rate based upon the total income including the loan forgiveness.

4. We calculated the federal and Arizona state tax rate without the loan forgiveness.

5. We calculated the difference between the total with loan forgiveness and the income without loan forgiveness to get the increased federal and tax liabilities that the borrower will owe as balloon payments when the loan(s) are forgiven.

EXAMPLE 1: Less-than-2-year Public

Average Loan Debt: $9,962* at 3.9% interest

Adjusted Gross Income (AGI): $28,995**

Family Information: Single, living in Arizona

Table 74: Example 1: Public Less-than-2-year Repayment Schedule Options (DOE screenshot)

Repayment Plan	Repayment Period	Monthly Payment Initial to Final Amounts		Projected Loan Forgiveness ❶	Total Interest Paid ❶	Total Amount Paid
Standard· ❶	120 months	$100 to	$100	$0	$2,085	$12,047
Graduated· ❶	120 months	$56 to	$168	$0	$2,600	$12,562
Pay As You Earn·· ❶	121 months	$96 to	$100	$0	$2,110	$12,072
Income-Based Repayment (IBR)·· ❶	-	-		-	-	-
Income-Contingent Repayment (ICR)·· ❶	177 months	$64 to	$86	$0	$3,350	$13,313

Best Option for the Borrower: Standard Repayment Plan should be recommended with the PAYE or ICR only when necessary.

- ◌ The Standard and Pay-As-You-Earn Repayment Plans are virtually the same payments and total amount paid.

- ◌ The Graduated Repayment Plan

  - • Costs an additional $515 in interest

  - • Has such large increases in payment amounts that it sets the students up for failure (i.e. higher risk of default over the life of the loan)

- ◌ The ICR Repayment Plan

  - • Costs an additional $1,265 in interest

  - • Increases the repayment period from 10 to 15 years

EXAMPLE 2: Less-than-2-year Private, Not-for-profit

Average Loan Debt: $13,356* at 3.9% interest

Adjusted Gross Income (AGI): $16,756**

Family Information: Single, living in Arizona

Table 75: Example 2: Private Less-than-2-year Repayment Schedule Options (DOE screenshot)

Repayment Plan		Repayment Period	Monthly Payment Initial to Final Amounts			Projected Loan Forgiveness ❶	Total Interest Paid ❶	Total Amount Paid
Standard•	❶	120 months	$135	to	$135	$0	$2,795	$16,151
Graduated•	❶	120 months	$75	to	$226	$0	$3,486	$16,841
Pay As You Earn••	❶	240 months	$0	to	$83	$16,734	$7,040	$7,040
Income-Based Repayment (IBR)••	❶	300 months	$0	to	$135	$6,985	$12,321	$18,692
Income-Contingent Repayment (ICR)••	❶	240 months	$69	to	$103	$0	$6,494	$19,850

Best Option for the Borrower: Standard Repayment Plan should be recommended initially, using PAYE only if necessary.

- If the goal is to collect on the student loan debt and minimize interest paid, the Standard plan is the best option.

- The Graduated Repayment Plan

  - Costs an additional $691 in interest

  - Has such large increases in payment amounts that it sets the students up for failure (i.e. higher risk of default over the life of the loan)

- If looking for the lowest payment, the Pay-As-You-Earn plan is best; however, the lower payments come with high costs and risk

  - It costs an additional $4,245 in interest

  - It doubles the repayment period from 10 to 20 years

  - It will have an estimated additional tax liability of $3,769 at 20 years. This calculation is as shown on the following page:

Table 76: Example 2: Private Less-than-2-year PAYE Calculation

$ 29,381.75	20 Year Earned Income with 3% increase per year
$ 16,734.00	Loan Forgiven
$ 46,115.75	Taxable Income

Tax Liability with Loan Forgiven

$ 6,822.69	Federal Tax Liability	
$ 1,549.49	3.36%	State Tax Liability
$ 8,372.18		

Tax Liability without Loan Forgiven

$ 3,616.01	Federal Tax Liability	
$ 987.23	3.36%	State Tax Liability
$ 4,603.24		

Increase in Tax Liability (Balloon Payments)

$ 3,206.67	Additional Federal Tax Liability
$ 562.26	Additional State Tax Liability
$ 3,768.94	Total Additional Taxes Due at Tax Filing Date

○ The ICR Repayment Plan

- Costs an additional $3,699 in interest

- Doubles the repayment period from 10 to 20 years

EXAMPLE 3: Less-than-2-year Proprietary

Average Loan Debt: $14,149* at 3.9% interest

Adjusted Gross Income (AGI): $14,700**

Family Information: Single, living in Arizona

Table 77: Example 3: Proprietary Less-than-2-year Repayment Schedule Options (DOE screenshot)

Repayment Plan	Repayment Period	Monthly Payment Initial to Final Amounts		Projected Loan Forgiveness ❶	Total Interest Paid ❶	Total Amount Paid
Standard· ❶	120 months	$143 to $143	————	$0	$2,961	$17,110
Graduated· ❶	120 months	$80 to $239	〰	$0	$3,693	$17,842
Pay As You Earn·· ❶	240 months	$0 to $39	〰	$23,242	$1,943	$1,943
Income-Based Repayment (IBR)·· ❶	300 months	$0 to $116	〰	$19,455	$8,490	$8,490
Income-Contingent Repayment (ICR)·· ❶	267 months	$51 to $110	〰	$0	$8,050	$22,199

Best Option for the Borrower: Standard Repayment Plan should be recommended initially, using PAYE only if necessary.

- If the goal is to collect on the student loan debt and minimize interest paid, the Standard plan is the best option.

- The Graduated Repayment Plan

  - Costs an additional $732 in interest

  - Has such large increases in payment amounts that it sets the students up for failure (i.e. higher risk of default over the life of the loan)

- If looking for the lowest payment, the Pay-As-You-Earn plan is best; however, the lower payments come with high costs and risk

  - It doubles the repayment period from 10 to 20 years

  - It will have an estimated additional tax liability of $5,254 at 20 years. This calculation is as shown on the following page:

Table 78: Example 3: Proprietary Less-than-2-year PAYE Calculation

$ 25,776.54	**20 Year Earned Income with 3% increase per year**
$ 23,242.00	**Loan Forgiven**
$ 49,018.54	**Taxable Income**

Tax Liability with Loan Forgiven

$ 7,548.38		**Federal Tax Liability**
$ 1,647.02	3.36%	**State Tax Liability**
$ 9,195.41		

Tax Liability without Loan Forgiven

$ 3,075.23		**Federal Tax Liability**
$ 866.09	3.36%	**State Tax Liability**
$ 3,941.32		

Increase in Tax Liability (Balloon Payments)

$ 4,473.14	**Additional Federal Tax Liability**
$ 780.93	**Additional State Tax Liability**
$ 5,254.09	**Total Additional Taxes Due at Tax Filing Date**

The IBR Repayment Plan also comes with long-term risks as follows:

- It has large increases in the payment amounts that it sets the students up for failure (i.e. higher risk of default over the life of the loan)

- It costs an additional $5,529 in interest

- In increases the repayment period from 10 to 25 years

- It will have an estimated additional tax liability of $4,419 at 25 years. This calculation is as follows:

Table 79: Example 3: Proprietary Less-than-2-year IBR Calculation

$ 28,166.72	25 Year Earned Income with 3% increase per year
$ 19,445.00	Loan Forgiven
$ 44,231.54	Taxable Income

Tax Liability with Loan Forgiven

$ 7,199.18		Federal Tax Liability
$ 1,600.09	3.36%	State Tax Liability
$ 8,799.27		

Tax Liability without Loan Forgiven

$ 3,433.76		Federal Tax Liability
$ 946.40	3.36%	State Tax Liability
$ 4,380.16		

Increase in Tax Liability (Balloon Payments)

$ 3,765.42	Additional Federal Tax Liability
$ 653.69	Additional State Tax Liability
$ 4,419.11	Total Additional Taxes Due at Tax Filing Date

The ICR Repayment Plan

- Costs an additional $5,089 in interest

- More than doubles the repayment period from 10 to 22 ¼ years.

EXAMPLE 4: 2-3-year Public

Average Loan Debt: $9,962* at 3.9% interest

Adjusted Gross Income (AGI): $29,902**

Family Information: Single, living in Arizona

Table 80: Example 4: Public 2–3 year Repayment Schedule Options (DOE screenshot)

Repayment Plan		Repayment Period	Monthly Payment Initial to Final Amounts			Projected Loan Forgiveness ❶	Total Interest Paid ❶	Total Amount Paid
Standard•	❶	120 months	$100	to	$100	$0	$2,085	$12,047
Graduated•	❶	120 months	$56	to	$168	$0	$2,600	$12,562
Pay As You Earn••	❶	-		-		-	-	-
Income-Based Repayment (IBR)••	❶	-		-		-	-	-
Income-Contingent Repayment (ICR)••	❶	174 months	$65	to	$86	$0	$3,281	$13,244

Best Option for the Borrower: Standard Repayment Plan should be recommended with ICR only if necessary.

○ If the goal is to collect on the student loan debt and minimize interest paid, the Standard plan is the best option.

○ The Graduated Repayment Plan

• Costs an additional $515 in interest

• Has such large increases in payment amounts that it sets the students up for failure (i.e. higher risk of default over the life of the loan)

○ The ICR Repayment Plan

• Costs an additional $1,196 in interest

• Increases the repayment period from 10 to 14 ½ years

EXAMPLE 5: 2-3-year Private, Not-for-profit

Average Loan Debt: $13,356* at 3.9% interest

Adjusted Gross Income (AGI): $29,837**

Family Information: Single, living in Arizona

Table 81: Example 5: Private 2–3 year Repayment Schedule Options (DOE screenshot)

Repayment Plan	Repayment Period	Monthly Payment Initial to Final Amounts		Projected Loan Forgiveness ❶	Total Interest Paid ❶	Total Amount Paid
Standard• ❶	120 months	$135 to $135	————	$0	$2,795	$16,151
Graduated• ❶	120 months	$75 to $226	⌐⌐⌐	$0	$3,486	$16,841
Pay As You Earn•• ❶	131 months	$103 to $135	∿∿	$0	$3,193	$16,549
Income-Based Repayment (IBR)•• ❶	-	-		-	-	-
Income-Contingent Repayment (ICR)•• ❶	174 months	$87 to $115	∿∿	$0	$4,405	$17,761

Best Option for the Borrower: Standard Repayment Plan should be recommended with PAYE only if necessary.

○ If the goal is to collect on the student loan debt and minimize interest paid, the Standard plan is the best option.

○ The Graduated Repayment Plan

  • Costs an additional $691 in interest

  • Has such large increases in payment amounts that it sets the students up for failure (i.e. higher risk of default over the life of the loan)

○ The Pay-As-You-Earn Plan

  • Costs an additional $398 in interest

  • Increases the repayment period from 10 to 11 years

○ The ICR Repayment Plan

  • Costs an additional $1,196 in interest

  • Increases the repayment period from 10 to 14 ½ years

EXAMPLE 6: 2-3-year Proprietary

Average Loan Debt: $14,149* at 3.9% interest

Adjusted Gross Income (AGI): $19,937**

Family Information: Single, living in Arizona

Table 82: Example 6: Proprietary 2–3 year Repayment Schedule Options (DOE screenshot)

Repayment Plan		Repayment Period	Monthly Payment Initial to Final Amounts			Projected Loan Forgiveness ❶	Total Interest Paid ❶	Total Amount Paid
Standard·	❶	120 months	$143	to	$143	$0	$2,961	$17,110
Graduated·	❶	120 months	$80	to	$239	$0	$3,693	$17,842
Pay As You Earn··	❶	240 months	$20	to	$143	$6,946	$10,139	$17,342
Income-Based Repayment (IBR)··	❶	234 months	$30	to	$143	$0	$7,995	$22,144
Income-Contingent Repayment (ICR)··	❶	219 months	$76	to	$117	$0	$6,174	$20,324

Best Option for the Borrower: Standard Repayment Plan should be recommended initially, using ICR only if necessary.

○ If the goal is to collect on the student loan debt and minimize interest paid, the Standard plan is the best option.

○ The Graduated Repayment Plan

   • Costs an additional $732 in interest

   • Has such large increases in payment amounts that it sets the students up for failure (i.e. higher risk of default over the life of the loan)

○ If looking for the lowest payment, the Pay-As-You-Earn plan is best; however, the lower payments come with high costs and risk.

   • It costs an additional $7,178 in interest

   • It doubles the repayment period from 10 to 20 years

   • Has such large increases in payment amounts that it sets the students up for failure (i.e. higher risk of default over the life of the loan)

- It will have an estimated additional tax liability of $3,769 at 20 years. This calculation is as follows:

Table 83: Example 6: Proprietary 2-3 year PAYE Calculation

$ 34,959.65	20 Year Earned Income with 3% increase per year
$ 6,946.00	Loan Forgiven
$ 41,905.65	Taxable Income

Tax Liability with Loan Forgiven

$ 5,770.16		Federal Tax Liability
$ 1,408.03	3.36%	State Tax Liability
$ 7,178.19		

Tax Liability without Loan Forgiven

$ 4,452.70		Federal Tax Liability
$ 1,174.64	3.36%	State Tax Liability
$ 5,627.34		

Increase in Tax Liability (Balloon Payments)

$ 1,317.47	Additional Federal Tax Liability
$ 233.39	Additional State Tax Liability
$ 1,440.85	Total Additional Taxes Due at Tax Filing Date

- The IBR Plan

  - Costs an additional $5,034 in interest

  - Increases the repayment period from 10 to 19 ½ years

  - Has such large increases in payment amounts that it sets the students up for failure (i.e. higher risk of default over the life of the loan)

- The ICR Repayment Plan

  - Costs an additional $3,213 in interest

  - Increases the repayment period from 10 to 18 ¼ years

EXAMPLE 7: 4+ -year Public

Average Loan Debt: $26,946* at 3.9% interest

Adjusted Gross Income (AGI): $42,027**

Family Information: Single, living in Arizona

Table 84: Example 7: Public 4+year Repayment Schedule Options (DOE screenshot)

Repayment Plan		Repayment Period	Monthly Payment Initial to Final Amounts			Projected Loan Forgiveness ❶	Total Interest Paid ❶	Total Amount Paid
Standard·	❶	120 months	$272	to	$272	——	$0	$5,638	$32,585
Graduated·	❶	120 months	$152	to	$455		$0	$7,032	$33,979
Pay As You Earn··	❶	133 months	$204	to	$272		$0	$6,619	$33,565
Income-Based Repayment (IBR)··	❶	·		·		·	·	·
Income-Contingent Reoayment (ICR)··	❶	149 months	$209	to	$260		$0	$7,338	$34,284

Best Option for the Borrower: Standard Repayment Plan should be recommended initially, using PAYE only if necessary.

- If the goal is to collect on the student loan debt and minimize interest paid, the Standard plan is the best option.
- The Graduated Repayment Plan
  - Costs an additional $1,394 in interest
  - Has such large increases in payment amounts that it sets the students up for failure (i.e. higher risk of default over the life of the loan)
- The Pay-As-You-Earn-Plan
  - Costs an additional $981 in interest
  - Increases the repayment period from 10 to 11+ years
- The ICR Repayment Plan
  - Costs an additional $1,700 in interest
  - Increases the repayment period from 10 to 12 ½ years

EXAMPLE 8: 4+ -year Private, Not-for-profit

Average Loan Debt: $29,214 at 3.9% interest

Adjusted Gross Income (AGI): $34,257

Family Information: Single, living in Arizona

Table 85: Example 8: Private 4+year Repayment Schedule Options (DOE screenshot)

Repayment Plan		Repayment Period	Monthly Payment Initial to Final Amounts			Projected Loan Forgiveness ❶	Total Interest Paid ❶	Total Amount Paid
Standard•	❶	120 months	$294	to	$294	$0	$6,113	$35,327
Graduated•	❶	120 months	$165	to	$494	$0	$7,624	$36,838
Pay As You Earn••	❶	182 months	$140	to	$294	$0	$11,164	$40,378
Income-Based Repayment (IBR)••	❶	136 months	$209	to	$294	$0	$7,466	$36,680
Income-Contingent Repayment (ICR)••	❶	163 months	$207	to	$256	$0	$8,859	$38,072

Best Option for the Borrower: Standard Repayment Plan should be recommended initially, using IBR or ICR only if necessary.

- If the goal is to collect on the student loan debt and minimize interest paid, the Standard plan is the best option.

- The Graduated Repayment Plan

  - Costs an additional $1,511 in interest

  - Has such large increases in payment amounts that it sets the students up for failure (i.e. higher risk of default over the life of the loan)

- The Pay-As-You-Earn Plan

  - Costs an additional $5,051 in interest

  - Increases the repayment period from 10 to 15+ years

  - Has such large increases in payment amounts that it sets the students up for failure (i.e. higher risk of default over the life of the loan)

○ The IBR Repayment Plan

  • Costs an additional $1,353 in interest

  • Increases the repayment period from 10 to 11 1/3 years

○ The ICR Repayment Plan

  • Costs an additional $2,746 in interest

  • Increases the repayment period from 10 to 13 ½ years

EXAMPLE 9: 4+ -year Proprietary

Average Loan Debt: $34,722* at 3.9% interest

Adjusted Gross Income (AGI): $32,027**

Family Information: Single, living in Arizona

Table 86: Example 9: Proprietary 4+ year Repayment Schedule Options (DOE screenshot)

Repayment Plan		Repayment Period	Monthly Payment Initial to Final Amounts			Projected Loan Forgiveness ❶	Total Interest Paid ❶	Total Amount Paid
Standard•	❶	120 months	$350	to	$350	$0	$7,265	$41,988
Graduated•	❶	120 months	$196	to	$587	$0	$9,062	$43,784
Extended Fixed	❶	300 months	$181	to	$181	$0	$19,687	$54,409
Extended Graduated	❶	300 months	$113	to	$328	$0	$24,772	$59,494
Pay As You Earn••	❶	223 months	$127	to	$350	$0	$17,502	$52,224
Income-Based Repayment (IBR)••	❶	163 months	$191	to	$350	$0	$11,395	$46,117
Income-Contingent Repayment (ICR)••	❶	166 months	$241	to	$299	$0	$10,794	$45,516

Best Option for the Borrower: Standard Repayment Plan should be recommended initially, using Extended Fixed or ICR only if necessary.

  ○ If the goal is to collect on the student loan debt and minimize interest paid, the Standard plan is the best option.

  ○ The Graduated Repayment Plan

- Costs an additional $1,797 in interest
- Has such large increases in payment amounts that it sets the students up for failure (i.e. higher risk of default over the life of the loan)

- Extended Fixed Repayment Plan
  - Costs an additional $12,422 in interest
  - Increases the repayment period from 10 to 25 years

- The Extended Graduated Repayment Plan
  - Costs an additional $17,507 in interest
  - Increases the repayment period from 10 to 25 years
  - Has such large increases in payment amounts that it sets the students up for failure (i.e. higher risk of default over the life of the loan)

- The Pay-As-You-Earn Plan
  - Costs an additional $10,237 in interest
  - Increases the repayment period from 10 to 18 ½ years
  - Has such large increases in payment amounts that it sets the students up for failure (i.e. higher risk of default over the life of the loan)

- The IBR Repayment Plan
  - Costs an additional $4,130 in interest
  - Increases the repayment period from 10 to 13 1/3 years

- The ICR Repayment Plan
  - Costs an additional $3,529 in interest
  - Increases the repayment period from 10 to just under 14 years

Table 87: Example 9: Proprietary 4+ year Repayment Plan Options Summary

Repayment Plan	Repayment Period	Monthly Payment	Total Interest (based on Standard)	Total Amount Paid (based on Standard)
Standard	**10 years**	**$350 fixed**	**$7,265**	**$41,988**
Extended Fixed	Standard + 15 years **Total 25 years**	$181 fixed	Standard + $12,422 **Total $19,687**	Standard + $12,421 **Total $54,409**
Extended Graduated	Standard + 15 years **Total 25 years**	$113 to $328	Standard + $17,507 **Total $24,772**	Standard + $17,496 **Total $59,494**
Pay As You Earn	Standard + 8 ½ years **Total 18 ½ years**	$127 to $350	Standard + $10,237 **Total $17,502**	Standard + $10,236 **Total $52,224**
IBR	Standard + 3 ½ years **Total 13 ½ years**	$191 to $350	Standard + $4,130 **Total $11,395**	Standard + $4,129 **Total $46,117**
ICR	Standard + 4 years **Total 14 years**	$241 to $299	Standard + $3,529 **Total $10,794**	Standard + $3,528 **Total $45,516**

Possible Solutions:

Eliminate the Graduated Repayment Plan. The extreme increases in payment amounts with this program set borrowers up for failure and increases the risk of default even for those who are savvy borrowers. Other variable payment options better serve the borrowers' interest and the variation in payment amounts are more realistic for borrowers to make.

Design a program for the subprime and nontraditional borrows. For these at-risk borrowers, frequency with smaller loan amounts is essential and forms healthy fiscal responsibility habits.[79]

---

79. Repayment Frequency and Default in Micro-Finance: Evidence from India by Erica Field and Rohini Pande

INJUSTICE FOR ALL INSIGHT

Realistic Suggestions
To Correct the Issues

Weekly payments that are drafted from the borrower's account will make the payments more manageable for the at-risk borrowers as seen in micro-finance. Statistics show that a 96% repayment rate is consistently obtained when payments start within 1–2 weeks of the loan origination and when payments are made weekly. To truly fix the issue, Congress will have to think outside of the box. Here, we offer a few suggestions:

1. Education funding should be driven by reward for good behavior. For example, begin with "all loans" and convert portions of the loan into grants as the borrower makes on-time payments instead of giving free money in the beginning. Pay an interest payment match when the payment is made on time during periods of deferment and forbearance.

2. Make it mandatory to make a 5% or 10% down payment for the education. Default rates are less likely when the borrower is financially invested in the experience, whether it is mortgage or student loans.

3. Align the federal servicing contracts to be consistent with the good rewards offered to borrowers so that everyone is driving the bus in the same direction. Conflicting rewards will never have good outcomes.

4. Make the payment plans something that the taxpayers will support. The fact that several of the examples show students making all interest payments and most of the loans' principal is forgiven is a tragedy for taxpayers. Americans are funding 100% of the cost of higher education and Americans deserve to be paid back for their investments.

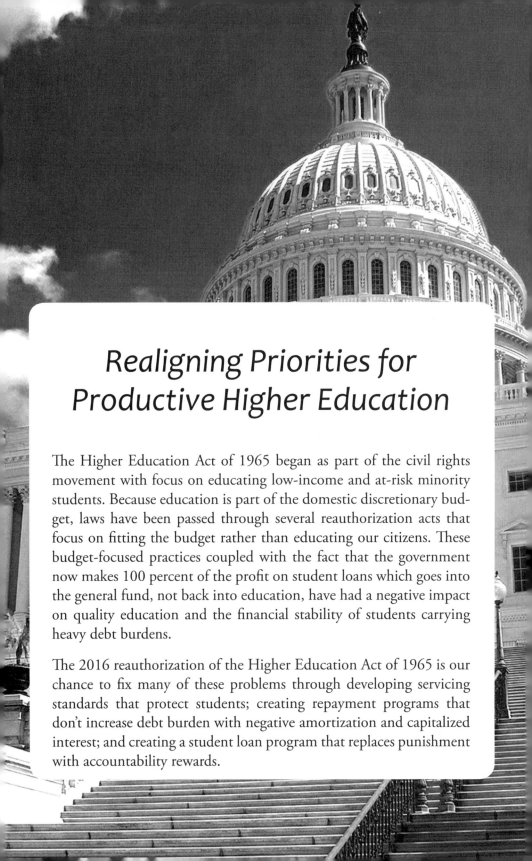

Realigning Priorities for Productive Higher Education

The Higher Education Act of 1965 began as part of the civil rights movement with focus on educating low-income and at-risk minority students. Because education is part of the domestic discretionary budget, laws have been passed through several reauthorization acts that focus on fitting the budget rather than educating our citizens. These budget-focused practices coupled with the fact that the government now makes 100 percent of the profit on student loans which goes into the general fund, not back into education, have had a negative impact on quality education and the financial stability of students carrying heavy debt burdens.

The 2016 reauthorization of the Higher Education Act of 1965 is our chance to fix many of these problems through developing servicing standards that protect students; creating repayment programs that don't increase debt burden with negative amortization and capitalized interest; and creating a student loan program that replaces punishment with accountability rewards.

IX. LEGISLATIVE SOLUTIONS THAT PROMOTE ACCOUNTABILITY

LEGISLATIVE SOLUTIONS *INCLUDING* A NEW STUDENT LOAN PROGRAM BASED ON ACCOUNTABILITY

Accountability versus Entitlement: where do we want to go? We ALWAYS have a choice: we can do what we've always done, we can do something different, or we can do nothing. Only one of those choices will make a difference and change the destiny of our children and our country.

Destiny Is a Choice

I grew up in an abusive home in a small town in Montana. My father's abhorrent actions could have broken me. My mother drank herself through the nightmare. And, I had a plan from a very early age to leave the "little house of horrors" using every bit of knowledge and education that I could get my hands on. I left home the day after I graduated from high school at the age of 17. I began taking college classes in the 7th grade so I "comped out" of many prerequisite classes in college and graduated with honors from college at the age of 19. I graduated from a proprietary school where, for the first time in my life, someone said they believed in me and many teachers mentored me—and that changed my destiny.

You see, this is why I stand up for the underdogs. I fight for the rights of the at-risk students because I am an at-risk student, not through poverty but through circumstances that could easily have broken my spirit. I chose to use my experiences as a reason for making a change.

And now, I ask lawmakers to support practices and programs that will improve the destinies of our children by teaching them accountability that fosters self-esteem, self-worth, and pride.

Legislative Solutions for Students: Teaching and Rewarding Financial Accountability

In the past, laws have been based upon manipulated data and reports put forth by the U.S. Department of Education that promoted better-than-actual results for public sector institutions while issuing worse-than-actual results for proprietary institutions. American citizens deserve to have quality metrics that are realistic and that apply to all institutions and auditing for government data and reports that ensures accuracy and integrity. These practices will drive a culture of accountability for ALL participants in federal college funding programs.

Solutions for students CAN happen in the 2015–2016 Reauthorization of the Higher Education Act of 1965. Members of Congress are currently working through this legislation and are determined to pass this bill during the 114th Congress in office at this time.

While I support several of the bills already introduced and some are a result of providing the information in this book to key members of the education committees, I am only including those legislative suggestions that are relevant to the subjects in the book and within my area of expertise.

Correcting the Reason for the CDR Adjustments in 2014

Conduit and PUT loan portfolios have experienced extremely high CDRs pushing 60% in addition to the FY 2011 FDSLP rate of 30.4%. These are directly related to colossal mistakes made by the DOE and numerous lenders and servicers. Many students had defaulted loans that NEVER should have occurred. The DOE thought this to be severe enough to correct the issue for a limited number of schools facing sanctions in September 2014 and 2015. They did not fix the problem for all schools nor did they fix the problem for ANY of the students. This is a tragedy that must be corrected.

The DOE's application to certain schools and not to others makes this decision arbitrary in nature which has been frowned upon in other applications, in addition to the fact that the students haven't been addressed at all.

We may not be able to change what has already happened but we certainly have the ability to correct the problem now.

Correcting the High DOE-Controlled CDRs for Students

The right thing to do is to bring these defaulted loans out of default, correct the bad credit that does not accurately reflect the borrower's intent or actions, and allow the borrowers to have a fresh start making timely payments. The loans should be placed with the servicer that has any other student loans on record since many of these students have or did have loans in good standing until this happened.

The Department's criteria for "adjusting" the default from being counted to not being counted was if the student had at least one other loan in good standing for a period of 60 consecutive days during the cohort period. I don't believe that this is expansive enough. Those students who did not have multiple loans but had loans subject to poor servicing during massive loan purchases and transfers should also be given a fair shot—they didn't really have a chance to make payments on time because their loans were in chaos for months. When you add chaos on top of first-time borrowers, it is truly a recipe for disaster.

These students shouldn't have to start their adult lives with a burden that is out of their control. This situation is a tragedy and the 114th Congress can change that. The benefits to our economy and working class will be enormous. The students with loans in the following categories should have the default status reversed:

1. ALL students who had at least one loan in good standing for a period of 60 days or more and who had one or more defaulted loans.

2. Any student who was part of the extended ECASLA student loan purchases (those with disbursements on or after October 1, 2007) who had one or more loans in good standing for 60 days or more.

3. Any student with one or more loans in the FY 2011 FDSLP portfolio who had one or more loans in good standing for a period of 60 days or more.

4. Any student loan that qualifies under items 1–3 above that has been consolidated.

These students' loans should be brought out of default and put into repayment AND any penalty and interest fees assessed should be applied to their principal to reduce their student loan debt. Their credit record also needs to be corrected so that it doesn't reflect any defaulted loans in the history. In other words, the credit history should not show these as a "bad debt resolved" because that still implies that the student has done something wrong—it needs to reflect no late payments and no default history. The student should also get a confirmation letter that confirms that these corrections are in process and, then, another when this has been completed.

All wage garnishments should immediately stop and interest should not accrue until the loans are placed back in repayment status. These students have been unduly punished enough already—this is the least the government should do for them.

Correcting the High DOE-Controlled CDRs for Schools

Additionally, the default rates of schools affected should be adjusted for all schools, not just those in jeopardy of sanctions. Many schools, good schools, rely upon the advantages of disbursement benefits by having three consecutive CDRs under 15%. All schools rely upon their reputation which is formed in large part by public opinion based on the cohort default rates publicly released each September. Schools also should have the benefit of having corrected data that accurately reflects their success and that of their students—not a failed process that devastated thousands of students both mentally and financially.

> *If your child was one of these affected students, wouldn't you want this wrong to be righted? I know that I would. Everyone deserves a fair chance and this should be done—because it's the right thing to do.*

Budgeting and Finance in the Students' Best Interest

Many students in college have little knowledge or experience in budgeting and finance. Some of them, even with the best intentions, get in over their heads when they are given their first experience with credit. I'm sure that many of us can remember overusing our first credit cards, thinking that it would be much easier to pay back the debt than it actually was. Usually, these first credit cards have low lines of credit and the inexperienced borrower gains a difficult but valuable lesson through this experience.

Student loans, however, are a different story. Not only is the credit amount high in many circumstances but it is also for a specific purpose—to obtain and complete an education so that the student can enter the workforce and become gainfully employed. When these inexperienced students, who often come from meager beginnings, get a large sum of money all at once, it is frequently misallocated and the student later finds himself or herself short of money before the end of the education funding period. This shortage of money often leads to students dropping out of school and taking a low paying job to put food on the table or keep their children in school or daycare. The purpose of getting an education—to enable the student to lift him or herself out of low-income circumstances and move the entire family into the middle class—has not been fulfilled. The student can become permanently discouraged.

I am proposing a system that revolves around monthly stipend disbursements rather than a lump sum along with support for learning how to manage that money. Monthly stipends prevent students from running out of money before the funding (loan period) ends and give them experience in budgeting, something that will benefit them for the rest of their lives. This approach teaches them how to manage money before their student loan payments are due. Practical application of financial literacy training drives long-term success.

All institutions would benefit from having the ability to help students manage their money while they are in school, especially schools serving at-risk students. For these reasons, we request that the following be included in the upcoming reauthorization of the Higher Education Act of 1965:

1. Give schools and financial aid offices the ability to limit student borrowing.

2. Give the schools the ability to disburse living expense money in monthly stipends during the loan period. Allow students to apply for "special circumstances" that can be granted under professional judgment by the financial aid office for those cases where more than an equal monthly payment is needed.

Payment Schedules That Promote Long-Term Success and Support the Federal Fiscal Interest

Now that student loans are directly funded by taxpayer money, we must protect the students' interest and the taxpayers and federal fiscal interest. I believe that there can be a balance in doing this where the repayment schedules promote borrowers' success and the fiscal interest is served by having a higher success of timely repayment.

There are many studies that show similar behaviors for at-risk student loan borrowers and subprime lending. Many of these studies consistently support the fact that repayment success is directly tied to stable and consistent payment amounts as seen with traditional mortgage loans. Many of these studies also show a direct correlation between fluctuating payments and higher failure rates as demonstrated in subprime ARM mortgage loans where payments are based upon interest rates. When the payments go up, borrowers are setup for failure. This is true for all borrowers and especially for at-risk borrowers.

In addition to the rewards outlined above, we believe that a combination of existing repayment options would best serve students with a few variations:

1. Interest rates should be fixed. Having moving payments that are adjusted and based on changing incomes in addition to changing interest rates is a recipe for disaster. If the interest rewards for on-time interest payments during school and timely payments during repayment are appropriately promoted with borrowers, the costs of the loans will decrease and the interest rate paid by students will be reasonable.

2. Income-based payments should be calculated for the first three (3) years of repayment and, then, the repayment schedule converts to a standard repayment with set payment amounts that can be easily budgeted. The length of the repayment would be determined and based upon the income of the borrower at the 3-year mark during the repayment. If the borrower experiences an increase in income and wants to make higher payments or request an adjusted repayment schedule, he or she may do so.

3. During the first three (3) critical years of repayment, the habits of the borrowers are formed. Most of these borrowers are just starting their adult lives or they are making an attempt to improve their lives. For

these reasons, capitalizing interest can paralyze them financially and emotionally by burdening them with overwhelming debt. A positive attitude about loan repayment is crucial to successful repayment so why would we want them to start off building more debt than what they began with? If the student's income is low enough to put them into a negative amortization, it is low enough to forgive some accruing interest in order to keep the student on track for successfully paying the loan in full over the long haul. Remember that these situations primarily affect at-risk students and those are the students we want to catapult to financial success so that they can raise above their circumstances and move into the middle and upper classes.

Poverty is not overcome by adding unmanageable debt to the mix. Give the students a chance to concentrate on and excel at their new trade or profession instead of worrying about a growing debt burden. By moving the "loan forgiveness" as seen in the Pay-As-You Earn or IBR Repayment Programs from the back end to the front end, borrowers are given hope that they can successfully pay their loans as opposed to feeling buried and overwhelmed by debt. When they give up, they stop paying.

Serving the Students' Best Interest

Charging interest into the future is strictly prohibited by law in some states but not in all states. Unfortunately, many students have been making additional payments on their loans in an attempt to pay them off early only to find out that the payments have been applied to future payments instead of principal reduction! Interest is supposed to be earned in the past before the payment is made and based upon the outstanding balance of the loan. The greedy practice of applying payments to future payments based on the amortization schedule forces the student to pay interest as if he or she is taking the entire repayment period to pay the loan. This is, simply put, wrong.

For this reason, we ask for legislation that prohibits these greedy practices and mandate that payments be applied in the following order:

- First, to late fees;

- Second, to outstanding interest; and

⊙ Third, to principal with any payments above the scheduled payments applied to principal reduction.

The legislation will also need to include language to force lenders and ser-vicers to back out the misapplied payments and reapply them as outlined above within 30 days of the student's request to do so. If there is a way to mandate this without the students' request, this would be the optimal solution because many uninformed students do not have the financial savvy to correct this problem on their own.

Loan and Grant Programs That Reward Good Behavior

There is truth in the theory that most people will behave in the way in which they are rewarded. We've all seen this with children whose parents reward them for good behavior and who then get the desired behaviors. Parents who ignore their children, only paying attention to them when they misbehave, develop children who act out because they are starved for any kind of attention, even punishment.

We can apply those same theories to education funding using the fol-lowing system:

1. Determine the total funding amount based on income and assets.

2. Reward graduates with a "loan forgiveness" that is similar to what is now known as a Pell Grant. In other words, a portion of the loan is converted to a grant when the student completes the program in a timely manner (within 150% of the original course length.) Because the grant portion is tied to program completion, the students enrolling in a course of study will have a strong incentive to enroll in a program that is appropriate for them and to be fully aware of the commitment they are making before taking out these loans. Consideration may need to be made for those stu-dents who have to drop out of school for emergencies or medical condi-tions so that they can return and complete their programs without losing this benefit. This may be best handled through an application process.

3. Reward those who make timely payments on accruing interest while they are in school by matching the interest payment. Instead of cutting the interest in half for all loans, match the equivalent of half the interest

paid as a reward for making on-time payments. This reduces the loan burden for students when they graduate and it also instills the behavior and habit of making monthly payments as planned. In some third world countries where cottage trade funding or micro-funding is practiced, the repayment rates are close to 90% when the payments start within a couple weeks of the loan funding. The same can apply here.

4. Reward borrowers for timely payments when they leave school in the same manner by matching the interest payment when the payments are made on time.

5. Reward the borrowers for long-term payment commitment and success by forgiving portions of the loans at intervals during the repayment period. For example, forgive 5% of the loan when timely payments have been made for each 20% increment of the repayment period. If the student successfully completes this for the entire loan period, the borrower can earn up to 20% in loan forgiveness and have paid the loans off early. The loan servicing costs are also reduced and the money is paid back earlier.

6. Align federal loan servicer incentives with borrower incentives.

Timely Repayment	Accrued Repayment	Loan Reduction	Accrued Reduction
20% of repayment period	20% of repayment	5% reduction	5% reduction
20% of repayment period	40% of repayment	5% reduction	10% reduction
20% of repayment period	60% of repayment	5% reduction	15% reduction
20% of repayment period	80% of repayment	5% reduction	20% reduction

Keeping this benefit available even when the student has a rocky start is important so that the incentive is still there when the borrower gets on his or her feet and is able to change the behavior from untimely payments to timely and successful repayment. For some, this habit may form early on and for others it may take a few stumbles before they get there, and we want to make sure that the rewards are available at any time that the borrowers decide to change their destiny. A later start may mean that the student can only accrue 10% or 15% total loan reduction, but some is better than none and the incentive goes a long way in helping to encourage healthy financial behaviors.

Gainful Employment 2.0: Existing Regulations Are Based on Inaccurate and Misleading Reporting and Should Be Eliminated

Quality measures and metrics are a good idea when they are reasonably administered, are based upon fair and realistic measurements, and are applied to all institutions. If all institutions can't live by the laws and regulations, they are most likely not fair and equitable. Every institution has challenging students and this is not determined by tax status—it is determined by the location and the students served.

The Gainful Employment FY 2011 Informational Rates data analysis produced the following discoveries:

- A disproportionate number of schools from each sector were reported in the "FY 2011 Streamlined Informational Data" that was released to the public compared to the comprehensive "FY 2011 Final Informational Data";

- Data for certain programs, primarily public and private sector programs, were removed and, therefore, these programs were not reported;

- In the comprehensive "Final" FY 2011 GE Informational Rates data, the payment calculations for programs where all sectors are compared were the most accurately reported ratios including the Undergraduate Certificate and Post Baccalaureate Certificate credential levels.

- The payment calculations for credential levels where the proprietary schools had the only applicable programs (foreign programs excepted), were inaccurately calculated too high. This had the negative impact of inflating the debt numbers used in the debt-to-earnings calculations which made the results look much worse than they actually were. The miscalculations for payments had a significant effect on the debt-to-earnings ratios for ALL GE programs but the most damaging errors were to proprietary school programs.

⊙ The miscalculations for payments had a significant impact on all programs and especially on the debt-to-earnings ratios for the 193 programs named as "failing all three metrics";

⊙ For programs identified in the FY 2011 Streamlined Data as "Failed 3 Rates" (193 proprietary programs), payments were not calculated properly in compliance with the original regulatory definition for 10-, 15-, and 20-year repayment schedules. We could not identify a pattern except that they were grossly inaccurate—as much as over 1,000% higher than the annual payment calculation should have been;

⊙ Out of the 193 proprietary programs that were reported as failing all three rates (DOE file name: FY2011StreamlinedFailed3Rates), the corrected payments produced only 6 programs that failed all three metrics. I believe this is why the U.S. Department of Education defined a "zone"—because it didn't have enough failing programs using its own flawed rationale in the Preamble of the original GE federal regulations;

⊙ The GE 2.0 regulations took a path that totally dismissed the rationale for the original GE metrics by adding a "zone" definition to capture more failing programs because the correct calculations for the original GE data no longer produced the desired number of failing programs—if that's not arbitrary and capricious, I don't know what is; and

⊙ The GE 2.0 FY 2012 Informational Rates were missing the "median debt" amount in the publicly released data; therefore, the rates could not be verified for accuracy. If the rates were accurately calculated, why would the DOE withhold this vital information?

In summary, the DOE has gone to great lengths to manipulate data and reporting for all sectors of education to support the Obama Administration's agenda for eliminating the for-profit proprietary sector. The main points that are pertinent here are:

1. If the public and private nonprofit sectors were really outperforming the

proprietary sector, why is there a need to eliminate data and reporting for those programs that fall within the definition of GE programs?

2. If the public and private nonprofit sectors were really performing well, why wouldn't they support the GE metrics application to all programs regardless of their tax-filing status?

3. If the proprietary schools were actually as bad as the DOE and certain politicians are asserting, why is there a need to negatively manipulate data and reporting to support their elimination?

4. If the DOE's rationale was justified in several hundred pages of the Preamble, how can they justify a harsher standard in GE 2.0 without it being considered arbitrary and capricious? The "zone" standard exactly follows the metrics explained in the original GE Preamble where the harsher standards were not used.

There definitely are programs and schools that should be eliminated for many reasons—and those programs and schools exist in every sector of higher education, not just the proprietary sector.

Quality metrics and standards should apply to all schools and all programs to truly protect our students. ***When the objective is anything other than protecting all students at all schools, the quality standards are not up to par.*** All students can only be protected when every quality standard applies equally to all schools and all programs.

GE Bottom Line: Eliminate the Gainful Employment 2.0 regulations and develop quality metrics that apply to all schools and all programs equally.

Injustice or All Insight

WE ALL WIN!

Rewarding graduation, timely payments, and timely completion of the repayment schedule ultimately increases cash flow, reduces collection costs, reduces the student's loan burden, reduces tax burden for the taxpayers, and frees up education funds for future students of America. Productive behaviors can be learned through accountability rewards for education funding that will benefit students throughout their lives.

Creating a Student Loan Program with Accountability

We must remember that for some, good credit is a habit that has been passed down through generations and for others, it is a life-changing experience. When it changes lives, we elevate at-risk students and their families from poverty and government programs into the middle and upper class. This is the true sense of changing America from a culture of entitlement to a culture of empowerment and that is the America where I want my children and grandchildren to thrive!

Taxpayers have the right to ask for a loan program that holds everyone involved accountable because taxpayers are paying for everyone's student loans. With 100% direct loans, whether they are current or in default, taxpayers are funding the programs.

For the Taxpayers:

Federal student loans and grants are now a very large part of the federal budget because they are all made directly from the government. We are no longer using the lenders to fund the loans where taxpayers only covered the cost of defaulted borrowers—we are paying directly for them through our tax dollars.

Rewarding graduation, timely payments, and timely completion of the repayment schedule ultimately increases cash flow, reduces collection costs, reduces the student's loan burden, reduces tax burden for the taxpayers, and frees up education funds for future students of America. Productive behaviors can be learned through accountability reward for education funding that will benefit the students throughout their lives.

A student loan program with accountability facilitates educating America within a budget process tied to accountability instead of entitlement by:

1. Encouraging students to enroll in the right field of study prior to taking out student loans by giving students big financial incentives for reducing their loan burden when they graduate on time.

2. Providing financial incentives to encourage interest payments as interest accrues so that the interest doesn't get capitalized. Paying interest reduces loan debt where capitalized interest increases the total loan debt is increased and the student pays interest on the unpaid interest. *A portion of the national student loan debt is directly attributed to unpaid and capitalized interest.*

3. Creating disbursement schedules in smaller increments like 20% at a time where accruing interest is minimized and the students don't receive large sums of living expense money that tempts overspending and possibly leads to dropping out.

4. Encouraging students to pay the loans in full within the original standard repayment schedule.

5. Mandating that no loans will be forgiven except when accompanied by good behaviors. Currently, certain student loan balances are forgiven after 20–25 years of repayment. This places the financial burden of these loans on our children. Our children should not be responsible for someone else's debt.

For the Students:

For most students and people in general, the journey of success begins with rewards that promote good behaviors. By doing so, we create a culture of accountability from enrollment through successful repayment of student loan debt for students. The positive side effect is that it also serves in the best interest of taxpayers.

In over 26 years in business, specializing in default prevention, with prior experience in mortgage lending and student loan lending, we have discovered that there is one common predictable outcome that will occur:

If you define a bonus based on a behavior that does not match your long-term goals, you will fail in meeting those goals. If you define a bonus that promotes good behavior, good behavior will occur. For example, in my business, if our bonuses are solely based on call volume, we would have a large number of calls and, generally, the contacts and recoveries would suffer. When we base our bonuses on recoveries with payments having a higher reward than deferments/forbearances, we meet our goals as a company by reducing loan burden for our student customers and by delivering a larger number of recoveries that produce lower default rates for our school clients. The goal of payment program recoveries is what we have in practice for our entire company. Without the right goals, our student customers and school clients face failure and that, in turn, increases the failure risk for our company.

Historically, certain trends can be used as a basis for creating a program that is fiscally sound and promotes student success.

The most important trends are as follows:

- The most likely default is with the student who never makes the first payment.

- Approximately half of defaults during the life of the loan occur during the first two years of repayment. The recent economic situation has modified the recent data; however, for long-term planning, we will consider the trend as being half in the first two years as an indicator for developing a sound structure for servicing.

- Students with little to no experience in successful financial planning rarely have the administrative capabilities or life skills to manage changing payments either through PAYE, REPAY, IBR/ICR, graduated repayment, interest rate changes, or capitalized interest. Predictability is the key to everyone's success. Payments that fluctuate are difficult to manage and fixing the rate helps students budget their money for the long-term. If the interest rate is variable and the rate goes up, the risk of default goes up as the payments increase. A fixed interest rate facilitates long-term financial planning and stability in the best interest of the students.

* Remember that the most common foreclosures over the years are those with ARM loans—when the payments go up, people can't pay and lose their homes. My prior experience in mortgage lending during the mid 80s coupled with recent foreclosure trends show this to be true in any economy. The ARM loans have the same structure as the graduated payment schedule and set people up to fail when payments increase. The same can be true when payments go up with student loans. Change is NOT good for borrowers who are just in the learning stages of financial literacy. You can teach through electronic financial literacy courses or out of a textbook all day long, but the real lessons come in application of learned behaviors.

* Notice that the cost of administering these alternate repayment plans is also costly to servicers and the government. Savings will be found in simplifying and stabilizing the options as long as there are temporary relief options when students can't make full payments.

○ Accruing and unpaid interest is also a leading indicator of defaults. Students end up owing more than they originally budgeted and more than they can afford in the long term. Incentives should consider this indicator, offering a larger incentive for borrowers who pay interest as it accrues and who are paying down their principal balance.

○ Deferments and forbearance for specific conditions are important to students for long-term success and also important for fiscal responsibility. If these options are taken away, as some politicians would like, our country would have to pay for defaults on all of those loans. It would devastate the lives of many students and would be fiscally irresponsible. Over the years, we have seen that the most common causes of delinquencies include the following situations:

Unemployed or underemployed. In the current economy and with employers reducing hours because of Obamacare restrictions, we will see a larger percent of underemployed people. This doesn't show up in national unemployment statistics but it is a reality in America. The unemployment deferment should be expanded to include the underemployed and consideration should be given to the maximum benefits defined, possibly by defining an individual maximum for the unemployed and underemployed. It is a very important option for students to have.

Military leave could be restructured to payroll deduction while in the military. These folks are making a living and the payroll deductions will ensure that they don't have burdensome debt when they return and will reduce servicing costs while they are on active duty.

Temporary financial burdens should be considered. Generally, they are short in duration and based upon circumstances beyond the borrower's control. For example, there might be a health issue or car repair that must be considered. If the servicer helps create a budget to pay down the burden and stay on track with the student loan long-term repayment goals, everyone wins. Approved payments with interest being paid as it accrues should be rewarded at a higher rate than those with negative amortization. The situation and progress should be measured quarterly.

Incentives should reward good behavior that promotes and facilitates reaching long-term goals. For student loans, this includes:

1. Graduating on time (ultimately) or within a reasonable amount of time

2. Minimizing debt through graduation incentives

3. Minimizing debt through interest payment incentives

4. Reducing the cost of paying the loans by minimizing interest when payments are made timely

5. Successful repayment of loans that rewards students with lower

costs and great credit ratings for future financial security

Schools and their third-party servicers for borrower education and default prevention should have timely access to the student/borrower data needed to accurately and appropriately assist borrowers in making good long-term decisions for their financial stability and success. Schools would be able to help facilitate understanding of and implementation of these good behaviors.

Here's how it can be done for the students:

- The total federal aid awarded would all begin as a loan.

- The grant portion (equivalent of the current Pell Grant) is noted in the award letter as a potential "graduation incentive payment" (GIP) that will be made when the student graduates from the program within 150% of the usual and customary time for graduating in the applicable education level. For example, for a bachelor's degree, the baseline for graduating would be 4 years so the student would have to graduate within 6 years to receive the graduation incentive payment.

In addition to being in compliance with satisfactory progress standards, the terms for the GIP are as follows:

- 100% of the GIP is paid to those who graduate within the usual and customary time for graduating in that field of study. In other words, the student gets 100% of the GIP for graduating at 100% of the course length.

- 90% of the GIP is paid to those who graduate within 125% of the usual and customary time for graduating in that field of study.

- 80% of the GIP is paid to those who graduate within 150% of the usual and customary time for graduating in that field of study.

- If the student terminates or changes his/her field of study to an unrelated field of study, the GIP is forfeited for the loans associated with the course the student did not graduate from. This gives incentives to students choosing the right field of study before taking out student loans and reduces the likelihood of students becoming "professional students."

○ The loan has a fixed interest rate.

○ Subsidized loans are eliminated in lieu of interest incentives explained below:

Students who make timely monthly interest payments as the interest accrues will have an "Interest Payment Match" (IPM) from the federal government that is equal to half of the interest payment made. This would apply to loan statuses including enrollment, grace period, repayment, deferment, and forbearance. The incentive should encourage borrowers to make the entire interest payment as the interest accrues.

- For example, if the interest rate is 8% and the student is making timely monthly payments or 100% of the monthly accruing interest, the student would be responsible for 4% or half the monthly accrued interest and the government would pay the other half. For those with this good behavior, the interest payment is half of the accrued interest.

- If the student pays less than 100% of the accruing interest, the government matches the amount paid as the interest accrues and the student is responsible for the balance of accruing interest (a combination of paid and unpaid interest). The IPM is only for the amount of interest collected as it accrues.

○ Students with bank drafts and automatic payments and who are paying 100% of the accruing interest as it accrues receive an additional 0.5% interest rate reduction because it saves money by eliminating manual labor for processing payments.

- For example, a timely payment based upon a fixed 8% interest rate would receive a 0.5% interest rate reduction for the bank draft or automatic payment and a 3.75% IPM, reducing the borrower's net interest payment to 3.75%.

○ Students who pay their student loans in full either prior to the original standard repayment schedule final payment due date based upon the original anticipated graduation date or when the student has continued enrollment within the grace period in a higher education level will received an "Education Interest Rebate" (EIR) for 25% of the interest paid by the student during the life of the loan within 90 days of paying the loan in full.

Example A: Sally Student took out "Loan A" at "School A" and was assigned a standard repayment schedule based on the enrollment end date at School A. Sally pays the loan in full on or before the original last payment due date from the original standard repayment schedule. Sally will receive an EIR within 90 days of the date the loan was paid in full.

Example B: Stevie Student took out "Loan B" at "School B" and was assigned a standard repayment schedule based on the enrollment end date at School B. Stevie subsequently enrolls in another institution (School C) within his grace period to get a higher degree in a related field of study. Stevie makes timely monthly interest payments[80] on Loan B during his enrollment at School C. When Stevie graduates from School C, he makes timely monthly payments on all loans and pays the loans in full on or before the last due date from the original standard repayment schedule based on the enrollment end date at School C. Stevie will receive an EIR within 90 days of the date Loan B was paid in full.

For the Servicers:

Servicers should be compensated for good behaviors that are consistent with those rewarded to the students. This will create an alignment in the education funding programs that lead to success for all parties involved. Here's how federal servicers would be compensated:

Servicers receive compensation during the borrower's enrollment, grace period, deferments and forbearance periods as follows:

⊙ 20% of the monthly interest payment if 100% of the accruing inter-

---

80. "Timely payments" are defined as complete scheduled payments received by the servicer/lender within 10 business days of the payment due date.

est is paid timely as it accrues.

○ 15% of the monthly interest payment if less than 100% of the accruing interest is paid as it accrues (collected prior to capitalization).

Servicers receive compensation during repayment as follows:

○ 25% of the monthly interest payment when payments are timely payments and have made a principal reduction.

○ Additional 5% of the monthly interest payment when timely payments are made through a bank draft or automated payment and have made a principal reduction.

Servicers receive compensation based on date of processed payments during delinquent status:

○ 20% of the accrued interest if the loan is brought current between 11–60 days of the payment due date.

○ 15% of the accrued interest if the loan is brought current between 61–120 days of the payment due date.

○ 10% of the accrued interest if the loan is brought current between 121–180 days of the payment due date.

○ 5% of the accrued interest if the loan is brought current between 181–360 days of the payment due date.

○ Servicers would be charged back for insufficient funds on payments.

○ Servicers receive compensation for fully rehabilitated loans brought back into repayment status:

• 100% of the monthly accrued interest for the first 3 months of repayment (after rehabilitation) if the payments are made timely.

Table 88: A Student Loan Program with Accountability Student-earned Principal Reductions

Example of a $10,000 Student Loan with a $4,000 Grant Qualification

Original Principal Balance	Graduation Incentive Payments (GIP)	Loan Balance at Graduation	Graduation Incentive Payment Requirements
$10,000	$(4,000)	$6,000	Equivalent of 100% of grant amount forgiven from the loan balance when the student graduates on or before the original anticipated graduation date for the program associated with the student loan.
	$(3,600)	$6,400	Equivalent of 90% of grant amount forgiven from the loan balance when the student graduates within 125% of the original anticipated graduation date for the program associated with the student loan.
	$(3,200)	$6,800	Equivalent of 80% of grant amount forgiven from the loan balance when the student graduates 150% of the original anticipated graduation date for the program associated with the student loan.
Paid-in-Full Early		25% of the interest paid by the borrower during the life of the loan	Students who pay their loans in full prior to the standard repayment schedule final payment due date based on their enrollment end date in the related field of study receive an Education Interest Rebate (EIR) equivalent to 25% of the interest that the borrower paid during the life of the loan.

Table 89: A Student Loan Program with Accountability Borrower Interest Rates & Payments

Example of a Student Loan at 8% Interest Rate

Loan Status	Interest Rate	Borrower's Responsi-bility	Interest Payment Match (IPM)	Interest Reduction & Rebate	Interest Payment Match (IPM), Interest Payment Reduction, & Education Interest Rebate (EIR) Requirements
Applies to Enrolled, Grace Period, Repayment, Deferment & Forbearance	8.0%	8.0%	0.0%		Interest Payment Match only occurs when interest is paid timely as it accrues.
	8.0%	4.0%	4.0%		When timely payments for 100% of the accruing interest are received, the borrower pays half the interest and the government pays the other half.
	7.5%	3.75%	3.75%	0.5%	When payments are set up on bank drafts or automated payments, the borrower receives an additional 0.5% interest rate reduction.
	8.0%	1/2 of accrued interest paid & 100% of unpaid interest	1/2 of accrued interest paid & no match for the unpaid interest		When timely payments for less than 100% of the accruing interest are received, the borrower pays half the interest plus all of the unpaid interest (either paid in the future or capitalized) and the government pays the other half of the interest paid when due.
Deliquent	8%	8%	n/a	n/a	n/a

Table 90: A Student Loan Program with Accountability Servicer & Government Compensation

Example of a Student Loan at 8% Interest Rate

Loan Status	Servicer Compensation	Government Estimated Revenue
Enrolled Grace Period Deferment Forbearance		Interest as it is collected.
	1.6% or 20% of paid accrued interest when 100% of the accruing interest is paid on time as it accrues.	2.4% of 100% accrued interest as collected (timely & predictable).
	1.5% or 20% of the paid accrued interest when 100% of the accruing interest is paid on time as it accrues.	2.25% of 100% accrued interest as collected (timely & predictable).
	1.2% or 15% of accrued interest collected (less than 100% of accruing interest) when paid on time.	2.8% of interest collected if less than 100% of accrued interest (timely & less predictable).
Repayment		Interest as it is collected.
	2% or 25% of paid accrued interest when 100% of the accruing interest is paid on time as it accrues.	2.0% of 100% accrued interest as collected (timely & predictable).
	1.875% or 25% of the paid accrued interest when 100% of the accruing interest is paid on time as it accrues.	1.875% of 100% accrued interest as collected (timely & predictable).
	1.6% or 20% of accrued interest collected (less than 100% of accruing interest) when paid on time.	2.4% of interest collected if less than 100% of accrued interest (timely & less predictable).
	n/a	If the student pays interest as it accrued & has automated payments, this would be approximately 1% interest on the loan.
Delinquent	• 1.6% or 20% of paid accrued interest paid when collected between 11–60 days past due. • 1.2% or 15% of accrued interest paid when collected between 61–120 days past due. • 0.8% or 10% of accrued interest paid when collected between 121–180 days past due. • 0.4% or 5% of accrued interest paid when collected between 181–360 days past due.	While there is increased revenues to the government when delinquent loans are brought current, the compensation is consistent with carrying the loan burden with no payments being made. The risk on these loans is much higher than those paid on time.

Accountability Brings Strength to America and Its Citizens

In an effort to make life easier, we have lost the processes and lifestyles that make people accountable. Student loan funds are magically deposited into the student's account when we used to have to sign the actual check. Entrance and exit counseling for student loans used to primarily happen with face-to-face meetings or group meetings where, now, we rely on self-discipline to complete and understand the important information about student loan borrowing rights and responsibilities.

Entitlement programs have grown at enormous rates where over 15% of our country is on food stamps, where the unemployment problems became so bad that people stopped looking and are no longer counted in the unemployment statistics, and where entitlement programs have replaced good, hard work. With the loss of good hard work, we have also lost sight of the pride that it brings to those who participate and we have become a nation where complacency is the norm.

America can recover if we bring back accountability through creating situations where good behaviors are rewarded instead of focusing on the negative impacts. We must empower students to make good choices for paying student loans on time because that also builds good habits in the rest of their financial lives. When our citizens are empowered and financially stable, many of our country's problems will diminish.

The time has come for laws and regulations that serve students who need school loans, taxpayers who are funding the student loan program and the schools that are preparing students for successful futures in the workforce.

The DOE must improve its data integrity and audit procedures so that they accurately reflect reality for all types of schools. The statutory and regulatory suggestions made here will create a system that is fair and equitable and will prepare students for the realities of financial responsibility.

insure domestic

and our Poster

Section. All legislat

Section. The Ho

INJUSTICE FOR ALL

SUMMARIES AND CONCLUSIONS

While under the direction of the Obama Administration, the U.S. Department of Education has blatantly released inaccurate information leading Americans to form false opinions about student loan funding by private companies. The DOE has diverted attention from the true successes, failures, and challenges of higher education by falsely accusing private-sector student loan companies of having higher default rates than these companies actually have and training the public to believe that private-sector loans are a higher cost to taxpayers and students than direct loans.

The Obama Administration has started to successfully train the public to believe that for-profit is bad and that all Americans should have access to "free" education—all the while reaching into the pockets of poor students who are forced to pay back loans at inflated interest rates and putting the money back into the government's general fund. The DOE has overstated the performance of nonprofit sectors and exaggerated numbers to negatively skew the performance of the proprietary sector, leaving the public to believe that the nonprofit sectors outperform the proprietary sector. Morals teach us that the problem with lying is that the lie eventually catches up—as it has with the DOE's sector-level reporting. You can, now, clearly see in the data facts, even those that have been manipulated, that the public sector is responsible for the lion's share of defaults with 91,563 more defaults than the proprietary sector, most of which belong to community colleges.

The data, when properly analyzed, now shows that, as the reputation of the proprietary schools is ruined through the DOE's misreporting and data manipulation, at-risk students have begun to attend community colleges and the nonprofit colleges have inherited the same problems that proprietary schools have been faced with for decades—because default rates are influenced by at-risk borrowers at whatever school they attend.

For the financial recovery of America and today's students, the government needs to stop pointing fingers to lay blame, create quality metrics that apply to all schools regardless of their tax-filing status, and start collecting defaulted dollars from all sectors of higher education.

Simultaneously, the DOE has underreported and/or falsely reported its own poor performance in many arenas and has developed burdensome regulations; redundant and costly mandatory institutional reporting that gets passed onto the students in tuition increases; and repayment programs lauded as helping students but truly at a great cost to institutions, taxpayers and students. These "wonderful" repayment plans have had the following effects on American citizens:

Decades-long repayment schedules: The repayment period doubles or triples (from 10 years to 20–30 years) which adds burden to those trying to get ahead (i.e., the borrower feels like they will never get out from under their student loan debt);

An albatross of redundant paperwork that leads to non-compliance: These plans are administratively burdensome, requiring students and servicers to recertify income every year (in 2015, over 700,000 students fell out of income-based repayment programs like PAYE because the borrowers failed to complete the required paperwork to remain in the program—this increases servicing and collection costs because the students become delinquent); and

Forgiveness comes with a lump-sum tax payment but taxpayers also lose: There are long-term adverse implications for the students' and America's federal financial interest because 20–25 years from the time borrowers enter the IBR, PAYE and REPAYE programs, their balance will be forgiven so taxpayers will never be paid back for funding the loans and the students will owe taxes, at their current tax rate, for the loan amount forgiven, leaving them with a lump sum payment that, most likely, they cannot afford.

Facts Recap on the Reasons for Plan to Eliminate FFEL Program

Here's a recap of the actions taken to carry out AGENDA ITEM #1— Eliminate the FFEL Program:

The Obama Administration eliminated the FFEL Program so it would have total control over student loans and would make 100 percent of the profit, then allowed the DOE to purchase "conduit loans" for approximately 12 million students from the FFELP lenders but then rehired these "greedy and unethical" companies (government words, not mine) to service the same loans that the FFELP lenders just made a huge profit on. *And, how does playing ping-pong with conduit loans serve the federal fiscal interest?*

As a result from the mass exit of FFELP participants, other FFELP portfolios needed to be assigned to new lenders and servicers because hundreds of FFELP companies went out of business. The catastrophic combination of Conduit, Put, and FFELP loan transfers directly caused the default rates to skyrocket. Whoops! *But because our economy was in such terrible shape, the DOE easily laid blame on the economy and the DOE also launched a full-on attack to ensure that the average American would lay the blame for the rising default rates on proprietary schools.*

When DOE officials were made aware of the tragedy that was unfolding for students who had correctly filed and been approved for deferments, forbearances, and payment options and whose status was not correctly transferred to the new federal conduit servicer, *the DOE officials chose to do nothing to correct the situation and allowed innocent students who had properly managed their student loans to go into default.*

Table 91: FY 2009–2012 Conduit & Put CDRs ABOVE the National Average

COHORT YEAR	CURR RATE	CURR DEF	CURR REP
FY 2009-3YR	21.2%	148,171	697,298
FY 2009-3YR	27.1%	19,598	72,201
FY 2009-3YR	59.8%	26,774	44,769
FY 2009-3YR	54.3%	1,294	2,381
FY 2010-3YR	56.7%*	25,433	44,872
FY 2010-3YR	18.2%	148,636	815,265
FY 2011-3YR	58.6%	14,455	24,666
FY 2012-3YR	56.0%	3,916	6,998

*Correct Calculation—DOE published 56.6%

Tragically, 388,277 students have been adversely affected! And, there may be more!

If the President really wanted to help students, why has he done nothing to help these wronged students?

When three official 3-year cohort default rates were in effect and schools were subject to sanctions under the new 3-year definition, the DOE chose to "adjust" rates that were defined in law without asking for Congressional approval. It directed data managers to accept Erroneous Data Appeals for changes in enrollment status "without regard to when the enrollment change occurred" that also isn't consistent with enrollment reporting guidelines and would otherwise call into question the institution's administrative capabilities. There is strong evidence that suggests the DOE made these changes *to avoid loan servicing appeals and government accountability—where schools, third-party servicers and consultants would see the trail of poor servicing that would bring into question the DOE's administrative capabilities and the tragedy for these students.*

Beginning in 2012, during the year Obama was running for re-election, the DOE manipulated information, underreported and falsely reported cohort default rates by loan program, and my findings are verified by Independent Accountants Reports, archived and detailed in this book. The misreported rates have been blatant lies either in the information publicly released or by data omission. The DOE has falsely reported the performance of the FFEL Program portfolios as being worse than the portfolios actually have performed to justify eliminating this private sector for student loans. *In every instance, the DOE has taken actions to mislead lawmakers and the public about the actual performance for student loan management by the DOE.*

Consider these facts:

- For FY 2009 and FY 2010, the DOE reported its own default rates **much lower** than the data show.

- The DOE also reported the FY 2009 FFELP CDR **higher** than the data show.

- The DOE **did not release** a FFELP Briefing for FY 2010 to my knowledge.

- The FY 2010 FDSLP Briefing was the last released by the DOE.

- For FY 2011 and FY 2012, the DOE posted Loan Holder Data for CDRs and **failed to include its own** direct loan default rates.

- The FY 2011 FDSLP CDR was 30.4% and the FY 2012 FDSLP CDR was 15.9%—**both were well above the national cohort default rate** reported in the institution cohort default rates (iCDR) (Details of these manipulations can be found in Chapter I. Manifesto and Chapter III. CDR Misreporting Inaccuracies.)

By eliminating the private sector for student loans, taxpayers transitioned from funding ONLY those loans that went into default to the financial burden of funding ALL student loans. The burden of student loans has vastly contributed to the national debt. *Were taxpayers asked if they wanted to fund everyone's student loans or manipulated into this situation?*

U.S. National Debt: $18 trillion and counting!

Student Loan Debt: $1.47 trillion and counting!

While writing this book I realized that a good portion of the drastic rise in student loan debt is attributed to the unpaid and capitalized interest—for example, the PAYE only requires a maximum payment of 10% of the borrower's discretionary income. In most cases, this puts students into a negative amortization where accrued and unpaid interest is added to the principal (capitalized) and the student pays interest on interest. After examining many different scenarios for all sectors at all credential levels, I have found that the majority of students with "loan forgiveness" will have a "loan amount" higher than the students' original loan amount. Translation: It takes decades to get out from under the student loan debt and then owe a "lump sum payment" to the IRS when the loan is "forgiven"—and this happens at a time when they are most likely sending *their own* children to college. And, somehow, the Obama Administration and the DOE have gotten America to think that this is good for students and America.

The Obama Administration and the DOE promoted these repayment programs to the point of forcing students into the programs *even when the students say no* because the students have the discernment to know that there are many adverse consequences of doing so. *And, why would the Administration and the DOE do this? We can clearly see this is because most or all of the payments are interest and this "profit" offsets the national debt.*

DOE 2013 Profit on Student Loans: $41.3 Billion!

Is it surprising that the DOE hasn't released its profit numbers for 2014?

While the DOE has blamed the FFELP community for being greedy and unethical, everything that has happened since FFELP was eliminated points to the DOE itself being greedy and unethical. The Obama Administration has swept catastrophic events for students and taxpayers under the carpet to keep the student lending world status quo—so that profits will keep growing as America slides into a sinking hole of debt.

The following pages include a timeline of events in regards to Agenda #1 to give you a synopsis of all that led to the elimination of the FFEL Program and also what has happened since that decision was made.

Table 92: FFELP Elimination Timeline

NOV 2008	**OBAMA ELECTED AS PRESIDENT** **AGENDA ITEM#1: Eliminate For-profit Lending in Student Loans**
FEB 2009	Obama's first President's Budget announced his intent to eliminate the FFEL Program.
MAR 2010	As part of the "Obamacare" bill, the FFEL Program was eliminated and no new loans were made under this program starting July 1, 2010.
JAN 2009– JAN 2014	As part of ECASLA bill, the DOE is allowed to purchase FFELP loan disbursed on or after Oct. 1, 2007 to keep lenders from exiting the student loan program before the DOE was ready.
Original 2009 Renewal 2014	The DOE negotiated servicing contracts with some of the same "greedy and unethical" FFELP companies that the DOE just got rid of. Some of these FFELP companies laughed all the way to the bank because the DOE *purchased* the loans and then the servicers got paid a second time to service the loans.
JAN 2011 SEP 2011	The first loan transfer of the Conduit or PUT Loans (FFELP loans purchased by DOE) took almost 10 months and students on deferments, forbearances and alternate payment schedules were not properly transferred and were immediately put into default when the transfer data was loaded with the DOE servicer.
OCT 2011	Mary Lyn Hammer traveled to Washington, DC to meet with David Bergeron, the Acting Deputy Assistant Secretary for Postsecondary Education to discuss the loan transfers and wrongful default statuses for thousands of students. Bergeron said that he would investigate and correct the situation. The DOE did nothing.

SEP 2012 FY 2009 3-YR CDRs were published by the DOE in "National Official Briefings" by loan program. The Department published an inaccurate FFELP CDR of 14.6% when data shows it to be 10.6%. For the DOE, it published an inaccurate CDR of 8.6% when data show it to be 23.9%. There were two conduit loan portfolios with unacceptably high CDRs of 59.8% and 54.3%.

SEP 2013 FY 2010 3-YR CDRs were published and the DOE only provided a briefing for itself where it reported a FDSLP default rate of 12.8% when data show it to be 16.5%. There were high CDRs for several conduit loan portfolios with one unacceptably high CDR of 56.5%.

SEP 2014 FY 2011 3-YR CDRs were published and the DOE did not provide briefings for loan programs. The DOE did provide a full set of data for FY 2009–2011 iCDRs so audits of the briefings could be conducted. The DOE did not include FDSLP loans in the Loan Holder Data which represented a 30.4% DOE CDR.

The DOE published announcements for making "adjustments" to iCDRs for schools facing sanctions due to improperly serviced loans and for "exceptions" to appeals granted to schools that did not comply with timely enrollment reporting.

SEP 2015 FY 2012 3-YR CDRs were published, there were no briefings and the DOE did not report FDSLP loans in the Loan Holder Data which represented a 15.9% DOE CDR.

The DOE did not publish electronic announcements for iCDR adjustments for schools facing sanctions; however, individual schools received letters for such.

The collective misreporting, iCDR adjustments and waivers for appeals with untimely adjustments are a direct reflection of the DOE's inability to manage their monopoly on the student loan programs.

The Injustices of Implementing Plans to Eliminate For-profit Proprietary Schools

The Administration and the DOE have gone to even greater lengths to falsely accuse the majority of for-profit colleges of not providing quality education at an affordable price for students—all the while the government has reaped the benefits by adding more money to the general fund with lucrative profits from convoluted loan repayment plans.

All institutions in every sector, not just the proprietary sector, should be under scrutiny, yet the DOE has actively and purposely misreported and misrepresented results **to make itself look good and negatively against the FFELP and proprietary sectors in higher education; therefore, Americans are being trained to believe these for-profit sectors are "bad."** The consistency in reporting for institutions from the DOE has been two-fold:

1. *Make public and private nonprofit institutions appear to be performing better than they actually are; and*

2. *Manipulate the numbers to make proprietary institutions look like they are performing worse than they actual are based on available data.*

The truth is that the proprietary sector is the highest performing sector for on-time graduation of students as seen in the DOE's own College Navigator information.

COMMUNITY COLLEGES	ALL OTHER PUBLICS	PRIVATE	PROPRIETARY
26.6%	45.6%	55.6%	60.4%

The College Navigator also shows that the proprietary sector student loan debt is the least costly for students when you divide the average student loan debt by the average graduation rate.

COMMUNITY COLLEGES	ALL OTHER PUBLICS	PRIVATE	PROPRIETARY
$195	$150	$189	$117

The truth is that most proprietary schools do not leave students with debt the students can't afford. The proprietary sector performs consistently with the public sector as a whole and outperforms the community colleges in almost every quality indicator. This is shown in several sets of data for the institution cohort default rate.

Table 93: 2015 Official FY 2012 iCDR Good & Bad Quality Indicators

	2015 Official FY 2012 Institution Cohort Default Rate (iCDR) Data					
	Schools with N/A (No Loans)		30 or More Borrowers			Average of iCDRs for Schools with Borrowers
SECTORS and TOTALS			Good Quality		Bad Quality	
	# Schools with N/A (No Loans)	% of Total Schools with No Loans	# Schools Under 15%	% Schools Under 15%	% Schools with Loans Subject to Sanctions	
PUBLIC	301	16.1%	909	58.0%	<1%	13.9%
COMMUNITY COLLEGES	296	22.1%	425	40.8%	<1%	17.1%
PROPRIETARY	439	21.3%	930	57.3%	<1%	13.9%

2015 Official FY 2012 iCDR data show the following about proprietary schools:

- 439 institutions or 21.3% of all proprietary institutions have no loans in the iCDR data—more institutions than the public sector and a consistent percent with community colleges.

- 930 institutions or 57.3% of all proprietary institutions with loans have default rates *under* 15%—consistent with the public sector and outperforms the community colleges.

- Less than 1% of all proprietary institutions had sanctions imposed for one iCDR over 40% or three consecutive iCDRs over 30%—consistent in all sectors and subsectors.

- The average iCDR for all proprietary schools is 13.9%—exactly the same as all public schools and lower than the average of all community colleges.

- The DOE doesn't publish these good quality statistics because these statistics aren't consistent with the DOE's agenda that has been pushed on lawmakers and the public.

Here's a recap of actions taken to carry out the first part of AGENDA ITEM #2: Eliminate the For-profit Proprietary Schools using iCDR information:

Beginning in 2012 during the year Obama was running for re-election, the DOE manipulated information and falsely reported cohort default rates information at the sector level. The misreported numbers for borrowers in default and borrowers entered repayment along with miscalculated and misreported iCDRs have been blatant lies either in information released or by omission of pertinent data including the following 4 points:

1. The DOE falsely underreported nonprofit sector iCDR information and exaggerated proprietary sector iCDR information to give Americans the illusion that a bigger gap exists between nonprofit and proprietary performance metrics than is factual. This erroneous spin has also been used to solicit public support for funding two years of "free" community college education. (Note: Nothing is free: the taxpayers will fund the "free" education.) *The DOE has used every opportunity to take actions to mislead the lawmakers and the public about the actual performance of institution sectors. Details about these manipulated facts can be found in Table 6 in Chapter I. Manifesto.*

1. The DOE has manipulated the number of defaults and number of borrowers entered repayment within the sectors to support their stories that the proprietary schools represent half the defaults while representing a low percentage of borrowers entered repayment. *Details about these manipulated facts can be found in Table 5 in Chapter I. Manifesto.*

2. The net effect of these data manipulation has skewed iCDR results and information to support an agenda that can no longer be proven even with manipulated information. *The following portrays the total numbers involved in manipulating the number of borrowers in default and the number of borrowers entered repayment:*

Table 94: YOY Comparison of Defaults in DOE Briefings vs Data Reality for FY 2009–2012 iCDRs (Public vs Proprietary)

Year-over-year Comparison of iCDR Manipulation # Defaults from Official Briefings and Institution iCDR (PEPS300) Data				
	FY 2009 #DFLT 2012 Release	FY 2010 #DFLT 2013 Release	FY 2011 #DFLT 2014 Release	FY 2012 #DFLT 2015 Release
DIFFERENCE BETWEEN #BORR IN DEFAULT FOR PUBLIC vs PROPRIETARY				
DOE Reported Difference in # Borrowers in Default (Public vs Proprietary iCDR)	(33,283)	(26,427)	3,886	66,069
Actual Difference # Default (Public vs Proprietary iCDR)	**(4,230)**	**3,881**	**27,494**	**91,563**

4. In the last four years, the dynamics of the cohort default rate data have drastically changed in the public and proprietary sectors while the private sector has remained relatively the same. *The percent of total borrowers entered repayment tells a story—NOT one about the proprietary sector as a whole aggressively recruiting students and leaving them with debt they cannot afford—one about the public sector recruiting students and leaving them debt they cannot afford.*

    - **PUBLIC SECTOR:** The percent of total borrowers in default rose from 42.9% in FY 2009 to 50.8% in FY 2012 while the percent of total borrowers entered repayment stayed virtually the same (51.0% to 50.6% respectively). The dynamics for the defaults drastically going up while those in repayment going down slightly indicates ***a rapidly increasing sector iCDR.***

    - **PRIVATE SECTOR:** The percent of total borrowers in default and borrowers entered repayment both stayed virtually the same. The percent of total borrowers in default was 13.2% for FY 2009 and 13.5% for FY 2012. The percent of total borrowers entered repayment was 23.1% for FY 2009 compared to 22.1% for FY 2012. The dynamics for the defaults going up slightly and those in repayment going down slightly indicates an ***increase in the sector's iCDR.***

* **PROPRIETARY SECTOR:** The percent of total borrowers in default decreased from 43.8% for FY 2009 to 35.6% for FY 2012 while the percent of total borrowers entered repayment increased from 25.6% for FY 2009 to 27.1% for FY 2012. The dynamics for the defaults drastically decreasing while those in repayment are increasing indicates *a rapidly decreasing sector iCDR.*

Table 95: Comparison of Sector Percent of Total iCDR Data from FY 2009 to FY 2012

Comparison of % of Total from FY 2009 to FY 2012	FY 2009 3-year iCDR		FY 2012 3-year iCDR	
	% of Total Borrowers in Default	% of Total Borrowers Entered Repayment	% of Total Borrowers in Default	% of Total Borrowers Entered Repayment
PUBLIC	42.9%	51.0%	50.8%	50.6%
PRIVATE	13.2%	23.1%	13.5%	22.1%
PROPRIETARY	43.8%	25.6%	35.6%	27.1%

The percent of total defaults went up 7.9% for the public sector while the percent of total defaults went down 8.2% for the proprietary sector and represented an increase in total number of defaults for each sector:

101,711 more defaults or 54% increase for the public sector

6,069 more defaults or 3% increase for the proprietary sector

Again, I ask: If collecting student loan defaulted dollars serves the federal fiscal interest, why are the DOE and certain lawmakers hyper-focused on the proprietary sector instead of looking at institution performance as a whole?

Millions of dollars have been spent on drafting, defending, and implementing the data management of gainful employment based on the theory that ALL proprietary schools are predatory, take advantage of at-risk students and leave them with debt they cannot afford or manage. *The actual data do not support that story.*

It is blatantly obvious now that, as the reputation of the proprietary sector is ruined by false and misleading DOE reporting, the at-risk students will migrate to the public sector and that sector will inherit the same problems that the proprietary sector has ALWAYS had because student loan defaults are a student-centric issue, not a school sector issue. The socioeconomic background of the students directly affects their experience and attitude toward paying student loans.

Here's a recap of the actions taken to carry out the second part of AGENDA ITEM #2: Eliminate the For-profit Proprietary Schools using Gainful Employment Regulations and Information:

Within the first year that Obama was in office, the DOE took the definition for education programs having the intent "to prepare students for gainful employment" to literal definitions that programs outside the definition that are taught by nonprofit institutions would fail if they were held to the same standards. These original gainful employment regulations were thrown out in federal district court in June 2012 for being "arbitrary and capricious."

 ○ Beginning in 2012 during the year Obama was running for re-election, the DOE manipulated information, underreported and falsely reported gainful employment informational rates. These underreported and misreported rates have been blatant lies either in information released or by omission. The DOE has underreported and falsely reported the performance of education programs in every sector defined in gainful employment regulations. *In every instance, the DOE has taken actions to mislead the lawmakers and the public about sector-level performance.*

 ○ When the correct repayment definition was used to calculate annual payments for each sector's data, all but the Undergraduate Program Discretionary DTE passed the Annual DTE limit of 12% and the Discretionary DTE limit of 30%. The truth about proprietary sector debt-to-earnings (DTE) emerged as follows:

Undergraduate Program Averages

○ Annual DTE dropped from 5.64% to **5.44%**

○ Discretionary DTE dropped from 85.40% to **32.71%**

Associate Degree Program Averages

○ Annual DTE dropped from 8.81% to **4.40%**

○ Discretionary DTE dropped from 68.60% to **12.64%**

Bachelor's Degree Program Averages

○ Annual DTE dropped from 9.86% to **3.06%**

○ Discretionary DTE dropped from 40.19% to **5.79%**

Post Baccalaureate Certificate Program Averages

○ Annual DTE increased from 1.30% to **1.80%**

○ Discretionary DTE increased from 1.90% to **2.42%**

Master's Degree Program Averages

○ Annual DTE dropped from 4.76% to **2.41%**

○ Discretionary DTE dropped from 18.87% to **3.37%**

Doctorate Degree Program Averages

○ Annual DTE dropped from 3.40% to **1.19%**

○ Discretionary DTE dropped from 4.81% to **1.49%**

First Professional Degree Program Averages

○ Annual DTE dropped from 13.60% to **5.88%**

○ Discretionary DTE dropped from 62.72% to **9.62%**

The DOE grossly exaggerated proprietary annual payments for failing programs.

○ Undergraduate Certificate: **32% too high**

○ Associate Degree: **178% too high**

○ Bachelor's Degree: **311% too high**

○ First Professional Degree: **304% too high**

Only 6 of the 193 programs reported as failing all 3 measures actually failed when the correct repayment schedules were used to calculate annual payments.

After my testimony, when I spoke of the gross inaccuracies in the debt-to-earnings ratios, the DOE did not publicly rescind the false and misleading rates that tarnished the reputations and diminished the value of the ENTIRE proprietary sector.

56 of the 193 programs reported fell within the GE 2.0 Zone.

Instead, the DOE chose to define the "zone" in the second, more aggressive gainful employment regulations known as GE 2.0 because it no longer had their desired number of failing programs.

The "zone" was NEVER a part of the original gainful employment regulations. From the beginning of the "Negotiated Rulemaking," the introduction of the zone was controversial because the rationale behind the zone definition contradicted ALL of the rationale for GE thresholds set forth in several hundred pages of Preamble language in the first set of GE regulations.

Removing at least one piece of data in certain programs provided a devious way to avoid releasing all the information because the programs were not to be reported due to the language of the regulations that read that the DOE would publish gainful employment rates where data are available. *Only 3,787 programs were publicly reported in the Streamlined GE Data when there were actually a total of 13,587 programs in the DOE's Final GE Data. The unreported data was not consistent among sectors. Details about these acts of omission can be found in Table 11 in Chapter I. Manifesto.*

The missing data and unreported data made no sense. For example, certain schools had a repayment rate for student loans but were missing the program cohort default rate (pCDR) or missing the annual payment amount.

Was this information intentionally removed to avoid reporting certain programs?

In an attempt to tarnish the reputations of for-profit schools and cover up the performance of most public institutions, DOE's Deputy Undersecretary from 2009 to 2011, Robert Shireman, provided "inside information" about pending gainful employment regulations to short-sellers who stood to gain huge profits and was allowed to keep his government-paid benefits upon his departure from the DOE. Shireman remains under investigation for these activities.

As recently as last year, Robert Shireman was in the spotlight over these same issues as reported by *Roll Call* in an article[81] titled "Education Official Who Left Under Ethical Cloud Returns to Washington":

Citizens for Responsibility and Ethics in Washington…CREW believes Shireman's coziness with Wall Street short sellers, and his overall indifference to playing by the rules, should make government officials wary of working with him…

During his time (as a DOE official), he spearheaded the department's efforts to increase regulation of for-profit colleges to ensure that students had a fair chance of finding 'gainful employment' after graduation. This subject became controversial, in part because of Wall Street's efforts to influence education policy.

Using the Freedom of Information Act, CREW uncovered incriminating emails revealing that Education officials, including Shireman, were in contact with short sellers about the proposed regulation. Based on these records, CREW asked the Securities and Exchange Commission in 2011 to investigate possible market manipulation and twice asked Education Secretary Arne Duncan to examine the improper influence on Education's regulatory process. We also asked the department's inspector general (to) investigate Shireman.

More than three years after he left Washington, Shireman remains the subject of a long-running inspector general inquiry into whether he violated ethics laws by discussing sensitive government information with The Institute for College Access and Success, an organization Shireman founded and led before joining the Obama administration. TICAS refused to comply with an OIG subpoena for records regarding its interaction with Shireman, forcing the Department of Justice to file legal action. In March (2014), a federal court ordered TICAS to turn over documents. Why would TICAS have fought so hard to prevent the release of these records unless they reveal improper conduct?

---

81. http://www.rollcall.com/news/education_official_who_left_under_ethical_ cloud_returns_to_washington-234751-1.html

When Shireman left the department in June 2010, he was immediately hired as a consultant. Despite this change in employment status, documents show Education officials allowed Shireman to continue receiving health care, paid leave and retirement benefits although the department's personnel manual specifically prohibits consultants from receiving such benefits. When CREW sought details about Shireman's consulting agreement, Education redacted the identities of the officials who signed off on the arrangement.

When the DOE released the Notice of Proposed Rulemaking for the GE 2.0 federal regulations, it released the FY 2012 GE Informational Rates. This set of data only reported 7,934 of the 13,587 programs reported in the FY 2011 GE Final data and was missing the "median debt" data so it could not be audited for accuracy.

If the rates were accurate, why wouldn't the DOE provide all of the data needed to verify the information?

The DOE has made voluminous attempts to cover up an underperforming public sector and blamed the entire proprietary sector of being greedy and unethical (sound familiar?) and taking advantage of at-risk students. All of the planning and orchestration of these events makes me ask—what are they covering up?

- Is it the fact that the proprietary sector delivers the highest graduation rate average of 60.4% compared to community colleges at 26.6% according to College Navigator information and this truth doesn't support two "free" years of education at community colleges paid by taxpayers?

- Is it the fact that the proprietary sector delivers the lowest cost of education among all sectors at $117.35 for the cost of student loans per percent of graduation compared to $194.82 for community colleges?

- Or, is it the fact that the DOE needed "someone" to blame for the drastically escalating default rates that were really a result of their poor management for the events related to the transition to 100% direct lending and inappropriate management of the FDSL

Program?

If we use the average federal student loan debt from the College Navigator FY 2010 data that we analyzed and apply those numbers to the FY 2012 iCDR data, the dollars in default that our lawmakers should be focused on recovering look like the following:

- PUBLIC SECTOR: **$3,989,699,996** (1,581 schools)

  - Traditional Colleges: $2,307,576,183 (629 schools)

  - Community Colleges: $1,682,123,813 (952 schools)

- PRIVATE SECTOR: $1,000,323,179 (1,557 schools)

- PROPRIETARY SECTOR: **$2,001,841,119** (1,714 schools)

These are estimates based on available data because the dollars in default are not published by the DOE. Why? Because the DOE doesn't want lawmakers and American citizens to know the truth. Again, if collecting student loan default dollars is the goal that protects the federal fiscal interest, why is the Obama Administration hyper-focused on only the proprietary sector when the public "nonprofit" sector represents the vast majority of dollars in default?

To bring perspective to the extent the DOE has gone to eliminate the proprietary sector, the following pages show the timeline of events documenting everything that has happened since 2008 when Obama was elected regarding Agenda Item #2.

Table 96: Assault and Defame Proprietary Sector Timeline

2007–2008	**OBAMA ELECTED AS PRESIDENT** **AGENDA ITEM #2: Eliminate For-profit Proprietary Institutions**
FEB 2009	Obama spoke about promoting community college education during his election campaign and chose a vice president with a wife who works at a community college.
NOV 2009	Negotiated Rulemaking began for Gainful Employment that targeted proprietary school programs. Consensus was not reached, giving the DOE room to write what it wanted; however, the DOE are to consider those parts of the negotiations where a consensus was acheived.
JUN 2010– DEC 2010	An orchestrated series of events between short sellers and two top officials at the DOE, Robert Shireman and David Bergeron, influenced the value of publicly-traded for-profit colleges. Requests under the Freedom of Information Act are tied to ongoing investigations of Shireman who eliminated the FFEL Program and was the driving force behind Gainful Employment. In his 18 months of DOE employment, Shireman brought down entire industries and somehow, his indictments have gone dark on several occasions since 2010.
JUL 2010	The GE NPRM was released and received a record number of public comments during the 45-day comment period.
AUG 2010	A set of GE informational data by school, *not programs* was released that included public schools and showed that many public and private schools would fail the same proposed GE regulations.

OCT 2010   Final GE regulations were published and contained numerous regulations that were NOT discussed in the negotiated rulemaking process, bringing the entire process into question.

JAN 2011   APSCU filed a lawsuit against the DOE about the Gainful Employment regulations.

JUL 2011   GE regulations went into effect. APSCU filed a second lawsuit.

JUN 2012   The DOE released TWO sets of GE data (first the "Streamlined Data" to the public and second the "Final Data" to specially selected group of Wall Street and press contacts). The streamlined data, or public set released, did not have the data details behind the rate calculations for 3,787 programs. The final set of data, released second, included details for 13,587 programs and also PROVED that the publicly-released rates were missing many programs (removed or manipulated data) and the rates for those programs included (primarily proprietary programs) were grossly exaggerated and inflammatory.

JUN 2012   The DOE hosted a webinar by David Bergeron that was announced *less than 24 hours before it occurred* so most schools were not included (see Chapter V.). The public streamlined rates were meant to fool the public into believing the **blatent lie** that most proprietary school programs left students with debt they couldn't afford.

A judge appointed by Obama in federal district court threw out GE as being arbitrary and capricious but upheld the DOE's authority to develop the rules. The "FY 2011 GE Informational Rates" had already been publicly released and the damage from inaccurate and inflammatory GE rates for proprietary schools had already occurred. The correct calculations for the 193 "failed 3 rates" proprietary programs proved that *only 6 programs had actually failed.*

2011–2012 President Obama used this false information in CDRs and GE to defame all for-profit colleges and promote education at community colleges whose information was "not reported" because of "missing data" in the FY 2011 GE Informational rates publicly released in June 2012.

SEP 2012 FY 2009 3-YR CDRs were published by the DOE in a "National Official Briefing" by institution sector and credential level. The DOE published public sector numbers that were 4% too low for the # defaults and # borrowers. The DOE also published proprietary sector numbers that were 10% too high for # defaults and 9% too high for # borrowers. The combination *gave the illusion* that there was a larger difference in sector performance than actually existed and increased the # defaults for proprietary schools to match the DOE's story that the for-profit schools represent half of all defaults in the country.

MAR 2013 The court threw out the DOE's request to reinstate portions of the GE regulations and allowed the reporting requirements to remain in effect.

APR 2013 The DOE announced an intent to form a negotiated rulemaking team including GE and provided a series of field hearings.

MAY 2013 Mary Lyn Hammer traveled to San Francisco to testify about the inaccuracies in the data and rates.

JUN 2013 The DOE announced a new negotiated rulemaking committee for GE.

AUG 2013 The DOE released the draft of the "new" GE regulations (GE 2.0) that were MORE damaging than the first set of GE regulations and included the "zone" that would eventually capture more failing programs *(only 6 ACTUALLY failed)* using the correct data under the original definition.

SEP 2013–DEC 2013 Negotiated Rulemaking for GE 2.0 began. The DOE's original intent was to have one session and publish final rules by November 1st according to the master calendar but ended up having three sessions in three months.

SEP 2013 FY 2010 3-YR CDRs were published by the DOE in a "National Official Briefing" by institution sector and credential level. The DOE published public sector numbers that were 4% too low for the # defaults and # borrowers. The DOE also published proprietary sector numbers that were 8% too high for # defaults and 7% too high for # borrowers. The misreported calculations showed the public sector lower than proprietary when the public sector was actually much higher than the for-profit sector. The briefing increased the # defaults for proprietary schools to match the story the DOE was selling to the public that the for-profit schools represented half of all defaults in the country.

MAR 2014 The GE NPRM was released with the more damaging version for defined programs, primarily proprietary programs. The FY 2012 GE Informational Data was released with 7,934 programs—again missing thousands of programs. The rates published were consistent with those in the FY 2011 GE Informational Rates and the data were missing the "median debt" so it could not be verified for accuracy.

SEP 2014 FY 2011 3-YR CDRs were published by the DOE in a "National Official Briefing" by institution sector and credential level. The DOE published public sector numbers that were 4% too low for the # defaults and # borrowers. The DOE also published proprietary sector numbers that were 4% too high for # defaults and 3% too high for # borrowers.

SEP 2014 (CONT)

The combination gave the illusion that a larger difference in sector performance existed than there actually was and increased the # defaults for proprietary schools to match the DOE's story that the for-profit schools represent half of all defaults in the country.

The DOE published announcements for making "adjustments" to iCDRs for schools facing sanctions due to improperly serviced loans and for "exceptions" to appeals granted to schools that did not comply with timely enrollment reporting.

OCT 2014

The DOE released the draft of the "new" GE regulations (GE 2.0) that were *more damaging* than the first set of GE regulations and included the "zone" that would eventually capture more failing programs since only 6 of them actually failed using the correct data under the original definition.

NOV 2014– MAY 2015

APC and APSCU, both representing for-profit colleges, filed lawsuits within a week. Both GE lawsuits were thrown out by two different judges at different venues. APC and APSCU didn't have all the facts straight and didn't focus on the bigger picture; therefore, the arguments presented were weak, and this contributed to the judges decisions.

JUL 2015

GE 2.0 went into effect and have been touted as the most damaging and over-burdensome regulations ever written to affect schools—including some community colleges and some private nonprofit institutions.

SEP 2015

FY 2012 3-YR CDRs were published by the DOE in a "National Official Briefing" by institution sector and credential level. The DOE published public sector numbers that were 2% too low for the # defaults and # borrowers. The DOE also published proprietary sector numbers that were 10% too high for # defaults and 6% too high for # borrowers. **The misreported calculations covered up the fact that the public sector now has 91,563 more defaults than the for-profit sector.** The briefing increased the # defaults for proprietary schools to match the DOE's story that the for-profit schools represent a large portion of the nation's default rate because it published a proprietary sector rate of 15.8% when iCDR data shows it as 15.4%.

For FY 2009–2011 3-year iCDRs, the private sector briefing rates matched the data calculations and numbers of defaults and borrowers were within 1%. For FY 2012, the private sector iCDR briefing did not match—significantly— where the DOE briefing reported the # defaults as 10% lower and # borrowers 5% lower than the data shows. The DOE published a private rate of 6.8% when data show it as 7.2%.

The DOE did NOT publish electronic announcements for iCDR adjustments for schools facing sanctions; however, individual schools received letters for such.

NOV 2015

Bills are moving through both the House and Senate to defund GE 2.0 or delay it until Congress can address the issue in the 2015 Reauthorization of the Higher Education Act of 1965.

Injustice for All Insight

Consistent Manipulation

The U.S. Department of Education has gone to great lengths to manipulate data and reporting EVERY year since Obama has been in office to:

- *Cover up failing public colleges to support Obama's agenda for community colleges for everyone whether they want to go there or not;*
- *Destroy the entire proprietary sector;*
- *Deflect blame for the high CDRs that are occurring under its management;*
- *Seal the fate of unknowing college students who think the PAYE and other payment programs that put loans into negative amortization and have a taxable "balloon" payment when loans are "forgiven."*

Barack Obama and his Administration want American citizens to believe these actions are ALL about helping students while Obama's administration covers up unacceptable management of federal education aid programs and rakes in BILLIONS in (interest) profit to cover up this Administration's outrageous spending habit!

Government sleight of hand—and, there may be more...

Third Party Servicer Audits: Are the Changes an Excuse for a Witch Hunt?

On October 23, 2014, I went to Washington, DC for a hearing and met with a former DOE official. I asked, "So did you know the data had been manipulated?" The answer was NOT one of surprise. In fact, it was a nervous reaction. After that, on more than one occasion, I was asked what I was going to do with the information. Each time, I said that I was going to move forward. I have chosen not to identify this person at this time for personal reasons and because there is an on-going investigation of the situation by Congress.

On January 9, 2015, the DOE issued a Dear Colleague Letter (DCL 15-01) expanding the definition of third-party servicers (TPS) and making substantive changes to the definitions for exemptions as explained in the Notice of Proposed Rulemaking and Preamble of the original federal regulations for TPS that were published on April 29, 1994. The original regulations required audits of "required functions," and this DCL letter expands this requirement to voluntary functions for certain TPS.

Is this a masked attempt to shoot the messenger?

The DCL also contains language that substantively changes the exclusions to only apply to software and data warehousing that DOES NOT contain student level information. Because these regulations are part of Title IV (federal financial aid), they specifically apply to student level information and always have. When the exclusions were originally published by the Secretary in 1994, they were explained as a "tool" for schools to carry out functions. These recent changes have made a 180-degree shift in the original intent for the exclusions and have, in essence, excluded the exclusions.

Substantive changes cannot be made in a Dear Colleague Letter—they must go through a negotiated rulemaking process as defined by law.

Additionally, the DOE has asked TPS companies defined in the letter to explain why they haven't had audits prior to the date of the letter. The DCL also acknowledges that "The Department is aware that some third-party servicers have not filed annual compliance audits due to an incorrect assessment of whether the entity meets the regulatory definition of a third-party servicer and/

or based on the omission of specific audit procedures in the OIG Audit Guide for some services or functions performed on behalf of an institution."

The changes specifically target and expand definitions to include all activities of default management which are valid when applied to those schools with mandated default management plans; however, most schools perform these functions on a voluntary basis. I happen to own a company that has been in business for over 25 years specializing in default management, and we perform primarily voluntary functions, have SAAS software for schools to perform their own functions, and we host the data for both SAAS and full-service clients.

> *While audits are a good idea in general, is it a coincidence that TPS audits have retroactive consequences and target companies like the one owned by the person who is coming forward with the evidence provided in this book?*

> **Wicked Witch:** *A-hah! (Laughs.) So! You won't take warning, eh? All the worse for you, then. I'll take care of you now instead of later! Hah! When I gain those ruby slippers, my power will be the greatest in Oz! And now, my beauties! Something with poison in it, I think. With poison in it, but attractive to the eye—and soothing to the smell! (Laughs.) Poppies! Poppies! Poppies!*

As of the date that I am writing this conclusion in December 2015, neither the DOE nor the OIG have provided audit guidance to those companies and individuals who they say are mandated to conduct audits for tasks never before covered in third-party audits. With the deadline for most of the audits due by the end of the 2015 calendar year, it is looking more and more like these new expanded definitions may be a set-up.

Where Do We Go from Here?

American citizens have two choices:

1. **Acceptance and Indifference.** We can sit back and accept what is going on while America's world ranking in education declines; employers have limited resources for obtaining employees with much needed professional and executive function and professional skills; and while at-risk untrained

students slip deeper into poverty and require more and more entitlement programs that yes, WE THE PEOPLE will be responsible for funding through exorbitant taxes.

2. **Involvement to Preserve Educational Freedoms.** Or we can get involved and take actions to stop the annihilation of America's education system so that students have an appropriate-level understanding of Math and English when entering college; so that students have the freedom to choose where to get proper training and education; so that trained workers have professional and executive function skills when entering the workforce; and so that the United States regains respect, financial stability, and high rankings for world-class education.

I, for one, want to go back to America, the land of opportunity where ingenuity and entrepreneurship are admired and embraced.

Dorothy: *There's no place like home. (clicks her heels three times) There's no place like home...*

I want to go back to an America where people from around the world work hard to get into our schools because we offer a superior education to what they can get in other countries.

I will fight and I won't be silenced because I want to return America to a place where our children grow up to say that they are proud to be Americans.

Will you join me?

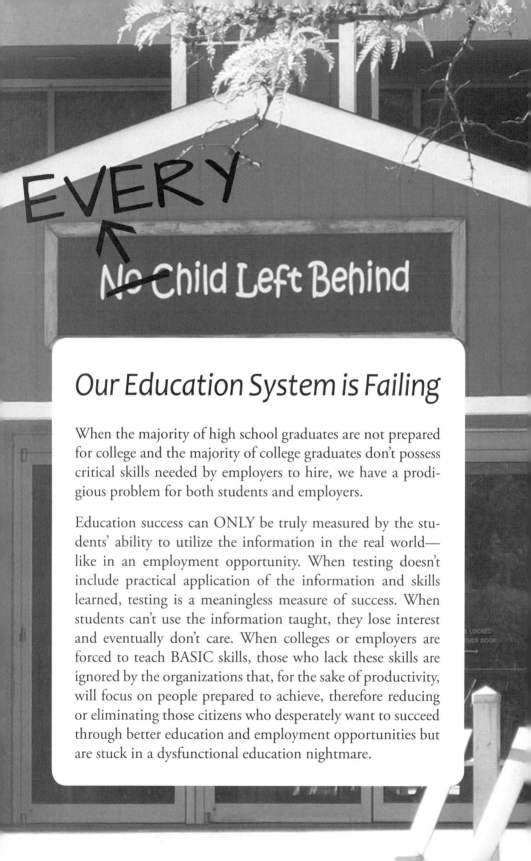

EVERY

No Child Left Behind

Our Education System is Failing

When the majority of high school graduates are not prepared for college and the majority of college graduates don't possess critical skills needed by employers to hire, we have a prodigious problem for both students and employers.

Education success can ONLY be truly measured by the students' ability to utilize the information in the real world—like in an employment opportunity. When testing doesn't include practical application of the information and skills learned, testing is a meaningless measure of success. When students can't use the information taught, they lose interest and eventually don't care. When colleges or employers are forced to teach BASIC skills, those who lack these skills are ignored by the organizations that, for the sake of productivity, will focus on people prepared to achieve, therefore reducing or eliminating those citizens who desperately want to succeed through better education and employment opportunities but are stuck in a dysfunctional education nightmare.

EPILOGUE: PRIMARY AND SECONDARY EDUCATION

Common Core, No Child Left Behind, and the 2015 Reauthorization of the ESEA

Education needs to transition from "teaching to pass standards" to "teaching to learn." Failure to teach where children learn can result in every child left behind. When we teach our children to learn and love learning, no child will be left behind.

Changing a Culture of Education That FAILS for Students

An old saying in the educational field tells us, "It takes a hundred years for anything in education to change—fifty years to get an idea accepted and fifty more to get it implemented." Another way of looking at this concept as we find it today is to realize that the educational system in the United States is designed for preparing students with life skills and knowledge suitable for the early part of the last century.

Thankfully, this enormous gap between workforce needs and schooling is being addressed, albeit clumsily. On January 8, 2002 the people were presented with the No Child Left Behind Act (NCLB) that was heralded to level our educational system and prepare American students to thrive in a global economy. But NCLB was flawed—if NCLB had been a computer program the developer would have sent all users a patch to fix the bugs in the system, but we are dealing with difficult-to-change laws. Nonetheless, as NCLB crashed and burned, it was replaced by Common Core that was supposed to fix the serious design flaws of NCLB.

During 2015, the U.S. House Education and the Workforce Committee members diligently worked on legislation to reauthorize the Elementary and Secondary Education Act of 1965 (ESEA). The House passed H.R. 5, known as Every Student Succeeds Act (ESSA) and the Senate passed S. 1177, the Every Child Achieves Act (ECAA). Through the conference that joins and amends the House (H.R. 5) and Senate (S. 1177) into one conference report (H. Rept. 114-354 filed on November 30, 2015), many important amendments were compromised or lost altogether. Amendments that minimized federal intervention in education, although states are getting more control over defining their standards and measures, reduced required testing of up to 112 tests for every student from pre-K through high school, and those aimed to enhance Title I portability and school choice have almost disappeared, leaving us with a reauthorization that continues BOTH NCLB and Common Core in part. ESSA was signed into law December 10, 2015

Unfortunately both NCLB[82] and Common Core[83] are attempts to create an educational system in the United States that would educate individuals for the 21st century but BOTH were inherently flawed because they are derivatives of the VERY system these programs were supposed to change. Lesson: if the foundation is cracked, the building will fall when stressed.

Learning, Teaching, and Testing

NCLB and Common Core assume that testing is THE way to determine if

---

82. No Child Left Behind Act of 2002 (http://www.gpo.gov/fdsys/pkg/PLAW-107publ110/html/PLAW-107publ110.htm)

83. Common Core (http://www.npr.org/blogs/ed/2014/05/27/307755798/the-common-core-faq#q5) (http://www.nytimes.com/2013/02/14/education/obamas-college-scorecard-needs-works-experts-say.html?_r=0)

a child is learning and if a teacher is really teaching. In fact, standardized tests only reveal which students are good at taking tests. Highly creative students, like the ones who develop new technologies, solve perplexing problems, develop and build new businesses, create lasting art, literature and music that enrich societies, typically do not perform very well on tests, especially the popular multiple-choice tests. Because so much is riding on test results, teachers are forced to teach to the test. The passion that good teachers have for imparting subject matter to students is fading. The connection between student and teacher that can nurture a lifetime love of learning is in danger of extinction when testing becomes the most important thing in the classroom.

Any system that attempts to measure the totality of both learning and teaching with an objective test that assesses a few easily measurable skills will result in a skewed image of both students' and teachers' accomplishments.

The Fix?

Common Core claims to remedy the lack of critical thinking skills emphasized through NCLB by introducing them as early as first grade without giving appropriate consideration to the physical maturity of first graders' brains. The developers of Common Core failed to include any early childhood professionals. Twenty-five individuals drafted the standards, a group made up of six test makers from the College Board, five from the test publishers at ACT and four from Achieve whose primary focus since its inception in 1996 has been the high school to college arena with more recent activities in K–12.

No teachers were involved. Feedback groups of 35 participants were composed mostly of university professors who typically do not have any kindergarten through 12th grade (K–12) teaching experience. We also question the lack of involvement in the Common Core development by neuroscientists who research childhood brain development. Expecting children to learn beyond their brain maturation not only frustrates both the child and the teacher, but it also has the potential for convincing the child that she or he is incapable of learning!

The 2015 Student Success Act[84] reauthorizing the Elementary and Second-

---

84. https://www.congress.gov/bill/114th-congress/senate-bill/1177/text

ary Education Act of 1965 strips down the Secretary of Education's authority a great deal and gives states, parents, and teachers more authority for creating and measuring education systems that cater to their particular student base. The concern, though, is that the states must also choose between NCLB and Common Core tests that will still be administered. While I acknowledge that this was a HUGE improvement, I still have concerns about how time consuming these tests are. We have yet to see whether continuing these tests diverts much-needed attention from developing new programs that are more successful for the students.

Technological and Practical Distractions

In addition to dealing with what is going on between each student's ears, teachers have always competed with outside distractions. Historically, students came into classrooms with a variety of experiences—family dynamics, hunger, too little sleep, exposure to violence, loving support, parental help with homework. Currently, many of those diversions are rooted in technology. While computers have opened the world to a different style of learning, the search engines deliver the most "popular" results first—not the best option for a well-researched answer. This lack of adequately researched information means that we and our children are forming beliefs based on what may well range from deliberate lies to stupidity to intentional propaganda designed to influence public opinion. We have become a country full of young people saturated with technology and, while in their classrooms, they are focused on memorizing measurable facts. The line between computer-generated fantasy and reality easily becomes blurred. Rote fact-based education neglects both critical and creative thinking, vital skills in discerning what is truth and what is fiction in the realm of massive amounts of computer-provided information.

With teachers forced to devote classroom time to making students test successfully rather than on learning, there is little to no opportunity for teaching objective, analytical thinking, which is a vital skill for creating empowered citizens. An individual who lacks the ability to step back from internet-based content to remind themselves that what they see or read could well be fantasy-based or even manipulative can easily allow a technological reality to become their total reality. A generation infused with people who believe that everything they read on Wikipedia, social media, or what they watch on 24-hour news channels is completely 100 percent factual is disastrous. That is a recipe for failure of such an epic level that we will NEED to create MORE entitlement programs to serve these disempowered citizens. Our goal is to provide education and life skills to a generation immersed in a complex cyber-world, like no other before, with dangers like predators, bullies, pornography, terrorism, financial scams, low self-esteem or self-worth—consider that much of our children's belief system about the world at large is now formed by a growing number of social media outlets that have ZERO accountability standards for delivering the truth. The fact that a more appropriate job title for teachers today is "testers" is just one more ingredient in this disastrous recipe. Many long-term negative consequences occur when people lack the basic skills to analyze life situations and make decisions based on that analysis. This next generation could be an easily manipulated one where delusional thinking dominates. Fans of NCLB tout the accumulated data that show where student deficiencies lie. Yet these data are relevant ONLY to the assessment of fixed factual information.

Teaching Discernment Is Critical

The skills necessary to life in the 21st century are largely unmeasured and overlooked in Common Core. Certainly reading and math are important. But in today's world of in-the-blink-of-an-eye communication, verbal and written interactions show the intelligence, beliefs, and opinions of the American population to the entire world. In addition to the basics of reading, writing, and arithmetic, the curriculum for students today must include a K–12 emphasis on thinking and creating skills built on the following three levels of discernment:

1. *What is fact?* The amount of information that daily inundates everyone is virtually immeasurable. The foundation of discernment rests on being able to pick out fact from opinion, fact from fiction. This skill must be applied to blogs, newscasts, search engine reports, social media, and to the sources for each of these. It must become part of every K–12 curriculum.

2. *How am I being persuaded or manipulated?* In the United States, we are bombarded daily with advertising seeking to convince us that some product is superior to all others and to persuade us that we need that product. Sometimes, this might be true. But more often we are simply

being manipulated for the sake of a sale. Children are especially vulnerable to such suggestions. The benefits of developing the ability to discern how we are being persuaded extends far beyond the obvious realm of advertising and reaches into most areas of our lives. This discernment skill is necessary for thriving in this century.

3. *What is the source for this information and what reasons does that source have for telling it to me?* Developing the patience and the search skills to pinpoint the source of information is the third level of discernment. Knowing the source for information can sometimes tell us immediately if it is worth considering. Once the source has been determined, we can ferret out the reasons behind disseminating that data.

Developing these three levels of discernment must be a part of school curricula at all grade levels if we are to have an empowered population capable of making sound decisions that are part of a productive life.

Applied Discernment

Discernment also becomes a necessity for valuing others' as well as our own unique gifts and abilities. Success in any workplace is just as dependent upon an individual's ability to work cooperatively with others as it is to exhibit the technical skills necessary for the job. We need to teach self-monitoring of personal accountability that is the basis for productivity and other measures of success in our internet-based work world. Developing emotional awareness skills is just as important to success in our global economy as is intellectual education. Emotional skills include the empathy necessary to understand and work with people from diverse cultural backgrounds. Students can be schooled in both intellectual and emotional intelligence starting in kindergarten, as long as the teaching methods are age appropriate. But teachers must be given the skills and classroom time for this type of education.

Discernment also includes teachers' sensitivity to the variety of learning styles that are present in every classroom. If our intention is to educate every American to their maximum potential, then each student's unique way of learning must be validated then expanded to include other, compatible ways of learning. When that happens, we have successful teaching and a culture that embraces a lifetime love of learning.

Our collective American creativity has kept us at the forefront of the global economy. But originality dies when test-only dominates. As long as attempts to "fix" our educational system grow out of the existing system that rewards limited-fact-based test results and includes punishment and public shaming for missing the expected target, our educational system will fail at developing our students into future leaders. Repairs to our school system must begin with identifying the skills students need to thrive NOW, followed by teaching those skills to teachers in all subject areas and developing ways to measure success in those skill areas. These measurements will likely include both objective and subjective assessments. The knowledge generated from this approach will be useful in understanding which students, teachers and school systems need additional support—not punishment—to fulfill expectations.

The Remedial Dilemma

One popular measure of teaching success is the rate at which college-bound high school graduates must take remedial courses to be ready for college-level work. The implication is that high school grads are also unprepared for today's workforce. The percentage of students needing remedial math, English and reading classes varies from state to state, ranging from 10% to as much as 60% at some colleges. Arguments about exact numbers are another diversion from the critical issue—too many high school graduates are unprepared for college level work or for full participation in the workforce. No matter which source is referenced, we as taxpayers are paying twice for educating young people, first in high school and secondly in remedial college classes. These are numbers we can track if we are willing to cope with the old adage that there are three kinds of lies: lies, damn lies, and statistics.

Being cautious about the source for our numbers, we refer to EngageNY. org, a site run by the New York State Education Department, for that state's numbers on this topic. Of high school graduates in New York State, only 34.7% are calculated to be college and career ready. This percentage varies widely for ethnic groups. Looking at numbers for first-time, full-time undergraduates, 51% of those entering two-year institutions need at least one remedial class while 11% of those entering a four-year higher education school must take at least one remedial class. The latter schools typically have more stringent admissions requirements than do the two-year schools. While these classes prepare students for the college level courses they want to take, no college credit is granted for them because they are below college level work. Students still have to pay for them and spend their time and effort getting to a state of readiness that their high school diploma ought to have given them. Taxpayers are providing the money for the instructors, classroom space and, often, tuition (in the form of grants and loans) for the students. The emotional impact on students who believe they are ready for college and who find out they are not can lead to discouragement and dropping out. These students may, in essence, feel lied to by the educational system that they were a part of for thirteen years. As a country, we cannot afford to lose the talents of any generation simply because young people have been poorly prepared for today's economic reality.

In a side note, Florida is considering eliminating remedial training altogether because of the costs. This brings up more concerns to students being pushed through the higher education system without the proper knowledge needed to successfully enter the workforce.

Unprepared high school graduates who want to enter the workforce directly upon graduating are much harder to track than those who attempt college. But we encounter them in stores when they do not know how to make change unless their computerized cash register tells them exactly how many of what denomination in cash to give back to us for a purchase. In the workplace we find ourselves in meetings with them where they cannot stay on task or contribute to problem-solving in a meaningful way. These skills are foreign to them. We come across them trapped in fear-mongering because they lack the ability to analyze or search for the truth.

For over two decades career researchers have been telling us that most newly created jobs require education beyond high school. Again citing EngageNY.org and studies from Harvard University and the Georgetown Center on Education and the Workforce, "Of the projected 47 million job openings [to be created] between 2009–2018, at least two-thirds will require workers to have at least some post-secondary education." Further, 14 million of those new jobs will require an associate's degree or occupational certificate. They will, naturally, pay more than jobs for high school graduates. Advanced education generally gives workers more flexibility to move from one job to another, learning new skills as the workplace grows and expands with jobs that don't even exist today.

Today in the United States we are presented with a unique opportunity. We must adapt our primary educational system to include a methodology that prepares our citizens to thrive in a world that is filled with misrepresented information. If we do not act, we will develop a populace ill-equipped for the demands of a global, fast-moving world. We can truly update our educational system to develop individuals who can maximize their potential for the betterment of themselves and this country.

Changing a Broken System to Save Our Children and Our Country

I have interviewed teachers all over the United States and the points that every one of them thought were important to tell me included:

- Teachers report spending the first third of the year assessing the students, which is time consuming with hard-stop deadlines. They spend the last third of the school year assessing the students, again time consuming with hard-stop deadlines. They spend the middle third teaching a year's worth of curriculum which can't be done in one-third of the year so they teach kids to pass their tests which gives short-term success measures but fails for long-term knowledge retention.

- Teachers are not allowed to be creative in their teaching so they don't have the ability to customize the learning experience to maximize learning. This is where much-needed passion is developed both for the teachers and the students and passion leads to successful learning of the materials.

- The ability of teachers to work and interact with students has been crushed by bureaucracy which has stifled enthusiasm for both teachers and their students. When passion is taken from the teachers and the students, we lose hope for success in both the teachers and the students—and they give up. This is a tragedy.

Our children are our most precious commodity. They are who bring love and passion to our lives. They are our future. Without successful learning taught by quality teachers, our children will be set up for failure that they don't want to face. We are already seeing the negative effects in rising alcohol and drug abuse and in the rapidly increasing suicide rate in teens and young adults.

Accountability prepares children for the real world. If everyone gets a ribbon and everyone "passes" tests without learning materials, children don't learn accountability for themselves and they expect good results without doing the work that it takes to actually learn and grow through failures and successes along the way. When children fail and learn how to use discernment to turn failures into learning experiences, they learn to survive with valuable life skills. I have never heard successful adults describe life-changing experiences from things that came easily for them.

We must create educational situations that allow our children to safely learn accountability and discernment. It starts with making good choices on the playground and grows into making good choices in life.

When children actually experience consequences that are appropriate for their failures and successes, they develop into creative survivors, capable of adapting to live happy, healthy, and enriching lives. Isn't that what we want for all of our children?

The answer, I believe, is LESS federal government interference; more creativity and rewards for teachers that are tied to learning and not solely to test results; more parental participation and not taking parental rights away; and a system that focuses on *accountability for everyone involved* which leads students to successful lives as adults.

When the government gives control of education back to states and citizens, we WILL see improvements in education and employment opportunities at all levels. And, we will have come full circle back to the days when education was meaningful and created opportunities for Americans to dream big and pursue their passions *and* cease reliance on governmental entitlement programs.

Let's bring optimism back to our citizens so we can rekindle the glory days of America when the majority of Americans were bright-eyed, happy, proud, productive and innovative citizens.

GLOSSARY

Index of Key Concepts

Every area of study has its own language and education is no exception. This is especially true when dealing with the government and its acronyms. Refer to these key concepts to become familiar with the specialized language encountered in this book.

Terminology

Borrower Education: institutions are required to educate and/or counsel students regarding student loan rights and responsibilities

Cohort Default Rates, aka CDR: defined by the 1990 Omnibus Budget Reconciliation Act as eligibility criteria for institutions to provide federal student loans to those in attendance at their institution; a 2-year CDR is the number of borrowers who began repayment in a given federal fiscal year divided by the number of borrowers who defaulted before the end of the subsequent federal fiscal year; the threshold for eligibility uses one (1) year over 40% or three (3) consecutive years of data and used 25% beginning in July, 1994 (it was originally higher); for 2-year CDRs, schools could earn "disbursement benefits" for having three (3) most recent CDRs under 10% which include a waiver of the 30-day-delayed-certification for first-time borrowers and an ability to pull down financial aid funds in one disbursement instead of several disbursements; in 2008, the Higher Education Opportunity Act redefined the CDR as a 3-year definition with thresholds of one (1) year over 40% and three (3) consecutive years over 30%; for 3-year CDRs, schools could earn "disbursement benefits" for having three (3) most recent CDRs under 15% which include a waiver of the 30-day-delayed certification for first-time borrowers and an ability to pull down financial aid funds in one disbursement instead of several disbursements; schools have certain appeal rights to correct erroneous data, remove defaults based on unacceptable loan servicing standards, and receive exemptions for having a large populous of economically disadvantaged borrowers, 30-or-fewer borrowers, a small percent of participants and an average rates. There are CDR measures for loan holders which have no related consequences, for institutions (iCDRs) which determine institution eligibility for both grant and loan participation under Title IV, and for program-level (pCDRs) measures which are currently informational and a required GE disclosure for schools

> **Disclaimer:** Because of the observations that the author has made through over 28 years of experience; for the purposes of the analyses in this book she used fewer-than-30 borrowers instead of 30-or-fewer borrowers because, more often than not, these schools go back and forth between CDR average rates (30-or-fewer) and stand-alone rates (over 30) based on fluctuating enrollment numbers. This also usually represents schools that are new to Title IV Eligibility (Pell Grants and federal student loans) and have fairly drastic increases in enrollment after the schools become eligible. Schools that consistently remain under 30 borrowers have limited use of federal programs.

Deferment: when certain requirements are met and approved by the Secretary through FFELP or federal servicers, it allows a student to temporarily stop making loan payments; the government pays the accruing interest during the deferment period on certain subsidized Stafford Loans; for unsubsidized loans, and certain graduate loans, and PLUS loans during periods of deferment, the borrower is responsible for paying interest; if the interest is not paid, it is added to the principal balance (capitalized); schools and their third-party servicers can assist student loan borrowers in requesting deferments but do not have the authority to grant a forbearance as that authority solely lies with the Secretary

Department of Education or U.S. Department of Education (ED, USDOE or DOE): established by Congress on May 4, 1980, under the Department of Education Organization Act (Public Law 96-98 of October 1979) with a "mission (is) to promote student achievement and preparation for global competitiveness by fostering education excellence and ensuring equal access... Under this law, ED's mission is to strengthen the Federal Commitment to assuring access to equal educational opportunity for every individual; supplement and complement the efforts of states, the local school systems and other instrumentalities of the states, the private sector, public and private nonprofit educational research institutions, community-based organizations, parents, and students to improve the quality of education; encourage the increased involvement of the public, parents, and students in Federal education programs; promote the improvements in the quality and usefulness of education through Federally supported research, evaluation, and sharing of information; improve the coordination of Federal education programs; improve the management of Federal education activities; and increase the accountability of Federal education programs to the President, the Congress, and the public." (Source: http://www2.ed.gov/about/overview/mission/mission.html)

DOE GE Final Data: contains detailed data behind the calculations for FY 2011 Informational Gainful Employment (GE) Rates that were NOT publicly released

DOE Briefing: cohort default rates and data are mandated to be released by the DOE no later than September 30th each year; there are briefings for eligible institutions published by sector and credential level that contain the three most recent fiscal years' data that determine institution eligibility; briefings for FFEL and FDSL loan programs were released by the DOE prior to 2014; loan program briefings have not been released for the 2014 or 2015 national official CDRs meaning that the DOE is no longer reporting its own results for direct loans which represent a growing majority of federal student loans

DOE GE Streamlined Data: released by the DOE as "the" GE FY 2011 Informational Data, this data lacks detailed data behind the calculations which covered up grossly inaccurate data being perceived as accurate; although DOE officials knew this information had been misreported and had misled lawmakers and the public about quality measures for schools, particularly inflammatory for proprietary schools, it never rescinded the information leaving lawmakers and the public with the false impression that the majority of proprietary schools left students with debt they could not afford

Discretionary Forbearance: under certain circumstances, the lender may choose to grant forbearance for administrative reasons or based on financial hardship or illness (see Forbearance) to bring a loan current; the Secretary's authority is very broad for this discretion and the borrower's approval is not required

Domestic Discretionary Budget: spending authorized by Congress and implemented through an appropriations bill; education is part of the domestic discretionary budget

Federal Direct Student Loan Program, aka FDSL, FDSLP, or Direct Loans: student loans made directly to students by the federal government; therefore, it is funded with money left over after all other federal expenditures are paid, which forces lawmakers to write laws to fit the budget instead of writing laws to educate American citizens

Federal Family Education Loan Program, aka FFEL or FFELP: federal Stafford, SLS, PLUS and Consolidation loans made by private lenders that are guaranteed by federal loan guarantee agencies; program ended on June 30, 2010 under the Affordable Care Act of 2010 (the same law that brought us Obamacare); taxpayers only paid for defaulted loans; however, money collected from defaulted loans goes into the federal general fund

Forbearance: when a student cannot meet requirements for deferment, he may be allowed to temporarily stop making payments, make smaller payments or extend the time for making payments; during periods of forbearance, the borrower is responsible for paying interest; if the interest is not paid, it is added to the principal balance (capitalized); schools and their third-party servicers can assist student loan borrowers in requesting forbearance but do not have the authority to grant the forbearance as that authority solely lies with the Secretary

Gainful Employment, aka GE and GE 2.0: extensive and burdensome federal regulations defined by the DOE without statutory language that broaden the definition of a program offered at an institution of higher education defined under 34 C.F.R. § 600.4(a)(4)(iii) that is at least a one-academic-year training program that leads to a certificate, or other non-degree recognized credential, and prepares students for gainful employment in a recognized occupation to 215 pages of regulatory language that applies primarily to proprietary institution programs. These GE regulations exclude most public and private nonprofit programs from these quality metrics. Programs included are defined under 34 C.F.R § 668.7(a)(3)(i) refers to any education program offered by the institution under § 668.8(c)(3) or (d) including all proprietary institution programs except (1) those with a Baccalaureate Degree in Liberal Arts that have been regionally accredited since October 1 2007; or preparatory courses of study that provide course work necessary for enrollment in an eligible program; (2) nonprofit, public, and private institution programs except those that lead to a degree; programs that are at least 2 years in length and fully-transferable to a bachelor's degree program; or preparatory courses of study that provide course work necessary for enrollment in an eligible program; and (3) teacher certification program exclusion applies if the program does not lead to a certificate awarded by the institution

GE Informational Rates: the DOE released informational rates for gainful employment for FY 2011 and FY 2012 to inform schools and the public of possible sanctions for unacceptable programmatic debt-to-income (DTE or D/E) and repayment rates; the FY 2011 GE Informational Rates released in June 2012 provided both DTE (D/E) and repayment rates but had two different data sets with a "Streamlined" data set that included rates without data details for 3,787 programs and a "Final" data set that included rates with data for 13,587 programs where there were obvious patterns of eliminated or revised data eliminating the reporting for most of the public and private sector programs; the FY 2012 GE Informational Rates released in March 2015 contained DTE rates for 7,934 programs and contained some data but were missing the "median debt"which is critical for verifying the rates provided; the FY 2012 GE Informational Rates were part of the Notice of Proposed Rulemaking for GE 2.0 and were incomplete and calculated differently than final regulations mandated and, therefore, were invalid as a method of determining the effect the GE 2.0 regulations would have on interested parties and stripping away the rights of those interested parties to accurately comment on correctly calculated data as determined in final GE 2.0 regulations

Higher Education Act of 1965, aka HEA: an education bill that was developed as part of the civil rights movement, focused on providing an equal opportunity for individuals to obtain an education beyond high school, that is, higher education

Historically Black Colleges and Universities, aka HBCU: institutions with a special designation from the DOE; allows for special considerations and funding, including an exemption from cohort default rate sanctions until July 1, 1994 and federal funding to help pay for their default management plans

iCDR: the term "iCDR" is not defined anywhere in federal regulations but has been used extensively in the gainful employment regulatory language and is now the industry standard abbreviation for "institution cohort default rates"

Mandatory Forbearance: when the student meets the eligibility criteria for the forbearance, the lender is required to grant it; schools and their third-party servicers can assist student loan borrowers in requesting forbearance but do not have the authority to grant the forbearance as that authority solely lies with the Secretary

pCDR: defined in federal regulations for gainful employment and is the industry standard abbreviation for "programmatic cohort default rates" that determined program eligibility for Title IV funding in the original GE regulations and is a reporting requirement in GE 2.0

PEPS300 Data: the file name used by the DOE for the cohort default rate data for all eligible institutions; PEPS is the Office of Federal Student Aid (FSA) management information system of all organizations that have a role in administering student financial aid and other Higher Education Act programs; PEPS maintains eligibility, certification, demographic, financial, review, audit, and default rate data about schools, lenders, and guarantors participating in the Title IV programs (PEPS information at http://www2.ed.gov/offices/OSFAP/PEPS/index.html)

PLUS Loans: federal loans that graduate or professional degree students and parents of dependent undergraduate students can use to help pay education expenses

Repayment Plans:

1. **Standard Repayment Plan:** best option for minimizing interest paid and paying off the loan

2. **Graduated Repayment Plan:** adds additional interest and has large increases in payment amounts; sets students up for failure

3. **Pay-As-You-Earn, aka PAYE (FDSLP) and REPAYE (FFELP):** based on 10% of one's discretionary income, doubles the repayment period from 10 to 20 years, forgives any outstanding balance at 20 years and may have tax liability for the loan forgiveness

4. **Income Based Repayment Plan (IBR):** sets the monthly loan payment at an amount based on income and family size; depending upon when the loan was initially taken out, that may be 10% or 15% of discretionary income but never more than the 10-year Standard Repayment Plan amount; adds additional interest to the original loan

5. **Income Contingency Repayment Plan (ICR):** monthly loan payment is the lesser of 20% or one's discretionary income or what one would pay on a repayment plan with a fixed payment over the course of 12 years, adjusted to income; adds additional interest to the original loan

Stafford Loans: federal loans for undergraduate and graduate students; subsidized or unsubsidized; FFELP or FDSLP

TIVAS as the group of FedLoan Servicing, aka PHEAA, Great Lakes Educational Loan Services, Inc., Nelnet, and Sallie Mae, aka SLMA: federal loan servicers subject to a set of performance metrics that includes customer satisfaction scores and default prevention statistics

Concepts or Terminology Originated by the Author

Education Interest Rebate, aka EIR: a 25% refund to a student who has paid his loan in full prior to the original standard repayment schedule or who has continued enrollment within the grace period in a higher education level in his field

Graduation Incentive Payment, aka GIP: that portion of a student loan that becomes a grant when the student graduates within 150% of the usual time for graduating

Interest Payment Match, aka IPM: a proposed program in which students who make timely interest payments would have half of those monthly interest payments made by the federal government

Latin Words (front cover)

Libertas: freedom, liberty, independence/frankness, candor (Source: University of British Columbia)

Praecipio: to instruct, advise, warn, anticipate (Source: University of British Columbia)

Prudentia: foresight; knowledge; sagacity, discretion (Source: University of Notre Dame)

ABOUT THE AUTHOR

MARY LYN HAMMER
EDUCATION ADVOCATE, CEO & ENTREPRENEUR

*Mentoring Champions One
American at a Time*

Ms. Mary Lyn Hammer is a seasoned education advocate, and the entrepreneurial founder, president and CEO of Champion College Services. Her belief that *education is the vehicle for making dreams come true* has led her into a life-long passionate fight, beginning in 1987, rectifying problems in the higher education industry to insure future participation for all students. During her career in higher education, she has touched more than 3 million students' lives through her companies and advocacy. Ms. Hammer's company Champion College Services (now it its 26th year of business) offers default prevention for federal and private student loans, job placement verification, skip tracing, consulting services, and custom surveys for students, alumni, and employers.

Her accomplishments include numerous state, regional, and national awards and recognitions over the years in both the higher education industry and in professional business arenas. She has participated in training sessions and workshops for numerous state, provincial, regional, national, and private associations in both the U.S. and Canada in a continued effort to share her experiences and knowledge. Ms. Hammer has had several hundred articles published in numerous higher education magazines.

Her experience specific to the contents of this book include the following:

1. **1988–1989** Hammer turned evidence over to Congress and the U.S. Department of Education (USDOE) and testified numerous times regarding a student lending corruption ring in California that put several companies out of business and cost the government an estimated $750 million to rectify.

2. **1989** Her innovative "Hands On" Default Management Program was recognized by the USDOE for its remarkable results and was used as the basis for default management in what became known as "Appendix D." Ms. Hammer was active in aiding the USDOE in drafting regulatory language for default management that was mandatory for high default rate schools from 1989 until 1996 and still exists today in rewritten regulations under "Subpart M" and "Subpart N."

3. **1990–1993** As part of several laws affecting higher education and cohort default rates, Ms. Hammer helped draft statutory and regulatory language for cohort default rate appeals.

4. **1993–1995** Hammer helped draft the Cohort Default Rate Guide and several revisions thereof.

5. **1994–1998** Hammer worked with Congressional members on school-based loan issues and cohort default rate matters that became statutory language in the 1998 reauthorization of the Higher Education Act of 1965.

6. **1999** She served as an alternate negotiator for school-based loan issues in the 1999 Negotiated Rulemaking.

7. **2000** She served as a primary negotiator for school-based loan issues in the 2000 Negotiated Rulemaking. The original default management regulations under "Appendix D" were rewritten into "Subpart M" in addition to other loan issues.

8. **2002–2008** Hammer worked with Congressional members on school-based loan issues and cohort default rate matters. Although she was opposed to increasing the cohort default rate definition, she was instrumental in correcting what was originally written as a 4-year CDR definition to a 3-year CDR definition and helped draft the increased threshold and appeal rights for sanctions under the new definition.

9. **2009** She served as a primary negotiator for Loan Issues—Team 2 and provided expert witness testimony for Team 1 Loan Issues. Default management regulations were written into "Subpart N" for the 3-year CDR definition along with conforming language for appeals in addition to other loan issues.

10. **1988–2014** Hammer has testified many times at Congressional and USDOE hearings and has worked closely with Congressional members, education committee professional staff, and key staff at the USDOE on many issues during her career to insure program integrity and access to quality higher education for at-risk students.

Ms. Hammer has been elected four times to the Board of Directors for the Career College Association, now known as APSCU, and she is the Charter Member, former Chairwoman for the Higher Education Allied Health Leaders (HEAL) Coalition, and has served as an Advisory Board Member for the Career Education Review. Additionally, she currently serves on the Board of Directors for the Private Career Colleges and Schools (PCCS, 3rd term) Regions XIII, IX & X and for the Northwest Career College Federation (NWCCF, 16th term), as Director of the Board for Champion for Success (a nonprofit mentoring and advocacy for at-risk kids), and on the Board of Directors for eMed, a medical research center for Chinese medicine.

Injustice for All, Ms. Hammer's first book, is written to provide us with detailed evidence on corruption in education reporting to protect the future of our country.

For More Visit MaryLynHammer.com

INDEX